THE COMPLETE WORKS OF

W. R. BION

VOLUME VI

Californian swimming pool
Watercolour painting by WRB

THE COMPLETE WORKS OF

W. R. BION

VOLUME VI

Edited by Chris Mawson

Editorial consultant Francesca Bion

Routledge
Taylor & Francis Group
LONDON AND NEW YORK

First published 2014 by Karnac Books Ltd

2 Park Square, Milton Park, Abingdon, Oxfordshire OX14 4RN
52 Vanderbilt Avenue, New York, NY 10017

Routledge is an imprint of the Taylor & Francis Group, an informa business

First issued in paperback 2019

British Library Cataloguing in Publication Data

A CIP record for this collection is available from the British Library

The Complete Works of W. R. Bion
ISBN (Complete set): 978–1–85575–603–8
ISBN (Volume VI): 978–1–82202–349–1 (hbk)
ISBN (Volume VI): 978–0–367–32286–1 (pbk)
This volume not to be sold separately

Edited, designed, and produced by Communication Crafts

CONTENTS

The Grid (1963)

	1 Defini- tory Hypo- thesis	2 ψ	3 Nota- tion	4 Atten- tion	5 Oedip.*	6 Action	. . . n . . .
A β-Elements	A1	A2				A6	An
B α-Elements	B1	B2	B3	B4	B5	B6	Bn
C Dream Thoughts Myth, Dream, Model	C1	C2	C3	C4	C5	C6	Cn
D Pre-conception	D1	D2	D3	D4	D5	D6	Dn
E Conception	E1	E2	E3	E4	E5	E6	En
F Concept	F1	F2	F3	F4	F5	F6	Fn
G Scientific Deductive System	G1	G2	G3	G4			
H Algebraic Calculus		H2					

*Later changed to 'Inquiry'. See 'The Grid' (1971) (Volume X, p. vii).

MEMORY AND DESIRE

1965

'Memory and Desire' was given without notes and without a pre-circulated version of the paper at a Scientific Meeting at the British Psychoanalytical Society on Wednesday 16 June 1965, but it was never published. In 2014, a recording of the 1965 presentation was found, which I transcribed. I am indebted to the Archivist of the British Psychoanalytical Society, Joanne Halford, for making the recording available to me to transcribe. The paper was published in the May 2014 issue of the *Bulletin of the British Psychoanalytical Society* (for Members, Candidates and Guests of the Society only).

EDITOR'S INTRODUCTION

> Even the simple act which we describe as 'seeing someone we know' is, to some extent, an intellectual process. We pack the physical outline of the creature we see with all the ideas we already formed about him, and in the complete picture of him which we compose in our minds those ideas have certainly the principal place. In the end . . . each time we see the face or hear the voice it is our own ideas of him which we recognize and to which we listen.
>
> Marcel Proust, *Remembrance of Things Past: Swann's Way*

Bion's original presentation of his ideas on memory and desire, given on 16 June 1965 at a Scientific Meeting of the British Psychoanalytical Society, was not published at the time because he gave it without notes, apologizing to his audience at the beginning and undertaking to provide a written version at some point. He said that if he had written down at that stage what he wanted to say about the two terms of the title that were the subject of his paper, he felt it would have made little sense. He preferred to speak it before expressing it in written language. In 1967 he published the bare bones of the paper as a two-page article, "Notes on Memory and Desire", in the *Psychoanalytic Forum*; it was reprinted in *Melanie Klein Today, Volume 2: Mainly Practice* (1988), edited by Elizabeth Spillius, and was also appended at the end of the 1994 edition of Bion's *Cogitations*. When Bion presented that cut-down, gnomic account, several analysts took part in the discussion of it, but only Bion's responses were published at the time. It is notable that in response to questions concerning the role of one of the terms he addresses in the paper, memory, Bion made a distinction between the kind of memory that interferes with analytic receptivity and a different kind, more akin to a suddenly recalled dream, which "swims into view". For this phenomenon Bion preferred the term *evolution*.

There are many references in Bion's work to the principles he articulated in such a condensed way in his brief, pithy "Notes on Memory and Desire". There is an extended treatment of the ideas in *Attention and Interpretation* (e.g., see the section 'Reality sensuous and psychic', p. 242, this volume).

Partly because the 1967 account was so brief, but also for other more complicated factors, the deep connection to Freud's thought on the subject of dreams, on psychoanalytic method, and on the nature of the ego-functions underlying memory and attention was not evident to many of those whose first reaction to Bion's presentation was one of rejection. Bion's ideas on the occluding effects of reliance in the analytic situation of memory and desire remain controversial in some quarters today, so the publication here of the original 1965 recording is valuable as it contains Bion's first presentation of these ideas, which were so important to him in his work and in his conception of a psychoanalytic attitude. I have written a longer introduction to this paper because of its important place in Bion's thinking and because of the many serious misunderstandings to which the short and pithy 'Notes on Memory and Desire' has given rise. One such source of misunderstanding is the emphatic and rather uncharacteristically dogmatic tone of parts of the 1965 presentation. In a paper presented to the British Psychoanalytical Society in 1967 on Negative Capability (later to form the basis of Chapter 13 in *Attention and Interpretation*, this volume), and which is a companion paper to 'Memory and Desire', Bion toned down this assertion and put it forward only as a suggestion for those experienced analysts who wished to try out the suspension of memory and desire as an experiment.

I think it is of particular interest that in the 1965 paper, Bion mentions the analogy of 'artificial blinding' to which Freud referred in his letter to Lou Andreas-Salomé on 25 May 1916 (in E. L. Freud, 1961). Although in the letter Freud referred to the act of writing when he said, "I have to blind myself artificially in order to focus all the light on one dark spot, renouncing cohesion, harmony, rhetoric and everything which you call symbolic", it is clear that he was referring to psychoanalytic attention itself – the conditions necessary for the evenly suspended attention that permits the analyst to "'turn his own unconscious like a receptive organ towards the transmitting unconscious of the patient" (Freud, 1912e, p. 115).

In his 25 May 1916 letter, Freud next refers directly to scotopic vision:

> . . . for my eyes, adapted as they are to the dark, probably can't stand strong light or an extensive range of vision.

The importance of this reference, with its hint of a psychoanalytic version of an easily disrupted Purkinjě Shift,[1] is significant for Bion's discussion of memory and desire in relation to Freud's own conjectures regarding the role of consciousness as a sense organ for the apprehension of psychic qualities. Freud (1900a) had suggested, essentially, that there were two 'sensory surfaces' or envelopes feeding awareness, one receiving impressions of external reality through the senses and the other sensitive to impressions emanating endogenously:

> . . . excitations from the periphery of the whole apparatus, the perceptual system; and in addition to this, it can receive excitations of pleasure and unpleasure, which prove to be almost the only psychical quality attaching to transpositions of energy in the inside of the apparatus" (Freud, 1900a, p. 574)

It is sometimes forgotten that Bion meant his comments about the importance of divesting oneself of past knowledge of the patient and of one's desires for his betterment to be understood not only in the context of Freud's recommendations, but also with the apophatic principle described by John Keats as 'Negative Capability' and termed by André Green in its application to psychoanalysis as 'the work of the negative'. Bion marked in his copy of *The Writings of St John of the Cross* the following passages, and he labelled them as being relevant to his ideas on memory and desire. In order to appreciate the particular use to which Bion was applying these principles, it is important to note that where there are references in such writings to God, or the 'Godhead', Bion is abstracting the term for use in his formulations in the realm of psychoanalysis to bring out what he feels are detectable underlying patterns common to both domains:

> All these sensory means and exercises of the faculties must be left behind and in silence. . . . As a result one has to follow this method of disencumbering, emptying, and depriving the faculties of their natural rights and operations to make room for the inflow and illu-

[1]The Purkyně effect or shift is what underlies dark adaptation in visual perception. It is named after the Czech anatomist Jan Evangelista Purkyně, who in 1819 discovered the principles at work. Purkyně reasoned that the eye has not one but two systems adapted to see colours, one for bright overall light intensity, and the other for dusk and dawn. The Purkyně effect occurs at the transition between primary use of the photopic (cone-based) and scotopic (rod-based) systems.

> mination. . . . If a person does not turn his eyes from his natural capacity, he will not attain to so lofty a communication; rather, he will hinder it. If it is true that the soul must journey by knowing God through what He is not, rather than through what He is, it must journey, insofar as possible, by way of the denial and rejection of natural and supernatural apprehensions. This is our task now with the memory. We must draw it away from its natural props and capacities and raise it above itself (above all distinct knowledge and apprehensible possession) to supreme hope in the incomprehensible. . . . The annihilation of the memory in regard to all forms (including the five senses) is an absolute requirement. . . . This union cannot be wrought without a complete separation of the memory from all forms. . . . Once he has the habit . . . he no longer experiences these lapses of memory in matters concerning his moral and natural life. ['The Ascent of Mt Carmel', Book 3, Chap. 2, #2; in Kavanaugh & Rodriguez, 1964]

Where the mystical thinkers were attempting to find terms for the objects of *their* contemplation, which they did – in the examples selected by Bion for his purposes – by considering what God was *not*, Bion is attempting to use an analogous process for contemplating the non-sensuous psychic reality of psychoanalysis. Bion thought that the problems in attending to the evolution of the transference often stem from there being a surfeit of ideas and theories, as well as an encumbrance of memories and desires.

Caper (1998) has pointed out that Bion's expositions of memory and desire and his concept of O have been misunderstood by some analysts as signs of Bion having turned to mysticism, but the formulations that Bion takes from mystical thinkers and applies to his formulations of container–contained (♀♂), the domain of O, and memory and desire constitute "a psychoanalytic model of mysticism, not a mystical model of psychoanalysis" (p. 420).

Finally, it is valuable to have available here the original 1965 paper "Memory and Desire" in order to appreciate properly the linkages left out in the writing of his peremptory 1967 "Notes on Memory and Desire", as well as offering further material that illuminates his discussions of psychoanalytic technique elsewhere in his work. It serves a similar bridging function in relation to his discussions in *Attention and Interpretation* and "Notes on Memory and Desire", as does his *Cogitations* in relation to the papers of the 1960s.

Memory and Desire

What I want to do this evening is something which is rather different from a scientific paper; it is a discussion of the subject in which I am interested, and I hope that it will interest you. The first point I would make is this: It is a paper about an event that hasn't taken place yet. The remarks I am making are addressed specifically to analysts who are seeing a patient tomorrow, or the day after. I think it would be helpful to focus not so much on what I am saying as on tomorrow's session; the one you are going to have tomorrow with the particular patient.

Now, to turn to the title of the paper: These two terms – memory and desire – I intend to use as what I have called elsewhere terms which bind a constant conjunction.[1] By a constant conjunction I mean that in certain circumstances you might notice that certain elements kept on turning up constantly conjoined – that you think, for example, that there is fur, claws, whiskers, and you bind the lot by saying "Cat" – the object of that being that once you have bound this constant conjunction you can then set about researching, as superficially or as deeply as you choose, into what you mean by this term. It is rather different from the ordinary views which are held philosophically about abstraction. I am really suggesting that you start with the unknown, that you note a constant conjunction, that you bind it by a term which is virtually meaningless, and then you proceed to investigate what you mean by that term – for the rest of your life if you are so inclined.

The first term, memory: the constant conjunction which I wish to bind by that is very much, probably, what we all understand by

---

[1]For example, *Elements of Psycho-Analysis* [Volume V].

that term in ordinary conversation. I think one might say that it also includes the ideas which Freud expresses when he speaks of Notation and of its relation to memory in the paper on the two principles of mental functioning[1].

It is also related to what we ordinarily mean when we talk about cases that we have seen, in scientific papers and elsewhere, and describe what we consider to be accounts of what took place. I think it is probably also the kind of thing that we try, at various times in our careers, to make notes about – so that we shall be able to know, or to remember, what has taken place in sessions, and then be able to report on them and to refer to these notes and so on. That, roughly speaking, is what I mean by the use of the term memory.

Similarly with regard to desire – again, it is a meaning which most of us are aware of in our ordinary conversation – I mean by it something rather positively covetous, as it were; something that one wants to have. It has a certain similarity to memory, in that one could say about memory that you tend to remember various things which you like to possess, and in this sense memory itself is very often used as if it were a container in which one keeps these objects that one desires.

I think that the term Desire is also – and I wish to include in it – something which Freud speaks of as wish-fulfilment and the expression of wishes in dreams; it is similar to that.

When we go into this matter further – and I am talking now specifically of the way in which I use these terms – the elements about which I am concerned are, really, sensuous images. That is, both desires and memories are spoken of in terms which are derived from a background of sensuous experience. Let us say that here are things which you can touch, or feel, or smell, which are felt to have a shape or a form, and so on. The fact that they are expressed and stored in

---

[1]Freud, S. (1911b),'Formulations on the Two Principles of Mental Functioning', p. 220. ["Consciousness now learned to comprehend sensory qualities in addition to the qualities of pleasure and unpleasure which hitherto had alone been of interest to it. A special function was instituted which had periodically to search the external world, in order that its data might be familiar already if an urgent internal need should arise – the function of attention. Its activity meets the sense-impressions half way, instead of awaiting their appearance. At the same time, probably, a system of notation was introduced, whose task it was to lay down the results of this periodical activity of consciousness – a part of what we call memory" (1911b, p. 220). *Ed.*]

terms of this kind also means that they are very closely related to the primitive background of senses, and very frequently to a phase in development in which the pleasure–pain principle is dominant. The consequence is that the terms in which these things are remembered or in which they are desired are suitable to objects which can be sensuously perceived and which can be regarded as painful or pleasant. Therefore the *scope* is relatively limited.

Now, I am aware that this is not the only meaning of memory; I am trying all the time to put a limit onto it, so it should apply to what I want to talk about, but for the sake of completeness I think that it is well for us to pay attention to the fact that one could say that even a mathematical formula can be used as a method by which you express or store a memory. I do not think, however, that when it comes to clinical work – when it comes to this session tomorrow – when one thinks of memory, that one is going to think of it in mathematical terms or anything like it. The terms will almost certainly be of this primitive kind, suitable for expressing sensuous experience; suitable for expressing experiences which are felt to be related either to pain or to pleasure.

The other elements which I want to touch on briefly I have thought of in terms of the Grid[1] which I drew up, in which one axis states, as it were, the genetic phase of a particular element that one is trying to categorize, and, on the other hand, the vertical axis, which expresses the use to which it is put. It is quite obvious that there can be highly developed formulations – thoughts, theories, ideas, even mathematical formulations – as I have said, which can be used in a highly sophisticated way; I am not concerning myself with that, for the reasons I have already given – because what I am concerned with are the terms in which we usually think about our cases.

At this point perhaps I ought to make clear that I have always been sceptical about what are called 'clinical accounts'. I have felt that they are, after all, only versions of what took place: they are transformations of what was a real experience. Most of us are critical, for various reasons, of a clinical description. I have felt increasingly disinclined even to pretend to give a clinical account of what takes place, because even if one is simply concerned with simplifying the events of a complicated situation, the distortion is really terrific.

[1][See p. vii, this volume. *Ed.*]

Nevertheless, as analysts we do know – and I think it is borne in on us more and more as experience builds up – that we really do deal with *something*; that the psychoanalytic experience, however sceptical we may be, is really an emotional experience and it really exists, even if we shall never know or be in a position to give even an approximately correct description of what takes place. For this reason, I think – and find it most useful to do so – of any clinical description as being by nature of a pictorial representation, or, shall we say, a sensuous representation (because I am thinking of what takes place in an analytic situation). I transform that situation into visual images and then a further transformation into verbal formulations, such as those with which we are familiar here. These transformations are of a kind in which one gets an increasing degree of sophistication, but the most comprehensible – the most easy to grasp – and therefore the reason why one frequently is asked, 'Can you give an example?', 'Can you illustrate this?', 'Can you give me a clinical account which matches this?', is because it is much easier to be able to grasp either a visual presentation or a verbalization of that visual presentation.

Now, while there is a gain in communicability of such a formulation, there is a loss of accuracy – for the reasons that I have given: one is using terms which come from a sensuous background to describe this, and there are other reasons with which I am not bothering tonight, but which are known to all of us through the experience of our own analysis.

My point is that this reality which we all know about, which we feel is unmistakeably borne-in on us in the course of analytic work, is something which cannot really be properly expressed, because if you take, shall we say, an anxiety state, most of us would expect to be able to recognize anxiety when we [meet] it,[1] but you can't smell it; it hasn't got a shape; you can't touch it; and so on. And by the time you *can* represent what is going on – in the terms which we ordinarily use – a very considerable development has taken place. The event itself – the thing itself, anxiety itself – has been transformed in a very striking way by the time you use a word like 'anxiety'.

This brings me to the point that any verbal description, any notes that we may make, practically any formulations are, really,

[1][On the tape: "most of us would expect to be able to recognize anxiety when we saw it"; for reasons that will be evident, 'saw' has been amended to 'meet'. *Ed.*]

distortions. I am not talking now about pathological states; I am not talking about this subject as it occurs looked at from the point of view of psychopathology, or from the point of view of the patient. I am considering it simply from the point of view of each one of us who has a patient to see tomorrow. Therefore, I am not concerning myself with either of these questions as being psychopathological manifestations, because on this I think that we all are in general agreement: it is considered to be absolutely essential, at least in our Society, that people should be analysed, and that we do not know of any better way of looking after this problem than by insisting that people should be analysed in order to deal with it.

What I am concerned with here is something much more conscious and under conscious control. I am concerned with the problem of what one should do in order to be ready for, and in condition for, the session tomorrow.

It is well known, in other realms, that it is possible to be in training. To take a trivial example: if someone is playing squash, or tennis, it is not felt to be advisable that they should play static ball games such as golf. Similarly, I am suggesting that there should be a consideration besides this matter of psychopathology – the matters dealt with by analysis and so forth – of what is the desirable state of affairs if you are a psychoanalyst and you have got a patient to see tomorrow. What can be done in the way of keeping in training?

Now, I want to remind you of the conventional view which crops up where there is a tendency to feel that it is important to remember what takes place in an analysis; that it is important to find some method by which you record it – to write notes or use a recording machine and so forth – and the more critical the situation becomes – the more cause you have for anxiety about any patient – the more important it is felt to be to be able to remember what took place today in that patient's analysis, what took place yesterday, and so on. The view that I am wanting to put is that this view is entirely mistaken. And not only mistaken, but positively bad for your analytic work.

With regard to desire, in which I want to include things like thinking 'How nice it will be when the session is over'; or 'How nice it will be when the Summer comes' – all ideas of that kind, including (and this is an important point) 'How nice it would be to cure the patient' – there is, as you know, a great deal of discussion as to what the aim of analysis is. I think that in fact it is a mistaken preoccupation, although a very interesting one, for an analyst *while he is analysing*. I think that the desire to cure the patient should have no place whatsoever in the consulting room, whatever place that it has in the make-up of the analyst or in his philosophical life; because, in my opinion, nothing will throw your judgement out more than to be concerned with trying to remember what the patient or you yourself have said, or wanting to cure the patient, or to entertain any other desire.

In my experience I find nearly always that the wish to remember what the patient said, or any desire to cure the patient, invariably seems to me to crop up in the situation, and in a formulation, that is intended to keep at bay and to keep out of mind certain other feelings.

I think that the point is brought home by those extremely brilliant (one might almost say) psychoanalysts – the psychotic patient – who, when he is concerned to break the link between the analyst and himself, will do his best to stimulate the analyst to remember something – that you will get floods of evocative words – and do his best to stimulate in the analyst a desire, if only a desire to get rid of him. This is because the stimulation of either of those two will virtually destroy the analyst's judgement. If the patient is successful in his aim, your judgement disappears. Therefore – harking back to tomorrow's session – what I would like to say is that you should spend your time banishing any memory of the patient whatsoever, in preparation for the session, and any aim or ambition as regard to his cure. I do not mean by this that forgetting is a good thing – that is just as bad as remembering. I think that it is something which is a positive discipline. I think it is a matter which you will find is extremely difficult, and you have only got to think of it for a moment to see how inherently improbable it is.

But so long as we are as we are – human beings – we shall entertain desires and we shall have memories. The view that I want to put is that our difficulty as analysts is not that we have such bad memories, or that we are deficient in a desire to cure our patients, but, on the contrary, is the intrusively powerful nature of these memories which, as I think you will realize, is quite compatible with views that Freud himself put forward with regard to the prominence in analysis of memories.

What I am suggesting, then, is that an effort is required which is an actual discipline, difficult to achieve; it cannot simply be achieved simply by contenting yourself with the fact that you have forgotten –

that is not good enough. It is a matter of trying to get out of the habit of remembering things, and trying to get out of the habit of desiring or wanting anything *while you are predominantly engaged on your work.* I am not expressing views about this as a philosophy of life or anything; it is simply an attempt to promulgate an actual rule – as if one could make rules for psychoanalytic training. This is the kind of rule that I would like to make.

I would like to stress once more that it is very different from the view that we are all used to – the view that we fall back into very easily: the more critical the situation, the more we try to remember something or other, even if it is only an appropriate theory – the direct contrary of what I think is desirable.

The consequences of this, insofar as I can speak of them, insofar as I am acquainted with them myself, are peculiar. I do not know how far I can go in an attempt to describe them. But one of the things about it is that in order to see clearly one really needs to be pretty well blind – metaphorically and literally. It is really a sort of positive lack of anything in one's mind, if one can put it like that; that the darker the spot[1] that you wish to illuminate, the darker you have to be – you have to shut out all light in order to be able to see it. Only in that way is it possible to get the conditions in which a real object – but one which is formless and not in any way appreciable to what we ordinarily regard as the senses – emerges, evolves, and becomes possible for us to be aware of.

If one can approximate to this situation, then I think that after a time it really does seem as if it is much clearer, as if one quite felt quite unmistakeably that what one was witnessing was, for example, anxiety, or hostility, and so forth.

---

[1][Bion here is following Freud, who wrote in a letter to Lou Andreas-Salomé on 13 May 1924: "I know that in writing I have to blind myself artificially in order to focus all the light on one dark spot, renouncing cohesion, harmony, rhetoric and everything which you call symbolic, frightened as I am by the experience that any such claim or expectation involves the danger of distorting the matter under investigation, even though it may embellish it. Then you come along and add what is missing, build upon it, putting what has been isolated back into its proper context. I cannot always follow you, for my eyes, adapted as they are to the dark, probably can't stand strong light or an extensive range of vision" (in E. L. Freud, 1961). He made this link to Freud's letter explicit in the discussion following the presentation of his 1967 'Notes on Memory and Desire' (see later, this volume). *Ed.*]

I said that I did not want to deal at all here with psychopathology, but just as an aside I would like to suggest that this view also perhaps gives an idea of what the infant or the child has to put up with in dealing with quite real things – real experiences – but which cannot be expressed beyond by saying, "I feel I've got a tummy ache". That is the kind of vocabulary, those are the sensuous terms that have to be employed in order to describe a thing which is in no way represented by that at all. There is a quite striking phrase in *Civilization and its Discontents* (1930a) where Freud, having given a description – a sort of model of the mind – then says that the striking thing about this, the thing you can really learn from it, is the utter inadequacy of a pictorial representation to provide a model for the mind. I think that this really sums up very well indeed what I am trying to say – namely, the fact that we are dealing with things which are real enough, which are absolutely real, even from earliest infancy on, but which cannot be expressed except in the kind of vocabulary which is quite unfitted for it by its derivation and characteristics.

When it comes to the actual progress of the analysis, I have found that it is very extraordinary – the way in which the experience, as it evolves in the analytic situation, is, over and over again, recognizable. That, over and over again, with the ordinary theories of analysis – whatever your school may be, whatever your private bent of mind may be, and the theories that you may hold – how much easier it becomes to be able to appreciate that what is happening in the consulting room is an actual approximation to one or other of the theories that you know, no matter how little you may feel that you know about psychoanalysis or psychoanalytic theories. It is extraordinary how much one does know, and how often the theories that have already been discovered which are a commonplace of psychoanalytic literature, swim into view, so to speak, irresistibly, because of what is happening in the consulting room. But the first, essential thing here is to be able to get into the state of mind in which these things which are not open to sensuous apprehension are nevertheless possible to apprehend.

The order in which this happens, however, seems to be different. I would not want to try to explain in what way it is different, but certainly it seems to me that a change takes place. There *is* a coherence about it, there *is* a respect in which the totality of the analysis hangs together, there *is* a way in which the pieces of the jigsaw can be seen to have a configuration which bears a relationship to the whole – even when you do not know what the whole is – but the order in which those events appear seems to me to be different when one tries to do analysis in this way, rather than in other ways with which one is familiar.

A further point is that I think it is quite a frightening way of doing it. For one thing, the cultural background to which we belong is the sort of background where, if anything went wrong, and you found yourself in a Court of Law or a Coroner's Court, it would be assumed as a matter of course that you really know something about your patient: that you know that your patient is married, has four children, say, and so on. And indeed, one feels that that is something one ought to know about. Now this is the dilemma: if you know that, and if you remember that, then it may take you quite a long time to appreciate the fact that your patient is talking in a way which is quite appropriate to his not being married at all, nor having any children. And the knowledge, the memory, that he is married and has children will easily distort one's view and interfere with one's judgement of the situation in which the interpretations are appropriate to his being unmarried and having no children, while one is tending to wish to make interpretations which would make allowance for the other facts. That is a crude example, but it is, roughly speaking, one aspect of it. On the other hand, there is a feeling that if it emerged that you did not even know that your patient was a married man, how very odd this would look, and what a queer light it would cast on any view of your professional competence, in the cultural background in which you belong.

One cannot do analysis on those terms, but at the same time I think that one cannot really do analysis on terms in which one is unaware of the risks that one is running and of the price that one has to pay if one is going to do analysis properly. If I am right in saying that this is *a* way of doing analysis properly, then, at the same time, one is going to pay the price of this in anxiety. So I think that there *is* an increase in anxiety; I do not think that one could say that it is an undesirable increase in anxiety; on the contrary I think, again, that it probably would mark the division between those who practise psychoanalysis and those who talk about it.

If you are a psychoanalyst, if you are seeing a patient tomorrow, then you are seeing that patient in a particular emotional situation:

not only in the consulting room but in the cultural situation, the cultural background. Therefore, it is important for the analyst to be both the analyst and also a member of the society, so that he is exposed to the emotional experiences and states of mind of the society to which he belongs. It is, however, as I say, somewhat disconcerting and at first not at all pleasing.

Again, with regard to the patient the situation is different, because what one is concerned to do, among other things, is to be able to observe the operation of his memories and of his desires. I think that it makes it very much easier when one keeps out of one's own mind these particular elements of memory and desire, because then it becomes possible to be able to 'see' what is operating in the patient's mind and what is actually going on in the analytic session.

I raised the point a little while back about the transformation. I would like to revert again to that for a moment. Perhaps I can express it best in this way: If you see a painting of a cornfield, most of us in this particular culture would recognize it for what it was. That must mean that there is something which is invariant – that there is something about the actual cornfield and there is something about the piece of canvas with the paint disposed on its surface which remains unaltered and which makes recognition possible. Another example, as you know, is that if you wish to represent a circular pond you have to draw an ellipse; if you wish to represent a path with parallel borders you have to represent it with lines which meet at a point.

What we are witnessing in an analytic session I don't think can ever *be* the real experience; we do not know what that is, but what we do know is the experience by the time it has been transformed – by the patient – into various forms of verbal representation. There is no reason why it should not be other representations except that analytically we usually conduct it in terms of verbal communication, but of course, as child analysts know, there are other methods of communication as well. If one ever analyses somebody who is by nature a musician, I think that it isn't a long time before you find yourself up against somebody who is opposed to your whole method of expression, that there is a feeling that if he were to be allowed to play the piano then he could say what he thinks, and considers that he is being restricted to a feeble sort of method of communication such as conversation. So in this way the number of transformations that we have to deal with are really very considerable. Again, when you are presented with a verbal account by a patient, one could make a parallel to this by saying that you might have to look at the painting – say Constable's *Hay Wain* – and you can regard that as being a record of a hay wain, that that's what it is, very simply: It is about a hay wain. Now that is not really good enough for the analyst, because if you stick to that then you stick to this state of affairs where you know *about* analysis, and you know *about* the patient – you know that the patient is married and so forth. But what you don't know is the patient. There has, therefore, got to be a quite different transformation.

Now, this other transformation is, I think, of a different sort of category altogether. It is to do with the actual emotional reality of the situation with which we are dealing. When you get onto that, then I think you are in difficulties because you are using language which is suitable for talking *about* something, but that is not a language which is necessarily suitable for an experience in which something is happening, a dynamic emotional experience which is not open to sensuous observation.

The final point, then, that I want to make is that as a prelude to this state of affairs where you are actually having to deal with, to psychoanalyse (whatever that may mean), a state of mind, these special steps have to be taken and they have to be steps of this nature, where the question of desires and the question of memory have to be dealt with as definite matters of discipline – the banishment of them from the mind.

CATASTROPHIC CHANGE

1966

'Catastrophic Change' was presented at a Scientific Meeting of the British Psycho-analytical Society on 4 May 1966. It was published in the *Bulletin of the British Psychoanalytical Society, 5* (1966).

EDITOR'S INTRODUCTION

On 4 May 1966, Wilfred Bion presented to a Scientific Meeting of the British Psychoanalytical Society his paper 'Catastrophic Change', which had been pre-published – unlike his 1965 presentation, 'Memory and Desire' – in the Bulletin of that Society, for members to consider and to bring with them for discussion. As was frequently the case, his spoken version of his ideas differed considerably from the written one, to the clear irritation of some of his colleagues, one of whom had prepared lengthy arguments in advance.

His spoken talk was short and to the point – an introduction only to the ideas put forward in the paper, on the assumption that everybody present had read it; he had wanted to allow plenty of time for a full discussion.

Bion introduced his topic by speaking about a pattern he had noticed that, as he put it, kept turning up. He emphasized that he was not putting forward a new theory but was describing and exploring an observable pattern, a configuration, that keeps on cropping up, both inside and outside the consulting room. At the end of the discussion Bion reiterated that detecting the underlying pattern was only the beginning of theorizing about it and its relationships to other phenomena, and that the status of the container–contained configuration, and ideas associated with it, were provisional: a model rather than a theory.

Bion gave four descriptions of ways in which the pattern he had observed manifested and the different forms it took in different contexts and at various levels of analysis. Something contains something else, and (a) simply houses it; (b) exerts confining, damaging influence or crushing force upon it; or (c) protects and stimulates its growth. In his paper these are referred to in terms borrowed from biology: *commensal* (etymologically: coexisting, sitting at the same table), *parasitic*, and *symbiotic*.

Bion observed the configuration as a constant conjunction, meaning elements which are observed to arise together reliably. The constantly conjoined elements he bound with a name, container–contained, making use of terminology and an instance of a pattern that he had retained from reading a 1925 paper by Carl Jung, 'Marriage as a Psychological Relationship'. Jung had used the term to contemplate the situation of one marital partner possessing a more complex personality than the other, with the less complicated partner feeling 'contained' or encapsulated by that of the other. Bion saw this as but one example of the underlying pattern that he wanted to explore further; in 'Catastrophic Change', and earlier in his treatment of the configuration in *Learning from Experience* (1962), Bion stated that he wished to retain the meaning of the male and female elements in sex, but not be restricted to it.

The following extract, from the transcription of the recording of the discussion at the Scientific Meeting devoted to discussing the paper, is included here because it illustrates so well both a valid criticism of Bion's mode of exposition of his ideas and an equally valid and interesting defence of it.

> *Donald Meltzer:*
>
> Now, when I listen to Dr Bion, I get drunk with a kind of delight because everything he says is so new, and so exciting, and I want to really express my resentment at this sort of drunkenness that he induces in me, and complain about how he does it, and why I think he shouldn't; and I want to agree with Dr Winnicott too, in that the chink is just where masterful chink detectors find it – it is when Dr Bion does not really condescend to inform us how it is linked with the things we have ordinarily been thinking, that he promotes in us a kind of excitement that takes us off, into new channels without providing us with an Anchorage, and seems to me it affects us as if he were announcing messianic ideas. Now, it seems to me that it is necessary to grasp what he's talking about in terms of the history of psychoanalysis; and particularly I was struck by the anomaly of his wondering how it linked with the paranoid-schizoid and depressive positions, because it seems to me that it has a very clear link. In the history of Melanie Klein's work, for instance, it starts with the investigation of the genetic problems, the early phase of the Oedipus complex, it then went on to this tremendous advance – I think the first advance in the economic aspect of metapsychology – the paranoid-schizoid and depressive positions, and this took her back

into dynamic problems, connected with the discovery of projective identification, and that led her into a new investigation of instinct and the elaboration of the problem of envy, and this is the way it goes – it goes metapsychologically, from one area of metapsychology to another, and Dr Bion is now taking us back to the problem of structure.

Now as soon as I can recognize it, that he is taking us the next logical step from the advances posed by 'Envy and Gratitude' (Klein, 1957), I stop being drunk and begin being really puzzled and worried about the quality of my work, and wonder what's wrong with it, that needs to be improved by what Dr Bion talking about. Now of course I don't know, but it has something to do with structure of the mental apparatus. It seems to me that Dr Bion is talking about the kind of things that I have found myself, in times of worrying about, such as, where are the objects? Does the ego contain the objects, or does an object contain the ego? Or does the self contain them all? Really, what is the structure of the mental apparatus, and what is the significance of the continual getting in and out of one another that goes on within the different elements of the structure of the mental apparatus.

Later in the discussion:

Elliott Jaques:

I only want to make one point: I believe that an inference can be drawn from what Dr Bion has said to us tonight for interpretive work – that is, the significance of what he's saying is that the ability of the analyst to apprehend, to appreciate the essence of the patient and his verbalizations at any particular moment is a function of the various relationships between the contained and the container, so that a correct interpretation, so to speak, would therefore be one which, in Dr Bion's terms, a symbiotic relationship pertains at the moment prior to the interpretation, and as Dr Bion pointed out to me when I discussed this with him, also at the moment after the interpretation, so that the patient with the analyst can proliferate and grow. Now the ways in which the analyst does this, and may develop the skill to do this, more effectively would make for a very important study, and I wondered if – in answer to Dr Meltzer's point, Dr Bion wouldn't say that you can only learn this, paradoxically, by giving up trying to understand the links between the known and the unknown beforehand.

Dr Bion:

To take up the point that Dr Meltzer made just now: I agree about this, and this is why when I spoke about the need to avoid the use of either memory or to allow desire, as it were, also to develop, it was

> because I felt that it got between oneself and the patient; that there is something peculiar about the operations of what are normally understood as memory and desire which leave one particularly unfitted to intuit what is actually happening in the session, and I think it is related to this question of the anchorage, in that if you try to do this, then I think you will have an unpleasant and anxious experience, in which you feel you lose your anchorage; and one is constantly trying to find it; one is constantly trying to fall back on something or other like a cure or something of that sort, something with which one is familiar, as a protection against what is really an unpleasant situation, a situation in which anything may happen. The patient that you see tomorrow is a patient you've never seen before – why? because if you have seen them before, the problem has been dealt with. If he hasn't understood what you have said to him – if you haven't been able to introduce him to himself – it will turn up again, and what one wants to do is to deal with it in the form in which it turns up again, and not in the form in which one thought it turned up at some predetermined occasion which one has probably forgotten or imperfectly remembered anyway. Therefore, it is important to see the patient tomorrow as if the patient has never been seen; it is a very difficult thing: It is much easier to talk about than to do; and the difficulty is made worse by this fact that one loses one's anchorage, and it's a nasty feeling, as you'll soon find out if you try that and if you have any success in trying it.
>
> Now, with regard to this feeling of excitement – well, the point is that this subject is actually an exciting subject. And I think it is something that we all object to . . .

Essentially this part of the discussion relates to two forms of the relationship between the pattern of existing knowledge and the impact of new perceptions or ideas. Meltzer, with his comment on mental 'anchorage', emphasizes the desire for *apperception*.

According to Johann Friedrich Herbart [1776–1841], apperception is the process through which a collection of presentations becomes structured by the accretion of new elements, from the direction of sensuous reality or from thoughts. In this process, there is an important quantum of reassurance stemming from the sum of antecedent experience, which compensates for the unsettling experience of new, unassimilated experience.

Apperception is thus a term for all mental processes in which a presentation is brought into connection with an already existing and systematized mental structure and can thereby be classified, explained, understood. A later formulation by William James [1842–1910], based on that of Herbart, is: "To unite and assimilate a new perception to a mass of ideas already possessed, and thereby to comprehend and interpret it."

Bion's formulations, on the other hand, stimulate the requirement of the reader or listener for Negative Capability, in which the links to a body of pre-existing knowledge – described in the paper as both possessed and protected by a conservative containing group (and by a corresponding part of the mind) called the 'Establishment' – are suspended. Bion quotes in *Attention and Interpretation* (p. 327, this volume) Keats's use of the term 'Negative Capability' as it features in a letter the poet wrote to his brothers:

> . . . several things dove-tailed in my mind, and at once it struck me what quality went to form a Man of Achievement, especially in Literature, and which Shakespeare possessed so enormously – I mean Negative Capability, that is, when a man is capable of being in uncertainties, mysteries, doubts, without any irritable reaching after fact and reason. [Keats, 1817]

In his recommendations on memory and desire, Bion is suggesting that the analyst tolerates the feelings consequent upon letting go, temporarily, of those facts and reasons forming the reassuring structure of existing theories and accepted facts, for the purpose of being receptive to new organizations of experience. This is what he has termed, borrowing from Henri Poincaré, a 'selected fact' – essentially, a fact that seems to select itself.

Parthenope Bion Talamo (1981) put it in the following terms:

> This Selected Fact is one which the thinking individual recognizes as unexpectedly harmonizing all the other scattered facts – it is one of them, but it allows the thinker to 'see' the meaning which had previously not been visible.

In his 1967 'Commentary' in *Second Thoughts* on the preceding chapters in it, Bion wrote:

> The analyst must discern the underlying pattern by a process of discrimination and selection. If the account given is a selection made to demonstrate the correctness of the original selection, it is clearly worthless. Only if the original experience is a genuine evolution of a psychoanalytic realization, i.e. a precipitation of coherence by a "selected fact", does the writer's conscious discrimination and selection become legitimate as a method of representation. [p. 172, this volume

In his contribution to the discussion (above), Meltzer highlighted the the characteristic disorientation precipitated by communications in which explanatory 'anchoring' links, which allow *apperception* of the underlying pattern, are absent.[1] By referring to a sense of 'drunkenness', he is conveying the 'heady' effects of combined excitement and irritation that, according to Bion, have to be tolerated in analysis and in clinical thinking of a particular kind, and the fact that the usefulness of doing so can be explored by the practising analyst if he wishes to.

A slightly amended and expanded version of 'Catastrophic Change' was published as Chapter 12 of *Attention and Interpretation: A Scientific Approach to Insight in Psycho-Analysis and Groups* (1970), which is included in this volume. A line-by-line comparison of the two texts is provided as Appendix C in Volume XV.

[1]André Green, in his review of Bion's *Cogitations* (see Volume XI), made a similar point, and he welcomed the notes forming *Cogitations* as supplying some of the missing links in Bion's earlier formulations.

Catastrophic Change

In this paper I describe a configuration which constantly recurs in psychoanalysis. Although I may resort to formulations which appear to be descriptions of events in psychoanalysis or history, I do not claim for them the status of historical narrative. They are what I call C category elements, descriptions made up of sensuous images derived from a background of experience or reported experience reassembled for my purposes. I shall give no psychoanalytic interpretations; these should be given only by the psychoanalyst in the course of a psychoanalysis when the facts which are to be interpreted are available and when he only is available to give them.

Description 1. This consists of two signs ♂ and ♀ which I call the contained and the container. The use of male and female symbols is deliberate but must not be taken to mean that other than sexual implications are excluded. These signs designate a relationship between ♀ and ♂: The link may be commensal, symbiotic, or parasitic.

Description 2. A word contains a meaning; conversely, a meaning can contain a word – which may or may not be discovered. This could be represented as the word (♀) containing the meaning (♂). Or *vice versa*, the meaning (♀) containing the word (♂). The relationship is established by the nature of the link. A constant conjunction of elements in a psychoanalysis can be bound by the attribution to it of a word, or a theory or other formulation. The word by which it is bound can have such a powerful pre-existing penumbra of associations that it squeezes the meaning out of the constant conjunction it is supposed to mark. Conversely the constant conjunction can destroy the word, theory, or other formulation which the formulation is intended to 'contain'. Thus ♀♂ can be so powerful that they destroy the meaning I want them to contain. Conversely the conjunction they are to represent may be so powerful that the sign cannot contain it. Equally the link may be symbiotic or commensal. Describing it in yet other C category terms: a man is attempting to express such powerful feelings that his capacity for verbal expression disintegrates into a stammer or becomes a meaningless and incoherent babble of words.

Description 3. The container (♀) extracts so much from the contained (♂) that the contained is left without substance. A psychoanalysis is so long continued that the patient can get no further meaning from it. A converse example would be the continuation until the patient had no more patience, tolerance, fortitude or money left. The container can squeeze everything 'out of' the contained. Conversely the 'pressure' may be exerted by the contained so that the container disintegrates. An illustration would be the word used as a metaphor until finally the genetic background is lost and the word loses its meaning. (See Fowler's *Modern English Usage* [2nd edition] for illustrations.)

Description 4. The marriage *in* which the sexual relationship ♀♂ plays such a part that there is *no room* for any of the other activities in which the married couple might engage. Conversely, the other (i.e. 'other than sexual') activities play such a part that there is *no room* for sexual fulfilment. (The metaphors used in this description exemplify the outside–the inside, container–contained, ♀♂ pattern).

Expansions of 1–4

Memory may be represented by ♀ or ♂. Thus regarding it as the container ♀ it is filled with 'memories' derived from sensuous experience. The sensuous background is dominant and 'memories' with such a background are tenacious. The memory ♀ is therefore saturated. The analyst who comes to a session with an active memory is therefore in no position to make 'observations' of mental phenomena because these are unknown and cannot be sensuously apprehended. Anxiety is known to us all but it has no shape or smell, colour or sound. An obtrusion of memory therefore obstructs intuition of the unknown phenomena. But, it may be said, do not analysts remember, and ought they not to remember, what has been said? There is certainly something which has often been called 'remembering' and which is essential to psychoanalytic work. But this must be sharply distinguished from what I have been calling memory. I want to make a distinction between (1) remembering a dream or having a memory of a dream and (2) the experience of the dream in which it seems to float into the mind as if it were a whole which was at one moment absent and at the next present. This experience, which I consider to be part of an evolution of the emotional reality of the session, is often called a memory, or remembering a dream, but is to be sharply distinguished from the dream remembered or the experience of remembering it. Indeed what I am describing is a good example of the meaning ♀ in which is embedded the unknown word or formulation ♂, for what I would like would be to find a word that most people would regard as appropriate to represent the meaning I want to convey. The term 'memory' I shall use with its ordinary conversational meaning and it represents something I consider to be out of place in the psychoanalyst's conduct of a psychoanalysis. A patient's close relatives are burdened with memories which make them quite unreliable judges of the patient's personality and unfit to be the patient's analyst.

So far I have examined the configuration as it appears in the limits of words themselves. I shall not spend time in detailed examination of its appearance in more complex formulation except to indicate the degree of its persistence. The psychoanalytic situation would be expected to evoke examples of the configuration and it does so. But it is also a situation in which it is likely that difficulties will arise for both analysand and analyst in finding methods of communication. Conversely there will be emotional experiences to be conveyed or represented, some of great intensity. It is likely therefore that we shall find in the subject matter instances of the configuration I mention and the same configuration in the psychoanalytic procedure designed to deal with it. Thus we arrive at another description.

Description 5. The patient will be at a loss to convey his meaning or, the meaning he wishes to convey will be too intense to express properly, or the formulation will be so rigid that he feels that the meaning conveyed is devoid of any interest or vitality. Similarly the interpretations given by the analyst, in this instance ♂, will meet with a reception from the patient which, by an apparently co-operative response of repeating the interpretation for confirmation, he deprives of meaning by compression or denudation. Which it is will depend on whether the link between ♀ and ♂ is commensal, symbiotic or parasitic. Failure to observe or demonstrate the point may produce an apparently inexplicable lack of progress in what is outwardly a progressive analysis. The clue lies in the observation of the fluctuations which make the analyst at one moment ♀ and the analysand ♂ and at the next reverse the roles. At the same time as this pattern is observed – worked out in words or persons – there must also be noted which link is operating, commensal, symbiotic or parasitic.

Expansions of 1–5

The more familiar the analyst becomes with the configuration of events, which I represent by the relationship between ♀ and ♂, the more often and the more readily will observe them. There is a difference between ♀ and ♂ which is I hope sufficiently clear to make it possible to distinguish between events in the session which approximate to these two representations. The essential experience for the analyst is not the reading of this paper but the matching of the real event in the psychoanalysis which approximates to these formulations. Aided by the frequent references made by patients and himself to events which occur 'in analysis' or 'in the past' or 'inside' or 'outside', it should be easy to recognize with increasing frequency the realizations to which these signs relate. The recognition of the category of link which is operating may be more difficult unless a lead-in can be obtained by considering the kind of event which takes the place of ♀ or ♂. Thus an extremely greedy patient may want to obtain as much as he can from his analysis while giving as little as possible: we should expect this to show itself by frequent events in which the container was denuding the contained object and vice versa. The patient might show that he made enormous demands on his family but resented doing anything for it. Many patients might show behaviour of this kind on relatively rare occasions but some might show it in many activities and in striking degree as, for example, by habitual incoherence while demanding great precision of interpretation from the analyst. This kind of patient cannot well be described in terms of narrative recording actual events, first, because any such formulation is suspect for reasons I have given in discussing memory, and, second, because it is impossible to predict what form his greed will take. Therefore the psychoanalyst, who may have such a patient, or a patient showing such patterns of behaviour relatively rarely, or anything between these extremes, needs formulations of theory that enable him to have as wide as possible a spectrum of observation so that these configurations do not pass unnoticed. If these formulations are too abstract they lack body. Therefore I give them body by using C category description but these are liable to produce so great a penumbra of association that the formulations become saturated and narrow the analyst's perspicacity.

Before leaving the expansion of descriptions 1–5 it will be as well to look at claustrophobia, agoraphobia and acting-out as illustrations of the appearance of the configuration. Acting-out, as it is ordinarily understood, takes place 'in' the analysis and the analysis is then itself a part of acting-out. In claustrophobia the patient identifies himself with an object which is inside a container. An ability to see the ♀♂ configuration in both these states reveals the relationships between one element and another of the patient's personality which otherwise would remain unknown. When a patient can be said to be acting-out the analysis is 'in' a situation of which the boundaries are unknown. If the behaviour characterized as 'acting-out' is brought to the analysis it can be accompanied by claustrophobic symptoms in the patient. The coherence of these symptoms may not be detected if the underlying configuration is not realized. As this last point touches on group behaviour I shall make my next description a formulation in terms of history. As I intend to broaden the scope of the configuration the description will appear to be complex but its complexity will be less if it is borne in mind that the description has the same fundamental configuration even if at first sight it appears that this is not so. It may help if I explain that new ideas may appear to be presented in this description; their novelty or otherwise is a function of the reader's personality and must not be supposed to inhere in the communication.

Description 6. From time to time men appear in history who are variously described as mystics or men of genius. Some attract notice as outstanding personalities but some must be supposed to attract virtually no attention because the conditions for their existence are not propitious. A similar fate attends upon ideas. A study of these conditions may at some time be carried out but I am only concerned here to formulate their existence. The idea which I consider to be a counterpart of the mystic or genius I shall call the 'messianic idea'. The idea that is messianic may be confused with the idea that he, she or it is the Messiah. The person I shall call 'the mystic'; the idea I shall call 'the messianic idea'. I shall use the terms 'mystic' and 'genius' as interchangeable.

Mystics have appeared in all religions, at all times, in all places and in all centres of scientific discussion. Such persons 'contain' the 'messianic idea', or the 'messianic idea' may 'contain' the person who is sought to incarnate, represent or manifest the Messiah in a manner analogous to the meaning which is felt to 'contain' the word which is to represent its. (See Expansion 1–4 and Description 2.)

The society in which the mystic appears has been described by Nietzsche as a body whose function it is to produce a genius. I shall adopt this view as part of my formulation. But I consider it also to be the function of the society to make the mystic or the messianic idea available to the members of the group. This is done by laws (in society), dogma (in religion), rules or laws (in mathematics or science). The governing body of the society I shall call the Establishment. The counterpart of this in the domain of thought would be the pre-existing disposition or pre-conception.

The mystic makes direct contact with, or – as with certain Christian mystics (one of whom, Meister Eckhart, I shall mention again) – is at one with, God. This is not possible for the ordinary member of the group. Hence the need for the Establishment to pronounce dogmatically, make laws or rules, by which the advantages of the mystic's communion with God or ultimate truth or reality may, as it were, be shared at one remove by the ordinary members. This the Establishment may fail to do either by lack of discrimination which loads to the furtherance of false views or by rigid adherence to an existing framework which sets up a parasitic link between mystic and group, ♂ and ♀. The life is then squeezed out of the mystic or messianic idea, or the society is disrupted. This brings me to catastrophic change and my next description.

Description 7. The conflict between the mystic and his group is exhibited in its most exaggerated, and therefore most easily studied, form in the account of Jesus and his relationship with the group. He himself claimed, in a manner typical of many mystics, that his teachings were in conformity with the existing Establishment: "Think not that I am come to destroy the law or the prophets: I am not come to destroy but to fulfil" (Matthew 5. 17. A.V.).

This claim is often associated with an awareness of the disruptive force which is being brought to bear upon the group from within. It was a charge which St. Augustine felt obliged to refute four centuries later in *The City of God* when the sack of Rome by Alaric was attributed to the pernicious influence of Christians and their doctrines. The mystic does not necessarily claim to conform to the group. He may appear in the guise of a destroyer from within or without. He does not claim peaceable intentions or methods.

It would be possible to make a distinction between the nihilistic mystic who disrupts the community which is his own creation and the creative mystic who appears to eschew violent methods particularly against his own group. We need not trouble about these claims because I wish to stress the disruptive quality of the mystic, whether he claims to be disruptive or not, for it is this disruptive quality which is associated with the group's hostility to the mystic and vice versa. It is, furthermore, the quality which I wish to emphasize in this description.

The reaction of the Establishment is to prevent the disruption and this it does as follows: It can load the mystic with such honours that he sinks without a trace. This is expressed in the biblical illustration by the temptation in the wilderness where the rewards of conformity are clearly stated. Conformity can be renunciation of the messianic ideas, or acceptance of the role of the messianic idea. Alternatively, the mystic can be destroyed and an attempt made to ensure the same fate for his ideas.

The failure of the rabbinical directorate had disastrous consequences for this group. The functions of containment – I use the word with its military implication of one force containing another – had to be assumed by the split factions of the group, one ostensibly against, and the other for, Jesus. Gradually a fresh group was formed and a fresh Establishment to contain the mystic, or rather the messianic idea. The Jewish group learned to handle the mystic with consequences which were less disastrous for itself. The Christian group, though finding a different solution of the problem, achieved a similarly satisfactory result. Neither system was free from recurrences of the problem. One Christian Establishment restored the disruptive structure and ensured its continuity by taking over the festivals of paganism and thus mollifying the hostility which might otherwise have followed the loss of holidays and feasts which were beloved and valued. The theme could be stated as bigger and brighter paganism with gods refurbished and rejuvenated as saints and devils. (Milton expresses this very clearly in his representation of Pandemonium in Books I and III of *Paradise Lost.*)

The problems of the Christian Establishment developed even in the lifetime of Jesus. The first were: delineation of the borders of the group, selection and training, and stabilization of the hierarchy.

To take the last point first: In the account in Mark's Gospel, Chapter 10, v. 35–45, the problem was clearly posed by James and John with their request for status. In his reply Jesus seems to suggest a kind of initiation or test, but the alacrity with which the two accept the conditions makes it hard to know what the initiation was, though it is clear that Jesus regarded its performance as beyond them. He also adumbrates a change in the function of the Establishment as it existed amongst the Gentiles of that time. The proposal put forward by James and John seems to be for status, and status appears to be a substitute for qualification. The point is that their desires were to be satisfied, as it were, 'ex officio'. The reply given by Jesus seems to indicate that the 'position' achieved *ex officio* was an alternative the pair produced to undergoing the experience of the mystic himself. In this respect the rejected solution meets one of the requirements of society, namely, to make the fruits of the mystic's work available to ordinary members who do not have the mystic's qualifications for atonement with the deity.

The problem of membership of the group and how to decide whether a man was to call himself a Christian or not also arose early. Characteristically it hinged on the question of the therapeutic efficiency of the Christian and his brand of Christianity. The problem was brought to a head through the apparently successful therapeutic effects obtained by persons who were not qualified members of the group (Mark 9. 38). In the instance quoted the criterion proposed by Jesus seems to be the successful cure and its attribution by the therapist to Jesus. The issues involved are: membership of the group as itself being a symbol of status; status – expressed by the locution, "In

Thy name" as a therapeutic agent; therapeutic result as a criterion of membership of the group. The solution was empirical but it accepted the criterion of therapeutic efficiency. For the time being the test of membership seems to be two-fold, namely, medical or therapeutic and capacity for achieving results. This last requirement always seems to have been something of a nightmare throughout history. It might be described as a demand that the group leader should (1) be able to foretell the future, (2) render adequate someone alleged to have been adequate in the past, and (3) guarantee continued adequacy to all future contingencies.

The Christian hierarchy soon found itself faced by the same problems that had defeated the rabbinical directorate. The same forces were involved: on the one side the need to control the messianic idea and make it available to ordinary people through dogmatic formulation, and on the other side the messianic idea or its incarnation perpetually breaking through the barriers intended to control it and threatening to disrupt the society in which it became manifest. The Reformation was a spectacular example of this but only one of many such. (See Knox on *Enthusiasm*.)

Expansion of 6–7

I have used for my 6 and 7 descriptions material familiar to all, for a configuration which is repeated in many forms and at many times.

It is not limited to religious societies, or therapeutic societies, or artistic societies, or scientific societies, but – as far as my limited experience can tell – is discernible in all societies. My intention, however, is not to express any opinion upon the nature of diverse groups. I must remind the reader that I am not purporting to write history but to formulate a pattern in picturesque C category terms. That is to say, to represent a configuration in terms which will give body to an idea which might otherwise seem to be a meaningless elaboration of abstractions. Naturally I suppose that people other than psychoanalysts would profit from a recognition of the configuration and the underlying group to which one suspects that it belongs. But here I am concerned only as an analyst with the configuration as it might be discerned by other analysts. Descriptions 6 and 7 must therefore not be supposed to have a sociological or political application but to be by way of fables or mythological constructs (C category) which, if formulated with greater precision and sophistication, represent a pattern to which the human personality would be found to approximate. The fable, constructed in terms of the group, must be regarded as a pictorialization of man's inner world. For those familiar with Kleinian theory my description can be seen as a dramatized, personified, socialized and pictorialized representation of the human personality. It may clarify my procedure to contrast this pictorial view with accepted morphology of classical analysis. The theory formulated in terms of ego, super-ego, and id differs in two respects: first, it is an F category formulation whereas the pictorialized formulation I am representing verbally is a C category formulation – primitive and based on sensuously derived terminology; second, it is a theory of which the realization that approximates to it is to be found in psychopathology and psychomorphology. The realization approximating to the C category formulation is to be found in material which is superficial and easily accessible to the conscious. Its unconscious roots are to be discovered through psychoanalytic investigation.

The Messianic idea

The nature of the messianic idea can be only very approximately represented by the C category formulations I have been using. In addition to Jesus I shall speak of Meister Eckhart and Isaac Luria. They represent in different ways the problem of reconciling the messianic idea and the Establishment. The rabbinical directorate appears to have learned caution so that when it had to adjust to the Lurianic doctrine and to the injuries which Lurianic doctrine was alleged by its opponents to have inflicted on Judaism, it did not contribute to an explosion. Luria for his part insisted on his conservatism and related all he said to older authorities. Significantly he left no writings and when questioned by a disciple about his reasons for not setting out his teaching in book form he replied, "It is impossible, because all things are inter-related: I can hardly open my mouth to speak without feeling as though the sea burst its dams and overflowed. How then shall I express what my soul has received, and how can I put it down in a book?"[1] Meister Eckhart wrote extensively but the obscurity of his writing and perhaps the matter led to the condemnation as heretical of some 28 propositions from his later writings. The main question seems to centre on his forthright statements of identity with the deity – "We are transformed and changed into God".[2] The fate of Jesus himself has been crucifixion as a criminal on the one hand and deification on the other. Both Isaac Luria and Jesus were alike in being followed by a proliferation of hagiographical biography, much of it, in the instance of Jesus, not being included in the canon. It is not necessary to pursue this topic for my prevent purpose but it can be followed in detail in *Enthusiasm* by R. A. Knox. The common features are the containment of the messianic idea in the individual, the containment of the messianic individual in the group and the problem for the Establishment that is concerned with the group on the one hand, and the messianic idea and individual on the other. It is now necessary to return to the word.

Description 2 (cycle 2). If it were necessary to express descriptions 6 and 7 by one word a choice could be made from terms such as 'religion' or 'Christianity' or 'God'. If none of these term is considered suitable an attempt could be made to find the suitable terms by introspection. This attempt is a search in the mind for the term supposed to exist or it is a search in the meaning for the term; the latter is an instance of the meaning containing the word. The difficulties attendant on finding the word are described in the terms used by Poincaré searching for a mathematical formula, or by Luria in the passage quoted above. A better idea of the problem is obtained by substituting the term 'statement' for 'word' and including in its definition any act of expression whatsoever. In C category terms the problem is analogous to that of the sculptor finding his form in the block of his material, the musician finding the formula of musical notation within the sounds he hears, the man of action finding the actions which represent his thoughts. One of the peculiarities of this discussion lies in its being an example of the problem being discussed. It is an attempt

---

[1]G. Scholem (1955), *Major Trends in Jewish Mysticism* (Thames and Hudson), p. 254.

[2]See J. Coplestone (1958–1963), *History of Philosophy*, Vol. VI, p. 193.

to find a verbal formulation to which psychoanalytic realizations approximate. I restate the problem thus: psychoanalysis, the thing-in-itself, existed. It remained for Freud to reveal the formulation embedded in it. Conversely, once formulated by Freud it remains for others (including Freud himself) to discover the meaning of the conjunction bound by his formulation.

It is necessary to postulate 'thinking' without supposing a thinker to be essential. I shall not at this point try to explain why. All thinking and all thoughts are true when there is no thinker. In contrast to this, for lies and falsities a thinker is absolutely necessary. In any situation where a thinker is present the thoughts when formulated are expressions of falsities and lies. The only true thought is one which has never found an individual to 'contain' it.

The messianic ideas may be supposed to have a counterpart, the absolute truth, to which a thinker is not necessary: this I shall mark by a sign O. Falsity is the characteristic of thought within an individual, or thought within a container. It follows that all thought as it is ordinarily known, that is as an attribute of the human being, is false, the problem associated with it being the degree and nature of the falsity. The lie is a falsity associated with 'morals'.

The messianic idea is a term representing O at the point at which its evolution and the evolution of a thinker intersect. The mystic, as seen in descriptions 6 and 7, is a thinker who claims the capacity for direct contact with O. The degree of falsity depends on whether the relationship with O is commensal, symbiotic or parasitic.

Commensal. The thought O and the thinker exist quite independently of each other. There is no reaction, or, as we should say ordinarily – identifying ourselves with the thinker – the truth has not been discovered though it 'exists'.

Symbiotic. The thought and the thinker correspond and modify each other through the correspondence. The thought proliferates and the thinker develops.

Parasitic. Thought and thinker correspond but the correspondence is category 2, meaning that the formulation is known to be false but is retained as a barrier against a truth which is feared as annihilating to the container or *vice versa*. The falsity proliferates until it becomes the lie. The barrier of the lie increases the need for the truth and *vice versa*.

The commensal position changes when thought and thinker approximate. In more usual terms, a critical situation arises when a 'discovery' threatens. It is commonly said that messianic hopes were more than usually active at the birth of Jesus, and it is a matter for remark that often more than one investigator seems to be approaching a discovery at the time when a discovery is made. The resistance of the thinker to the unthought thought is characteristic of category 2 thinking. The crucial problem appears to be the relative strength of the messianic idea and the personality who is to 'contain' it. We must therefore reconsider the personality. To do this I shall use the descriptions 6 and 7 as pictorial representations (C category) of the parts composing the totality of the individual, not the group. I am assuming that the reader keeps in mind existing theories of personality structure. It is not to be supposed that they are to be abandoned or even modified by what follows. Existing theories are F category formulations; what takes place in the consulting room is an emotional situation which is itself the intersection of an evolving O with another evolving O. The description I am giving is, as it has been through this paper, a C category formulation intended to bridge the gap between a unique event on the one hand and a generalized F category formulation on the other.

Description 3 (cycle 2). The messianic idea clothes itself, or is clothed, in a great variety of forms. There is no reason why it should not take any form, and yet there appears to be great difficulty for form and idea to achieve a symbiotic or commensal relationship. Therefore I shall not succeed in this description in finding a formulation by which I can convey my meaning to the reader. At most I can find a sign pointing him to the consulting room or other domain where he may intuit it for himself. Similarly I can direct him to seek out and carefully observe the word 'cure' when he hears it pronounced; for 'within' this word he may be able to intuit the messianic idea. He should allow his attention to dwell on formulations in which he himself is described in positive terms; for 'within' these statements he may be able to intuit the 'contained' messianic idea. Whether the statement appears outwardly to be representing a summer holiday or a car or a person or a state – in time he should be able by degrees to intuit the messianic idea with sufficient frequency to be persuaded of its reality and his ability to feel its presence.

When I said I might find a sign pointing the reader 'to the consulting room or other domain' I was deliberately restricting the field of search to provide a 'container' wherein the search might be pursued without too much difficulty. In this way the reader might experience the ineffable relatively quickly. Yet it is doubtful whether intuition of a constant conjunction occurring in the domain of psychic reality can ever be said to be attainable quickly or easily unless it is by virtue of exceptional capacity. It must be accepted therefore that there can be no short-cut for the psychoanalyst. He can hope that years of experience may enable him to intuit the messianic idea when he sees it or recognize that this hope is a formulation containing the messianic idea.

The idea that the messianic idea is contained within the analysis, or that descriptions 6 and 7 can be used as C category statements or formulations of the individual personality, implies that the personality can be represented by a ♀♂ relationship and that the personality has a ♀♂ relationship with a psychoanalysis. Such a formulation is useful if it assists the psychoanalyst to intuit, in the course of a psychoanalysis, a personality external to the psychoanalysis which is present in the analysis only by 'hearsay'. The patient becomes little more than a voice reporting that the messianic idea is abroad. I mention it as a typical complexity of the ♀♂ relation which is significant for its bearing on phenomena named collectively as 'acting-out'. I wish to relate these phenomena to beta-elements lying outside the domain of thought proper and only appearing to belong to it because they are represented 'in' the analysis by C 3 statements made by the analysand.

The psychoanalyst and his analysand therefore appear to be excluded from domain of action and confined within the domain of thought in such a way that they are not in a position to pursue their psychoanalytic aims by psychoanalytic means. What then *are* their psychoanalytic aims?

Psychoanalytic practice shows that the motives for any human activity are numerous and complex. They are derived from a background of sensuous desires; as fast as one is demonstrated it is apparent that further desires lie unknown. The aims of the psychoanalytic couple are arrived at by conjecture and formulated, at least as far as the analysand is concerned, in terms representative of sensuous experience. Even the objects of curiosity are formulated in terms suitable to a sensuous background. Insofar as the desires can be stated they will be sensuous desires and sensuous aims – the over-riding aim being to keep alive. Without exception these aims and desires are not relevant to psychoanalysis. Nor have they proved relevant either to Judaism or Christianity. It is true that their place has not been taken by any formulations which are more satisfactory. So long as thinking is regarded as subordinate to the senses there is no difficulty. If thinking is a primary activity the *aims* of contemplation or meditation are presumed to exist because thinking is associated with its genetic history as subordinate to muscular activity, and muscular activity is presumed to have an aim in accord with the dominance of the pleasure principle.

It is possible that the vacuity, produced by the subordination of sensuous aims to growth of a capacity for contemplation or meditation, was filled in the course of his teaching by Jesus. But as his teaching was subjected to the twin pressures I have described – namely, annihilation by physical destruction on the one hand, and divine honours on the other – we do not know what such a solution might have been. In practice the problem is shelved as thinking remains a function subordinate to the satisfaction of sensuous desires as a means to physical survival.

The consequence is that psychoanalysis is saddled with an aim which, according to their various desires, is attributed to it by both analyst and analysand. Both are debarred from fulfilling their aim when the aim is pursued in the domain of action and the analysis is confined to the domain of thought in which thought is the only means of fulfilment. The 'conflict' is between action and thought, the counter-part – in descriptions 6 and 7 – being the conflict expressed in St. Augustine's refutation of the responsibility of Christianity for the Fall of Rome. In the individual the demands for action and sensuous gratifications associated with physical survival conflict with the demand for mental 'activity'. The latter cannot justify itself in terms comprehensible to the former. The former cannot justify itself to the latter, for its apparatus of sensuous fulfilment is irrelevant to the domain of thought.

I have used the term 'conflict', in describing action and thought as a reminder of the accepted view. The object of using ♀♂ is to differentiate the states of containment which, as with thought and action, prevent conflict by containing thought and containing action in a mutually exclusive commensal state. In this condition thought and action do not modify each other but persist commensally in the same personality. Actions which appear to be compulsive are in reality beta-elements confined to the domain of action and thus insulated against thoughts which are confined to the domain of thought – which includes psychoanalysis. Similarly thoughts are within the domain of thought and cannot be influenced by beta-elements confined within the domain of action. An apparent exception, not real, is provided by C 3 elements in thought which appear to bring A category into the realm of thought but are only C category *records* of action; there is no conflict.

The domains of thought and action are so close, when the musculature used in talking is involved with beta-elements, that the distinction between them becomes confused. The same confusion arises if intolerance of frustration leads to a substitution of thought for action. The associated omnipotence of thought obstructs the proper use of the musculature, as a feeling of helplessness stimulated by ineffectual muscular action is often the genetic base of omnipotence: when one is active the other is present.

In the previous paragraphs I have given examples of ♀♂ associated with inside and outside: (1) the personality, (2) the analytic situation, (3) domain of action, (4) domain of thought. Although such instances have a psychological value in giving body to a formulation which might otherwise lack it, their use is bad if it encourages the reader to expect further instances instead of consulting his practice to provide them. According to his background a patient will name various objects as containers, such as 'his mind', the 'unconscious', the 'nation' and many others as 'contained', such as his projections, his money, his ideas. The objects are innumerable but the relationships are not.

The individual always displays some aspect of his personality which is stable and constant even though it may sometimes be very difficult to detect in the welter of evidence for instability; it may appear only in the regularity with which the patient attends his sessions. In this stability will be found the counterpart of what, in descriptions 6 and 7, I have called the Establishment. It will be maintained with great tenacity as the only force likely to contain the counterpart of the messianic idea. Reciprocally the messianic idea is the only force likely to withstand the pressures of the counterpart in the individual of the Establishment. Fears of megalomanic identification with the messianic idea are associated with an inability to be at one with the omnipotent Father. The counterpart of the Establishment in the individual is not related to father or mother but can be related to fragments of both.

In the ♀♂ configuration, decision is synonymous with selection for inclusion or exclusion. Thus the psychoanalyst has to decide whether to include or exclude himself from various groups, to include or exclude a patient from his practice, to include or exclude a given interpretation, to include or exclude given associations, ideas, experiences and so forth. The Establishment of the group has to decide to include or exclude certain individuals. The personality decides to include or exclude certain characteristics or, failing that, to include or exclude awareness of their existence. Dislike of the onus of decision, or of awareness of responsibility for the decision, contributes to the formulation of selection-procedures by which selection, like dogma, laws of science, are made to act as substitutes for judgement or scapegoats for the guilt attendant on overtly acknowledged exercise of responsibility.

The configuration to which I have drawn attention can be seen to have a penumbra of associations which retain an illuminating function in the circumstances on which they are brought to bear. At other times the light they shed distorts by over-emphasis of the past – and therefore irrelevant – elements, and occlusion of the unknown – and therefore relevant – elements. Once the constancy of the configuration is recognized its nature can be assessed and related to psychoanalytic theory. Reciprocally, theory can be reformulated when it requires readjustment.

The primitive formulation of ♀♂ in C category terms of breast and mouth, penis and vagina, has the simplicity of all C category formulations. Although descriptions 6 and 7 appear more complex, they too share the stamp of all C category formulations. Both appear to differ from the configuration represented by the Kleinian theory of paranoid-schizoid and depressive position interplay. I am unwilling to accept this apparent cleavage though I cannot suggest any satisfactory formulation which would display the underlying harmony. The approach to its discovery may lie through investigation of the disruptive effect of creative synthesis. Or, to put it in C category terms, the relationship between the mystic and his group.

SECOND THOUGHTS: SELECTED PAPERS ON PSYCHO-ANALYSIS

1967

Second Thoughts: Selected Papers on Psycho-Analysis was first published by William Heinemann Medical Books, London, in 1967; it was reprinted by Karnac Books, London, in 1984.

Chapter 2, 'The Imaginary Twin': Membership paper read to the British Psychoanalytical Society, 1 November 1950.

Chapter 3, 'Notes on the Theory of Schizophrenia': Paper read in the Symposium 'The Psychology of Schizophrenia' at the 18th International Psycho-Analytical Congress in London on 28 July 1953. *International Journal of Psycho-Analysis, 35* (1954): 113–118. A slightly different version appeared as 'Language and the Schizophrenic' in M. Klein, P. Heimann, & R. Money-Kyrle (Eds.), *New Directions in Psycho-Analysis*, London: Tavistock Publications, 1955, pp. 220–239.

Chapter 4, 'The Development of Schizophrenic Thought': *International Journal of Psycho-Analysis, 37* (4–5, 1956): 344–346.

Chapter 5, 'The Differentiation of the Psychotic from the Non-Psychotic personalities': Paper presented at a Scientific Meeting of the British Psychoanalytical Society on 6 October 1955. *International Journal of Psycho-Analysis, 38* (Parts 3–4, 1957): 266–275.

Chapter 6, 'On Hallucination': *International Journal of Psycho-Analysis, 39* (1958): 341–349.

Chapter 7, 'On Arrogance': Paper read before the 20th Congress of the International Psycho-Analytical Association, Paris, July–August 1957. *International Journal of Psycho-Analysis, 39* (1958): 144–146.

Chapter 8, 'Attacks on Linking': *International Journal of Psycho-Analysis, 40* (1959): 308–315.

Chapter 9, 'A Theory of Thinking': Published as 'The Psychoanalytic Study of Thinking', *International Journal of Psycho-Analysis, 43* (1962): 306–310.

EDITOR'S INTRODUCTION

Introducing his 1967 compilation, Bion wrote, "Now the time has come to reprint old papers, I find that the change in my views about psycho-analytic method makes me unwilling to let them go out without showing what that change is. For those who want the papers as they were originally printed, here they are, but I have added a commentary which involves an evolutionary change of opinion."

In publishing these clinically centred papers from the period 1950 to 1962, which have vital connections with the formulations to be found in the works that followed – *Learning from Experience, Elements of Psycho-Analysis, Transformations* and *Attention and Interpretation* – Francesca Bion suggested the addition of a numbering system (numerals in bold type before each section of each paper) – continuous across the eight papers – to facilitate a discussion of the shifts in his ideas published in the final section, the 'Commentary'. This reported Bion's 'evolutionary change of opinion' on various matters.

It is because of this that *Second Thoughts* appears here as an exception to the chronological structure of the *Complete Works,* since it makes sense to keep the papers together and to retain the numbering system that facilitates an understanding of the 'Commentary'.

Much of the clinical work informing these papers is from the analyses of patients in psychotic states of mind. Bion discussed his ideas concerning the relationship between what he observed in these cases, and the work of Melanie Klein, with Hanna Segal and, at length, with Herbert Rosenfeld. These two Kleinian colleagues were also accumulating clinical experience of analysing psychotic and borderline patients using an unmodified psychoanalytic technique.

The first chapter, the paper 'The Imaginary Twin', was Bion's Membership paper. It was first read to a Scientific Meeting of the British

Psychoanalytical Society on 1 November 1950, four months before Bion met Francesca McCallum, who was to become his wife. She reports that the original version of 'The Imaginary Twin' paper showed no sign of having been properly edited – certainly not by Bion himself, who, with few exceptions, did not re-read anything that he had written. No copy of the original paper has been found to date.

The other papers were prepared for the *International Journal of Psycho-Analysis* and required less editorial intervention. I shall not review the individual papers here.

A particularly important matter is discussed by Bion in 'Attacks on Linking'. Melanie Klein had, in her original formulation of the process of projective identification, emphasized pathological forms of splitting (many of which she felt remained to be discovered) and excessive projective identification. Bion introduced the notion of a normal degree of projective identification, which – in moderated conjunction with introjective identification – formed the foundation for normal mental growth. It is in this paper that Bion first describes what was to become his container–contained model:

> When the patient strove to rid himself of fears of death which were felt to be too powerful for his personality to contain, he split off his fears and put them into me, the idea apparently being that if they were allowed to repose there long enough they would undergo modification by my psyche and could then be safely reintrojected. [p. 147]

Bion considered the potentially disastrous consequences of a primary object felt to *deny* the infant this normal degree of projective identification. He presents clinical descriptions of a patient who, he came to feel from the evidence of his countertransference, had been denied the formative experience of a container for his more extreme fear and confusion; the patient appeared to have felt that this normal use of the mechanism had been obstructed, and refused, by his object. There had been no person to meet the expectation of a container – the essential helper whose attention would *contain* the projected part of himself felt to be dying, suffer the impact of it, reduce the fear to manageable proportions, and (eventually) return to the infant that part of itself rendered more tolerable to the infant's psyche. Bion states that, in his reconstruction, the patient's mother had needed to understand and experience the child's need, not only for her presence but for her to orient herself to her baby who was frightened of dying, and *to take this into herself,* and to feel the dread of it. Bion was putting this forward not as causative in the patient's problems, but as a crucial environmental factor. Bion saw that what would be of likely prognostic importance for such patients would be (a) that the analyst would have a capacity to bear and to understand this problem in the transference-countertransference, and (b) that problems of envious resentment arising from the analyst's capacity to do so could be worked with.

The 'Commentary' shows the evolution of Bion's clinical thinking since the original papers. Looking back at his papers and some of his notes, he shares with the reader – who is assumed to have some familiarity with these matters – his awareness of the limitations of referring back to his earlier writings:

> A special instance of the problem of communication between the psychoanalyst writing and the psychoanalyst reading, of which I have been reminded by preparing these papers for publication, arises when the writer and the reader is the same man. Here, one might suppose, are the perfect conditions for communication. Yet in the days when I used to write elaborate notes on my sessions with patients, I found that I was no more successful when the interval between writing and reading was relatively short than I do now when the interval is measured in years. At first I thought I could easily understand notes dashed off at speed, a squiggle here, an exclamation mark there, sometimes an interpolated conjecture or comment on my own feelings on what was happening. I will not say they were meaningless when I came to read them, but they did not convey the meaning I hoped to find. They resembled nothing so much as a sleepy note that I sometimes tried to make to pin down what I felt to be an important dream for study in the morning. [p. 165]

In a collegial manner he shares his feeling that he 'tolerates' many of his earlier formulations because he cannot find a more successful way of expressing himself – "what they communicate may not be worth communicating; conversely, what was, in the psychoanalytic experience, worth communicating may not in fact have been communicated".

In his commentary on the papers, Bion singles out the axiom he uses as a central heuristic device in his later formulations on thinking. For this axiom he uses the shorthand term, 'thoughts without a thinker'. Bion explores the consequences for a theory of thinking which stem from considering the existence of thoughts independent of the mind that houses them. He clearly was convinced of the value of working from this position:

> The ramifications of this attitude, more clearly discerned if the psychoanalyst postulates "thoughts without a thinker", are so considerable that I require another book to attempt elucidation. Inadequate though this formulation is, I hope it will help the reader to find the continuation of the developments which I have tried to sketch out in these papers.
>
> I would warn against the phrase "empirically verifiable data" . . . I do not mean that experience 'verifies' or 'validates' anything. This belief as I have come across it in the literature of the philosophy of science relates to an experience which enables the scientist to achieve a feeling of security to offset and neutralize the sense of insecurity following on the discovery that discovery has exposed further vistas of unsolved problems – 'thoughts' in search of a thinker. [p. 202]

Second Thoughts

Selected Papers on Psycho-Analysis

1

Introduction

It is customary to find in a book of collected papers on psychoanalysis, a number of case histories; this book is no exception. Ostensibly there is an account of the patient's history, some detailed reports of sessions with the patient's associations and the interpretations the analyst has given. It has always seemed to me that such reports are open to the objection that the narrative and the interpretations given are only two different ways of saying the same thing, or two different things said about the same fact. With the years my suspicion has ripened into conviction. I have attempted to formulate this conviction in three books, *Learning from Experience, Elements of Psycho-Analysis*, and *Transformations*, each one carrying the discussion a little further and making the formulations more precise.

Now the time has come to reprint old papers, I find that the change in my views about psychoanalytic method makes me unwilling to let them go out without showing what that change is. For those who want the papers as they were originally printed, here they are, but I have added a commentary which involves an evolutionary change of opinion. I do not regard any narrative purporting to be a report of fact, either of what the patient said or of what I said, as worth consideration as a 'factual account' of what happened. In the first place, I do not attribute to memory the significance it is usually given. The fact of involuntary distortions is so well established by psychoanalysis itself that it is absurd to behave as if our reports were somehow exempted from our own findings. Memory is born of, and only suited to, sensuous experience. As psychoanalysis is concerned with experience that is not sensuous – who supposes that anxiety has shape, colour or smell? – records based on perception of that which is sensible are records only of the psychoanalytically irrelevant. Therefore in any account of a session, no matter how soon it may be made after the event or by what means, memory should not be treated as more than a pictorialized communication of an emotional experience. The accounts of cases in this book, though sincerely supposed by me at the time to be factually correct (I exclude alterations made and acknowledged on account of discretion), should now be regarded as verbal formulations of sensory images constructed to communicate in one form what is probably communicated in another; for example, as psychoanalytic theory, either in the same paper or in some part of psychoanalytic literature. If this seems a harsh reassessment, I reply that progress in psychoanalytic work will cease unless this reassessment is seen to be essential; it should be the jumping-off point for a new attitude to scientific work – others no less than our own.

2

The imaginary twin

1. The patient from whose analysis I draw most of my material had had many years of psychotherapy which ended when the therapist advised leucotomy. In view of a shocking family history and the strains to which the patient had been subjected in early childhood the doctor who referred him thought the outlook bad.

2. The patient had a sister 18 months older than himself who died of a disease, from which both suffered, when the patient was one year old; both had severe diarrhoea during the course of the illness.

3. The family associated closely with their neighbours whose children, two girls, one two years younger than my patient, the other seven years younger, were his only playmates until he was ten. The younger died in an asylum before the war; the other still survives but in a state of incurable insanity, supposedly schizophrenia.

4. Disunited parents complicated his childhood. This was spent abroad in a country which was developing its football and other sports, so that when it was discovered that he was an athlete, and intelligent, the way seemed clear for a popular and successful career. But the family fortunes deteriorated and the domestic relationships with them, until at thirteen the boy had had a breakdown from which he made no adequate recovery though he returned to, and has continued in, work. His mother died after years of chronic and painful illness, when he was 17; the father, many years later. His circumstances were further complicated at the time of his mother's death by the need to leave his native land and start afresh here.

5. When he came to me I saw a man of 43, just under 6 feet in height, of wiry build, sallow complexion and dull expressionless features: by profession a teacher. The discussion of his difficulties was perfunctory, carried on for his part in monosyllabic listlessness. He agreed without enthusiasm to give analysis a trial.

6. My account of the next two years must necessarily be compressed. The central theme of the analysis was contamination: he had to protect his head from the pillow by resting his head on his hand; he could not shake hands; he felt that he contaminated the bath on which he relied to give him a feeling of cleanliness, and that it contaminated him back again.

7. He feared that he drank too much; he wondered if his penis was erect; he could not bear to have someone sitting behind him on a bus; it was equally contaminating if he sat behind someone.

He began to wonder if he felt sexual with his students; before long suspicion turned to certainty, and this made him feel unclean.

In his associations a big part was played by phantasied therapeutic injections which he had given, only to fear that his needle might not have been properly sterilized.

8. During the whole of the first two years, I had great difficulty in being able to determine, from his reactions, what validity to assign to my interpretations. I did, on two widely separated occasions, hear, from an extra-analytic source, that the patient was said to be greatly improved. I, myself, saw no improvement; nor was I able to remark, what I now believe to be true, that a change began to manifest itself in him at the end of this period. Till that time his intonation had been uniformly drained of emotion and his statements correspondingly difficult to interpret, for they almost always had the ambiguous character which admitted of different meanings if one considered them now with one emotional content, now with another.

9. There was plenty of oedipal material, produced on a most superficial level, which I duly interpreted, to meet with a perfunctory response or none at all.

My awareness of a change in the analysis developed over a period of some three months. At first it seemed as if my interpretations were only meeting with more than usually stubborn indifference, and then as if I was a parent issuing ineffectual exhortations and warnings to a refractory child. In due course I pointed this out to him and a change, not easily formulated, occurred. There was still the dreary monotone of associations but there was now a quality which derived from what I can best describe as the rhythm of his associations. It was as if two quite separate co-existent scansions of his material were possible.

One imparted an overpowering sense of boredom and depression; the other, dependent on the fact that he introduced regularly spaced pauses in the stream of his associations, an almost jocular effect as if he were saying "Go on; it's your turn".

10. Examining the matter still further, I noticed that the associations were all stale associations inviting a stale response. If I broke the rhythm, he showed signs of anxiety or irritability; if I continued to give the interpretations, which it now became clear he both invited and expected, there emerged a sense of having reached a dead-end. I was not surprised when he said to me in the early part of the next session, that he felt the treatment was getting nowhere and was doing no good: did I think, he very reasonably asked, that it was worthwhile going on?

11. I replied that though estimations of progress in analysis were difficult to make there was no reason why we should not accept his evaluation as correct. But, I added, before we pass on to consider what should be done about it, we need to know what is meant by treatment. It might mean psychoanalysis; in which case it would appear that some other method of approach to his problems would have to be sought. A perhaps more obvious meaning would be, psychoanalysis as practised by me, in which case the remedy would lie in a change of analyst rather than a change of method. There was, however, yet another possibility. We had already had reason to suppose that alleviation of symptoms was sometimes achieved by factors incidental to analysis; for example, the sense of security obtained from feeling there was someone to go to. It was possible that he was unconsciously referring to some factor of that kind.

12. There was a silence, and since we have now reached the point at which I must introduce the topic to be discussed, I shall take this opportunity to place before you some details of the analysis of the previous years, which are necessary for an understanding of what follows.

These details were not at the time important, but belonged rather to the periphery of the main stream of his associations. They derived from the point at which he introduced some new episode or anecdote that he was recounting. Thus he would say about some story that it had been told him by his homosexual brother-in-law. Or else that it was while visiting such and such a friend that he experienced particularly distressing symptoms. His circle of acquaintances was very great and as the theme of the analysis derived from the content of the story, I had no reason to pay much attention to the various characters thus casually mentioned. It is to this aspect of his associations, now become central and not peripheral, that I must retrospectively turn.

13. He would say, "I was thinking of talking to Mr X and telling him that etc., etc." One day my attention was arrested by some peculiarity of phraseology, or maybe it was the somewhat improbable character of the remark, and I asked if he meant he had actually said whatever it was he told me. "Oh, no", he replied, "I am just imagining it!" It then turned out that many conversations introduced by the phrase, "I was thinking of talking to "Mr X" or "Mrs Y" were imaginary conversations although not by any means all of them. I had mentioned then that it sounded as if no clear distinction was being made between the real and the imaginary, but at the time this feature had not the importance that it was now about to assume.

Among the characters to whom he had spoken, whether in fancy or fact, a considerable part was played by a man of his profession, of similar age, with the same symptoms as himself, married and with a family. He resided still on the Continent, worked full hours and with such success that no one even suspected he had any illness. This man was able to travel freely which my patient could not. My patient would seem to contrast himself unfavourably with him.

There was, as I have said, the homosexual brother-in-law, a man of the same age, perhaps stouter, but definitely homosexual and with an incestuous attraction, perhaps even relationship, with my patient's wife.

There was a man with whom my patient played tennis; of this character I heard no more than that he played tennis. There were a number of students of his, psychological cases he would remark, that had sent him other students. There was even one who had sent him a psychological case and he had wondered if he had realized that he was a psychological case when he sent him. (The ambiguity in the use of the relative pronoun is not a failure in grammar but rather a masterly expression of the patient's ability to convey much information, too much information, concisely).

There was an unpleasant colleague, whom he had known as a child and who had been contemporaneous with him in school, and now taught close by, who occasionally looked after his students, but he was so unscrupulously thrusting that my patient proposed not to use him again.

14. Let us now return to the patient whom we left silent after my summary of the issues confronting him before he could make a decision about treatment: I asked him what he was thinking about.

He replied that he was thinking about a woman with rheumatic pain. "She's always complaining about something or other and I thought", he said, "that she's very neurotic. I just advised her to buy some amytal and packed her off."

This, I said, was probably a compact description of the treatment he was having from me, treatment of which he doubted the efficacy. My interpretations were felt by him to be vague complaints to which he paid scant attention; his associations were many of them stale associations employed more for the soporific effect they shared with amytal than for their informative value, and designed to keep me employed without bothering him. But, I added, we should also consider how this situation was rendered tolerable for himself; I drew his attention to peculiarities in his behaviour, notably the rhythm of 'association–interpretation association', which indicated that I was a twin of himself who supported him in a jocular evasion of my complaints and thus softened his resentment. He could identify himself with any one of the three roles.

His response was striking. His voice changed and he said, in a depressed tone, that he felt tired and unclean. It was as if, in a moment, I had in front of me, unchanged in every respect the patient as I had seen him at the first interview. The change was so sudden as to be disconcerting. What on earth, I wondered, had happened to the twin and the complaining parent? It was as if he had swallowed them and was suffering the consequences.

That was the end of the session. When I had recovered from my surprise, I remembered that we had often had reason to suppose that he felt he had a poisonous family inside him, but that was the first occasion on which I had had quite such a dramatic exhibition of himself in the act of introjecting objects.

15. At the next session, the patient reported that he had had a terrifying dream. It was this: he was driving in a car and was about to overtake another. He drew level with it and then instead of passing it kept carefully abreast of it. The rival car slowed down and stopped, he himself conforming to its movements. The two cars were thus parked side by side. Thereupon the other driver, a man much the same build as himself, got out, walked round to his door and leaned heavily against it. He was unable to escape as, by parking his car near to the other, he had blocked egress from the far door, while the figure blocked egress from his door. The figure leered menacingly at him through the window. He woke in terror, to remain filled with anxiety throughout the waking day.

16. I interpreted the dream thus: the menacing figure was myself who was also the imaginary twin of which he had last spoken at the previous session. The twin was imaginary because my patient had prevented the birth of the twin – there was in fact no twin. His use of a twin as a means of alleviating anxiety was therefore illegitimate and the twin was determined that he, the patient, should not now be born or, to put it in other words, achieve freedom or independence. He was thus shut in, both by the twin and by his own act in parking his car so near the twin's car. The analysis had been the car from which I had not been allowed to emerge as a real being; the dream showed his fear that in the previous session I had become alive only to block his escape from analysis by using me as a personification of the bad part of himself from which he wished to be dissociated.

17. There now followed a period in which the prominent features of the analysis were exhibitions of introjection and projection, splitting, and, not least, personification of the split-off portions of his personality. In a sense there was nothing new about all this, but as at the same time his analysis became far more integrated and his fear of his mechanisms less pronounced, we were the more able to see them clearly for what they were. In retrospect, I could see how much the anxiety produced by interpretations, made before the emergence of the twin, derived not only from the content of his associations, but from the mere fact that I was drawing attention to his intra-psychic processes.

18. One result of the increased. integration of his analysis was that I was able to see that certain of his associations announced the theme around which the work, probably of several sessions, would centre. I shall take advantage of this fact to confine the discussion to two associations only, leaving the reader to assume that the material on which I based my interpretations was infinitely more copious than this necessarily compressed account would suggest.

19. The first association was produced before a week-end when he was going away to stay with friends. Week-end holidays, and even annual holidays, had not been thought of as possible until some six months previously when he had taken his first holiday for many years, but they had now become fairly regular occurrences. He said, "I am leaving a locum in charge of my students: he is not very experienced – the same age as myself but I don't feel sure he will be able to cope. There is a girl who may become ill and she may have to be admitted to hospital. That would be fairly straightforward except that you have to know the ropes a bit or you may not get the child into hospital. Usually I have an arrangement with a doctor I know well by which he helps when I am away, but this has been mucked up by a misunderstanding."

From the subsequent working through of this, it emerged that I had been the person who had messed up the understanding between the two doctors by my interpretation of the twin and the consequent forcing back into himself of the twin. The locum was a split-off portion of himself lacking in some essential qualities and in particular the ability to introduce the girl into hospital. I suggested that the part of himself that he left in charge of the girl was a genitally impotent part.

20. After the week-end he told me that the locum had made a mess of things and had frightened one of the parents. My patient felt you had to be very careful what you said to parents and the locum had made her anxious by talking too openly about her child's illnesses. The result was that she wanted him in future and not the locum; he felt it was hardly worth employing a locum because you only had to do the work yourself anyway. In reply to a question of mine he agreed that even before the week-end he had worried about the locum. So, in a sense, the employment of the locum had not relieved him of any anxiety or responsibility. He objected that the parent made a lot of demands on him and half implied that she was sexually attracted to him.

I interpreted that I was the parent who complained about being left in charge of the inexperienced locum. As a result of his leaving me in charge of his inexperienced self I, in turn, had been able to say things which had very much upset him. His anxiety was that if he came to me as an experienced man, that is to say potent, then I made demands on him, particularly sexual demands, which he felt unable to meet.

21. He shifted uneasily on the couch and became tense; after a moment he replied, "I feel curled up and I am afraid that if I stay like this I shall have cramp. If I stretch out I shall become rigid and touch the pillow and contaminate it and get contaminated back again. I feel as if I were in the womb".

I said that the uterus here represented the limitations he felt he imposed upon himself by being compelled to come as the locum. We had throughout his analysis seen that he feared that with him violence and aggression took the place of sexuality. The fear of his aggression, closely linked in his mind with faeces, caused him to retreat to a position in which he felt constrained and confined and thus secure from the hatred that a less cramped position would release. In fact all that happened was that he resented more than ever a relationship which imposed these limitations on him. We might take it that his association indicated that he had retreated into the womb and feared being born; but it was necessary to consider what this meant in present terms; I suggested that it meant that he could not rely on the use to which he would put his capacity if he permitted himself to develop by reuniting the various splits in his personality – particularly in allowing hatred to return as a part of himself in his relationship with me. Nor did he feel sure of my response to this. He feared that if he were to have a relationship with me, both of us being experienced, it would be bound to issue in mutual hatred.

22. The session ended: and that night he had a dream with which he started the next session. I will only give a portion of it: a man had presented him with a bill and then left the house. The bill was far too large; he followed to expostulate but the man rapidly disappeared, disregarding my patient's attempts to arrest his attention by tapping him on the shoulder. My patient felt overwhelmed with rage such as he had never felt before and awoke in terror. I reminded him of the previous session and his fear of what would happen if he left his cramped curled up position – this was the split-off hatred of me, and the demands, financial and otherwise, that I and the analysis made upon him.

He went on to speak of a psychiatrist whom he had met that day. The man had during the war been on a Board which my patient attended for re-categorization on psychiatric grounds but he had not recognized my patient. My patient had questioned him and elicited that he treated patients and considered some 50 sessions enough. My patient formed a very poor opinion of him and decided that he could never have done anything for my patient's troubles had he tried to cure them in 50 sessions. During this overtly friendly questioning he had felt an intense hatred of him. My patient added that he still felt tense. I said that he was comparing me favourably with the psychiatrist, but the incident was produced as a warning of the interrogation to which I would be subjected were our roles reversed.

23. By this time, his relationship with me had become altogether more realistic and he showed every sign of cooperating in the investigation of his problem. It was possible, as it had never been before, to question him about details and to ask for an expansion of his associations whenever it seemed necessary for a clearer grasp of the material he was presenting.

He now commenced a series of associations in which he emerged as sending various students for opinion to consultations with a specialist.

The next association was the second of this kind: he said, "I have a student whose eye has become infected; an eye man said he thought it was an infection. Anyway nothing could be done about it, but her father said he wanted another opinion, so I had to send her to another eye man and now I have got landed with a whole lot of work I don't want to do; she's a nuisance. I have to give a whole series of interviews. The second eye man doesn't think it's much different clinically from what the first eye man says, but he thinks it's worth doing something. The first man didn't think it worth bothering and that is why her father thought him a bit slack I suppose. Anyhow I have to do this now. She must get a blood test done to see if she has syphilis. She should have done it before".

24. This association may be considered as the starting point of an investigation which illuminated two problems: first, the unconscious material that it expressed and, second, the manner in which the patient was able to bring this material into consciousness.

As his analysis unfolded it was possible to demonstrate that his association, with its subsequent variations, compactly expressed the following themes:

1. I was the first eye man who said, in effect, that the injured girl was an internal object, infected by the bad objects inside him, for which nothing could be done. I was also the second eye man who said

that the girl was injured by his faeces, spirochaetes and bacilli, all varieties of bad penes, for whom nothing could be done but for whom he would have to do it just the same. He would have to cure her with his penis, since I would not repair damage done by him and it was his object in any case; and he would have to cure her without any pleasurable gain. I was also the eye surgeon who threatened him with castration. He had spent some anxious hours on correspondence to see that no question of jealousy or friction marred the relationship between the two eye men and between them and himself. So the twins were to be brought into harmonious co-operation.

2. The first, passive, eye man represented his previous psychotherapeutic experiences which had left him and his objects more or less in peace. The second eye man was psychoanalysis that was giving him increased insight, and seducing him into genital sexuality and the threatening situation that went with it.
3. The first, passive, eye man was the mother, and the second, active, eye man the father whom he tried to harmonize by his correspondence with both.

25. I will now consider the light his analysis threw on the second problem – the manner in which the patient brought this material into consciousness.

My first point is that with his association we are back again on the theme of contamination. The girl has an infection, be it tubercular, syphilitic, or obscure. He himself noted spontaneously that he had not mentioned, although in the actual case it had been canvassed, the possibility of diabetes. We were thus rehearsing a topic which had already been well tested, as it were orally, in the past 2½ years of analysis, but which was now to be re-investigated by other means.

The consultation of two eye men indicated an ocular method of investigation. Furthermore, a modification of the twin theme, the two eye men, was again in evidence.

26. The result of this re-investigation had been increase of hope, but also of fresh burdens and responsibilities; amongst these was the possibility of genital sexuality, a further essay in the oral sexuality which he had neglected, withdrawal of blood, possibly contaminated, from the object, and the giving of injections.

The eye men, particularly the second, also represented the reinforcement of the investigating weapons by something like intellect: they were supposed to know more than himself.

Throughout this period it was clear that I was felt to be present and indeed my presence was even regarded as necessary. But I was not to interfere. Any interpretation which had in it the least tincture which the patient could interpret as an incursion into the realms of diagnosis and treatment was resented; but I could be myself, not just a twin to be fashioned into a shape he desired. If I observed the manifestations presented to me by my patient in the consulting room in terms of play therapy with a child, then I could consider the two eye men as parts of his body, possibly his two eyes that were to be harmonized into binocular vision. The injured girl was some object, recovered from his inside, which was to be subjected to the scrutiny of both his eyes and a developing intellect, a scrutiny thus exercised on an externalized object.

The results of this scrutiny were not altogether reassuring, for one thing the two eye men were not completely harmonized, for another the diagnosis remained obscure, or, in other words, the intellect had not solved the problem, and finally, there had been foreshadowed the imposition of further and burdensome responsibilities, namely a revision of oral sexuality and an exploration of genital sexuality. At this last point, I noticed that he had begun to call the eye man an eye surgeon. When I drew his attention to this, he said the surgeon had not thought an operation necessary.

I was not surprised when at the next session another student had to be sent for a consultation, this time to an ear, nose and throat surgeon, and again at the request of the father. In recounting this episode, he expressed persecutory feelings towards the ear, nose and throat man. A retreat to auditory, olfactory and oral levels had taken place. I interpreted that his advance had been felt to be impossible to sustain and that he felt persecuted not only for the reasons already educed but also because psychoanalysis, a method that involved examining his problems with all his senses, including sight and intellect, was far more burdensome than psychotherapy; it involved (1) painful co-ordination, which he had not been able to accomplish (2) the acceptance by himself of all the splittings of his personality which he had personified and externalized (3) the imposition of responsibilities which he could not shoulder and (4) the threatened punishment of castration which he could not sustain. I reminded him of the dream of the painter who presented too large a bill, and said that I was thus the object of his hatred both because I was imposing on him these responsibilities and punishments, and forcing him to retreat to levels which he had already found unendurable. I pointed out to him that it looked, since he said the ear, nose and throat surgeon had agreed that his treatment was correct, as if all levels indicated that he was responsible and should restore the injured object.

27. I told the patient that we must consider that the one component that remained unaltered, whatever happened, was his conscience and that this seemed so exacting that he was driven by it from one frightening and demanding situation to another.

The patient's oscillations helped him to try out his methods of reality testing by enabling him to compare his findings in oral and ocular phases. The injured object had been very thoroughly explored on an oral level before being submitted for scrutiny by the "eye men". Nevertheless the change to the eye men aroused great anxiety and tension because, instead of simply solving the problem of the injured object, they revealed the presence of the Oedipus situation which he could not tolerate. The subsequent succession of advances and regressions served the purpose of enabling him to strengthen the ego; he could therefore deal with the Oedipus situation, now become emotionally powerful which it never was before the emergence of the imaginary twin. I have already remarked on the way in which the analysis seemed to have no effect whatever on oedipal material of the early phase. At this point in his analysis there seemed to go together an increase of confidence in his methods of reality testing, in reality, and in his ego.

28. I have now completed my account of all the clinical material I propose to present from the analysis of this patient. In the discussion that follows I shall have to refer to associations from two other patients, and in order to keep the material distinct I propose to call the patient of whom I have so far spoken, A, and the other two B and C respectively.

The first point I would discuss is the mastery and confidence displayed by patient A in his use of the mechanisms of introjection, projection, splitting and the personification of his splits. His reactions contrasted, during the period I have described, with those of patient

B, a real twin and a more disturbed personality, who resorted to phantasies of an identical twin, phantasies which seemed intended to serve the same functions as A's imaginary twin. This patient seemed always to be struggling with the intractability of his material. Introjected objects were described as cubes of burnished steel: he complained during sessions of pain in mouth, stomach and anus. Sustenance had to be drawn through a hair-fine tube, and the associations by which he strove to obtain relief in analysis were tenuous and fitful to match. His real twin seemed as intractable as material for phantasy as food appeared to be for sustenance. Patient A personified his splits with such success that in some sessions, as I have said, one might almost imagine one's self watching a session of play therapy with a child. B seemed to feel as inadequately equipped for the exploration of intrapsychic tensions as he did for contact with reality and I could not help feeling that A, particularly in the sessions devoted to the consultants, when he seemed able to tolerate my presence as a person in my own right, was demonstrating, by his personifications, his attempt to bridge the gulf to reality, and displaying, in doing so, one factor that contributed to hopefulness about the outcome of his analysis. In his testing of reality the patient was also testing, apparently with growing confidence in the results, his mechanisms for testing reality.

29. In this respect he seems to me to differ from patient C, whose association, which I shall now give, indicated no such confidence either in reality or in his means for testing it. He told me, after returning to analysis from hospital – where his treatment by deep X-ray therapy had been canvassed only to be rejected on the grounds that it might be dangerous, on account of possible destruction of genital function – that he had been next to a patient who was being transfused with blood, the donor of which was his cousin. The cousins had mothers who were twin sisters, he said, and added, reflectively, that his sister had twins. His doctor, he went on, had the same name as the doctor who had treated him some time previously when he had been abroad and suffered from indigestion. He paused; and then said one of his eyes was weak. Furthermore, if he used this eye alone he saw double. His defect in vision could be corrected with glasses but he hated wearing his glasses, which in fact did correct his sight, because they made him feel cross-eyed. I made the interpretation that the two cousins were parents in intercourse whom he wished to destroy with his penetrating, sadistic, X-ray gaze and that he felt in consequence that his genitality was menaced by the destructive scrutiny of the parents. He replied with an all-embracing pun, 'I am unreliable'. No sooner had he said it than he began to complain of indigestion, expressed his fears of having to return to hospital and spent the rest of the session in fears about his food. This patient frequently complained that it was equally disturbing whether he concluded that his observations were correct, in which case the reality was terrifying, or whether he concluded they were incorrect, in which case his mental state was terrifying. His pun indicated that, unlike A, he felt he could not rely on his instruments of investigation, the eye and all it stood for, the parents that his eye revealed, and the ego that had to incorporate the result of the investigation. He, like A, regressed to an oral level.

30. I now turn to a session with the patient B whom I mentioned earlier. He said: "I saw your last patient I think. I came early and have been waiting. Last night my twin kept me up all night telling me some long-winded rigmarole the way these people do. I was wanting to go to my bed all the time. Thanks to psychoanalysis I can see right through the mind of the man who works at the next table to mine. I can laugh at him."

I interpreted that the twin was my last patient who had kept him out with his rigmarole. But he could laugh at him now as he knew what he must be feeling now he was excluded.

B went on, "My lab. man likes using the ordinary microscope but I prefer the binocular. There's no doubt at all you can see far better. Mind you he partly agrees with me. I've just been thinking how much better treatment you can get when you have more money and that of course makes you better."

I said psychoanalysis or myself gave him binocular vision. As a result he had more knowledge, and increased knowledge was felt to bring healing.

He went on, "Life is very complicated. You just go and make things difficult for me."

I replied, "You are now feeling that the better vision that two eyes give you, analysis being one of them, shows you more than poor monocular vision; it makes you realize life is very complicated and difficult. It has made you see the other patient who comes to me."

He continued: "I could not eat my lunch. It looked very nice but it made me feel sick."

I replied, "Your eyes made you think when you saw the other patient was here that the analysis was very nice. Now you find it is poisoning you and you do not feel able to take it. There is a feeling that the other patient's rigmarole, as you called it, is something he has left behind to poison you."

He continued: "Of course the binocular microscope is very difficult to use at first. You have to learn how to use it and then it is much better than the ordinary one."

I replied, "You are feeling that if you use your analysis to see right through people to laugh at them you have not learned to use it properly, and then others you look at attack you back again."

31. Subsequent analysis showed that the doubt he had about his ability to use the binocular microscope straight away was partly based on his fear that it might make a very small twin look like a very big father. At the time of this association he was not prepared to see a father and a mother together although his association showed that such a scene might be revealed – if his instruments of investigation, and ability to use them, improved. This warning too was implicit in the statement that I made things very difficult for him. His claim that he possessed psychoanalytic insight indicated that I was in the role of the identical twin – this patient's imaginary twin.

The session I have described indicated to me that B had now reached a point where interpretations of myself as the identical twin had become possible. Up to this point oedipal material, though quite apparent was, as with A in the early phase, on a superficial level and interpretations had little effect. His statements about the need to become skilled in the use of the binocular microscope indicate a growing sense of reality towards his means of establishing contact, and growing confidence in his ability to explore intra-psychic tensions, whereas all through the earlier part of his analysis I had come into the picture again and again as his brain that had to do his exploration for him; and this brings me to the next point I wish to discuss. How was it that with A, the emergence of the imaginary twin was so important? And if it was so important, why had the phenomena associated with it remained peripheral, and not central, for so long?

The answer I suggest is that the imaginary twin goes back to his very earliest relationship and is an expression of his inability to tolerate an object that was not entirely under his control. The function of the imaginary twin was thus to deny a reality different from himself.

With this denial of external reality there co-existed his inability to tolerate the internal psychic realities, and a great deal of work had to be done before any increase in tolerance occurred. As his fears of his psychic mechanisms decreased, it became possible for him to allow their presence to manifest itself by a movement of their representation in his stream of associations into a more central position. Only when I had been able to demonstrate how bad I was on all levels of his mind did it become possible for him first to recognize his mechanisms of splitting and personification and then to employ them, as it were in reverse, to establish the contact which they had originally been used to break. After the demonstration of the imaginary twin I began to be allowed existence as a real person and not a thing created by himself until the point, already mentioned, when I felt I was allowed to exist more or less passively watching his play, and finally as a consultant. In the session I have described with B, despite some appearances to the contrary, I was still only an identical twin.

32. I have left till last two speculations which pose questions I do not propose to attempt to answer. The first concerns the personification of splits to which I have drawn attention. Is it possible that the capacity to personify splittings of the personality is in some way analogous to a capacity for symbol formation to which Mrs Klein has drawn attention in her paper 'The Importance of Symbol-Formation in the Development of the Ego' (1930b); had it a similar value in the development of A in the period I have attempted to describe?

My second question is concerned with the part played by vision in these three patients' associations. In each of them it seems to be linked with the development of intellect, witness the consultant in A, myself as the brain with B, and in a similar role, though I had no time to bring it in, with C, and in each with the emergence of genital sexuality and the Oedipus situation. Furthermore, each patient in his individual way seemed to have similar problems that obtruded themselves almost as if concerned with vision itself. A stressed how much work he had thrust upon him to keep the relationship with the two eye men harmonious; B compared the merits of monocular and binocular microscopes; C the need for glasses to correct his sight. Each seemed to feel that new burdens had been imposed; A by the second eye man, B by myself making things difficult for him, and C by saying the glasses made him feel cross-eyed.

In each case I have mentioned, the visual power has represented the emergence of a new capacity for exploring the *environment:* it has been possible to show that in this respect the analysis was being felt as an addition to the patient's armoury for investigation and was likely therefore to be reactivating emotions associated with very early advances in psychological development that had a similar effect in increasing capacity. The increase of power was felt to demand an increase in intellectual grasp.

33. In each case the newly achieved powers were used to solve an already existing problem, but were found to reveal still other problems that demanded solution. Thus A, who seemed preoccupied with the problem of an internal injured object, and brought to bear on it his fresh powers, found himself threatened by the relationship between father and child. B showed the same development expressed in terms of the discovery of a by no means identical twin that had a relationship with a mother. C likewise – but in terms of a cousin being transfused with the blood of another.

All three patients seemed to feel that the problem had been there all the time but that its revelation had depended on increased capacity for awareness.

The regression in each case could thus be stated as being away from (1) the increase in capacity produced by psychological development; (2) the phenomena brought into awareness by the increased capacity; (3) the physiological development, associated with the psychological development which revealed the relationship between the external parents.

In each case I had the impression that the patient felt that sight produced problems of mastery of a new sense organ. This had its counterpart in a feeling that development of the psyche, like development of visual capacity, involved the emergence of the Oedipus situation. With A, the change from a perfunctory and superficial treatment of the Oedipus situation to a struggle to come to terms with an emotionally charged Oedipus complex was extremely striking.

I have found it impossible to interpret the material presented to me by these patients as a manifestation of purely psychological development divorced from any concurrent physical development. I have wondered whether the psychological development was bound up with the development of ocular control in the same way that problems of development linked with oral aggression co-exist with the eruption of teeth. If this is so, we would have to ask ourselves if these psychological developments, ushering in the Oedipus complex, come close to the first four months in the individual's life. The relevance of this to assessment of the correctness or otherwise of Mrs Klein's view of the earliness of the oedipal phase is obvious; if the experience of other observers appears to confirm my impressions, it may provide incidental reasons for favouring an early date for the pre-oedipal phase.

3

Notes on the theory of schizophrenia

A. Introduction

34. In this paper I shall discuss the schizophrenic patient's use of language and the bearing of this on the theory and practice of analysis. At a later date I shall acknowledge my indebtedness to, and discuss the views of, the psychoanalysts who have contributed to the growth of my own views. I cannot do that now, but I must make it clear for the better understanding of what I say that, even where I do not make specific acknowledgement of the fact, Melanie Klein's work occupies a central position in my view of the psychoanalytic theory of schizophrenia. I assume that the explanation of terms such as 'projective identification' and the 'paranoid' and 'depressive positions' is known through her work.

By approaching the subject through consideration of verbal thought I run the risk of appearing to neglect the nature of the schizophrenic's object relations. I must therefore emphasize now that I think that the peculiarity of the schizophrenic's object relations is the outstanding feature of schizophrenia. The importance of the points that I wish to make lies in their capacity to illuminate the nature of this object relationship of which they are a subordinate function.

35. The material is derived from the analysis of six patients; two were drug addicts, one an obsessional anxiety state with schizoid features, and the remaining three schizophrenics all of whom suffered from hallucinations which were well in evidence over a period of between four and five years of analysis. Of these three, two showed marked paranoid features and one depression.

I did not depart from the psychoanalytic procedure I usually employ with neurotics, being careful always to take up both positive and negative aspects of the transference.

B. Nature of the observation on which interpretations are based

Evidence for interpretations has to be sought in the counter-transference and in the actions and free associations of the patient. Counter-transference has to play an important part in analysis of the schizophrenic, but I do not propose to discuss this to-day. I shall therefore pass on to the patient's free associations.

C. Schizophrenic language

36. Language is employed by the schizophrenic in three ways; as a mode of action, as a method of communication, and as a mode of thought. He will show a preference for action on occasions when other patients would realize that what was required was thought; thus, he will want to go over to a piano to take out the movement to understand why someone is playing the piano. Reciprocally, if he has a problem the solution of which depends on action, as when, being in one place, he should be in another, he will resort to thought – omnipotent thought – as his mode of transport.

At the moment I want to consider only his use of it as a mode of action in the service either of splitting the object or projective identification. It will be noted that this is but one aspect of schizophrenic object relations in which he is either splitting or getting in and out of his objects.

The first of these uses is in the service of projective identification. In this the patient uses words as things or as split-off parts of himself which he pushes forcibly into the analyst. Typical of the consequences of this behaviour is the experience of a patient who felt he got inside me at the beginning of each session and had to be extricated at the end of it.

Language is again employed as a mode of action for the splitting of his object. This obtrudes when the analyst becomes identified with internal persecutors, but it is employed at other times too. Here are two examples of this use of language: the patient comes into the room, shakes me warmly by the hand, and looking piercingly into my eyes says, "I think the sessions are not for a long while but stop me ever going out." I know from previous experience that this patient has a grievance that the sessions are too few and that they interfere with his free time. He intended to split me by making me give two opposite interpretations at once, and this was shown by his next association when he said, "How does the lift know what to do when I press two buttons at once?"

My second example has wide implications, which I cannot take up here, because of their bearing on insomnia. The technique depends on the combination of two incompatible elements thus: the patient speaks in a drowsy manner calculated to put the analyst to sleep. At the same time he stimulates the analyst's curiosity. The intention is again to split the analyst, who is not allowed to go to sleep and is not allowed to keep awake.

You will note a third example of splitting later on when I describe a patient splitting the analyst's speech itself.

To turn now to the schizophrenic's difficulties with language as a mode of thought, here is a sequence of associations all in one session, but separated from each other by intervals of four or five minutes.

I have a problem I am trying to work out. As a child I never had phantasies.

I knew they weren't facts so I stopped them. I don't dream nowadays.

Then after a pause he went on in a bewildered voice, "I don't know what to do now." I said, "About a year ago you told me you were no good at thinking. Just now you said you were working out a problem – obviously something you were thinking about."

Patient. "Yes."

Analyst. "But you went on with the thought that you had no phantasies in childhood; and then that you had no dreams; you then said that you did not know what to do. It must mean that without phantasies and without dreams you have not the means with which to think out your problem." The patient agreed, and began to talk with marked freedom and coherence. The reference to the inhibition of phantasy as a severe disability hindering development supports Melanie Klein's observations in her paper, 'A Contribution to the Theory of Intellectual Inhibition'.

37. The severe splitting in the schizophrenic makes it difficult for him to achieve the use of symbols and subsequently of substantives and verbs. It is necessary to demonstrate these difficulties to him as they arise; of this I shall shortly give an example. The capacity to form symbols is dependent on:

1. The ability to grasp whole objects.
2. The abandonment of the paranoid-schizoid position with its attendant splitting.
3. The bringing together of splits and the ushering in of the depressive position.

Since verbal thought depends on the ability to integrate, it is not surprising to find that its emergence is intimately associated with the depressive position which, as Melanie Klein has pointed out, is a phase of active synthesis and integration. Verbal thought sharpens awareness of psychic reality and therefore of the depression which is linked with destruction and loss of good objects. The presence of internal persecutors, as another aspect of psychic reality, is similarly unconsciously more recognized. The patient feels that the association between the depressive position and verbal thought is one of cause and effect – itself a belief based on his capacity to integrate – and this adds one more to the many causes of his hatred of analysis, already well in evidence, which is, after all, a treatment which employs verbal thought in the solution of mental problems.

The patient at this stage becomes frightened of the analyst, even though he may concede that he feels better, but, and this is where the kernel of our problem lies, he shows every sign of being anxious to have nothing whatever to do with his embryonic capacity for verbal thought. That is felt to be better left to the analyst; or, as I think it more correct to say, the analyst is felt to be better able than he to harbour it within himself without disaster. The patient seems, despite all the work done, to have reverted to the use of language that I have described as characteristic of the schizophrenic before analysis. He has greater verbal capacity but prefers to employ it as he did when it was slight.

D. *Development of capacity for verbal thought*

38. To explain why the patient is so chary of using his increased capacity, I must report an experience which seems to have peculiar significance for him. The patient said to me, "I am a prisoner of psychoanalysis"; later in the session he added, "I can't escape". Some months later he said, "I can't get out of my state of mind". A mass of material, to which quotations cannot do justice, had accumulated over a period of three years to give the impression that the patient felt unable to escape from a prison which seemed sometimes to be me, sometimes psychoanalysis and sometimes his state of mind which is a constant struggle with his own internal objects. He thus shows the same attitude to verbal thought as he has to his potency and his equipment for work and love.

The problem to which I am addressing myself can best be understood if it is seen to appertain to the moment when the patient feels he has effected his escape. The escape appears to contribute to the patient's feeling which he occasionally reports, that he is better; but it has cost him dear. The same patient said, "I have lost my words", and meant by this, as further analysis disclosed, that the instrument with which he had effected his escape had been lost in the process. Words, the capacity for verbal thought, the one essential for further progress, have gone. On expansion it appears that he thinks he has reached this pass as a penalty for forging this instrument of verbal thought and using it to escape from his former state of mind; hence the unwillingness I described to use his greater verbal capacity except as a mode of action.

Here now is the example I promised you when I was speaking of the difficulty that schizophrenic splitting caused in the formation of symbols and the development of verbal thought. The patient was a schizophrenic who had been in analysis five years; I describe some essentials of two sessions. I must warn you that compression has compelled me to leave out many repetitive formulations which in fact would mitigate the baldness of the interpretations as I report them here. I think interpretation should be in language that is simple, exact and mature.

Patient. I picked a tiny piece of skin from my face and feel quite empty.

Analyst. The tiny piece of skin is your penis, which you have torn out, and all your insides have come with it.

Patient. *I* do not understand . . . penis . . . only syllables.

Analyst. *You* have split my word "penis" into syllables and it now has no meaning.

Patient. I don't know what it means, but I want to say, "If I can't spell I cannot think".

Analyst. The syllables have now been split into letters; you cannot spell – that is to say you cannot put the letters together again to make words. So now you cannot think.

The patient started the next day's session with disjointed associations and complained that he could not think. I reminded him of the session I have described, whereupon he resumed correct speech; thus:

Patient. I cannot find any interesting food.

Analyst. You feel it *has all been eaten up.*

Patient. I do not feel able to buy any new clothes and my socks are a mass of holes.

Analyst. By picking out the tiny piece of skin yesterday you injured yourself so badly you cannot even buy clothes; you are empty and have nothing to buy them with.

Patient. Although they are full of holes they constrict my foot.

Analyst. Not only did you tear out your own penis but also mine. So to-day there is no interesting food – only a hole, a sock. But even this sock is made of a mass of holes, all of which you made and which have joined together to constrict, or swallow and injure, your foot.

This and subsequent sessions confirmed that he felt lie had eaten the penis and that therefore there was no interesting food left, only a hole. But this hole was now so persecutory that he had to split it up. As a result of the splitting, the hole became a mass of holes which all came together in a persecutory way to constrict his foot.

This patient's picking habits had been worked over for some three years. At first he had been occupied only with blackheads, and I shall quote from Freud's description of three cases, one observed by himself, one by Dr Tausk and one by R. Reitler, which have a resemblance to my patient. They are taken from his paper, 'The Unconscious' (Freud, 1915e).

Of his patient Freud said, "he has let himself withdraw from all the interests of life on account of the unhealthy condition of the skin of his face. He declares that he has blackheads and that there are deep holes in his face which everyone notices". Freud says he was working out his castration complex on his skin and that he began to think there was a deep cavity wherever he had got rid of a blackhead. He continues: "The cavity which then appears in consequence of his guilty act is the female genital, i.e. stands for the fulfilment of the threat of castration (or the phantasy representing it) called forth by onanism". Freud compares such substitute formations with those of the hysteric, saying, "A tiny little hole such as a pore of the skin will hardly be used by an hysteric as a symbol for the vagina, which otherwise he will compare with every imaginable object capable of enclosing a space. Besides, we should think that the multiplicity of these little cavities would prevent him from using them as a substitute for the female genital".

Of Tausk's case he says, "in pulling on his stockings he was disturbed by the idea that he must draw apart the knitted stitches, i.e. the holes, and every hole was for him a symbol of the female genital aperture".

Quoting Reitler's case, he says the patient "found the explanation that his foot symbolized the penis; putting on the stocking stood for an onanistic act".

I shall now return to my patient at a session ten days later. A tear welled from his eye and he said with a mixture of despair and reproach, "Tears come from my ears now".

This kind of association had by now become familiar to me, so I was aware that I had been set a problem in interpretation. But by this time the patient, who had been in analysis some six years, was capable of a fair degree of identification with the analyst and I had his help. I shall not attempt a description of the stages by which the conclusions I put before you were reached. The steps were laborious and slow even though we had the evidence of six years' analysis on which to draw.

It appeared that he was deploring a blunder that seemed to bear out his suspicion that his capacity for verbal communication was impaired. It seemed that his sentence was but another instance of an inability to put words together properly.

After this had been discussed it was seen that tears were very bad things, that he felt much the same about tears which came from his ears as he did about sweat that came from the holes in his skin when he had, as he supposed, removed blackheads or other such objects from the skin. His feeling about tears from his cars was seen to be similar to his feeling about the urine that came from the hole that was left in a person when his penis had been torn out; the bad urine still came.

When he told me that he couldn't listen very well I took advantage of his remark to remind him that in any case we needed to know why his mind was full of such thoughts at the present juncture, and I suggested that probably his hearing was felt to be defective because my words were being drowned by the tears that poured from his ears.

When it emerged that he couldn't talk very well either I suggested that it was because he felt his tongue had been torn out and he had been left only with an ear.

This was followed by what seemed to be a completely chaotic series of words and noises. I interpreted that now he felt he had a tongue but it was really just as bad as his ear – it just poured out a flow of destroyed language. In short it appeared that despite his wishes and mine we could not, or he felt we could not, communicate. I suggested that he felt he had a very bad and hostile object inside him which was treating our verbal intercourse to much the same kind of destructive attack which he had once felt he had launched against parental intercourse whether sexual or verbal.

At first he seemed to feel most keenly the defects in his capacity for communication or thought, and there was a great deal of play with the pronunciation of tears (teers or tares) the emphasis being mostly on the inability to bring together the objects, words, or word pronunciation, except cruelly. But at one point he seemed to become aware that his association had been the starting-point for much discussion. Then, "Lots of people" he murmured. On working this out in turn it appeared that he had swung away from the idea that his verbal capacity was being irretrievably destroyed by the attacks to which our conversation was being subjected, to the idea that his verbal communication was extremely greedy. This greed was ministered to by his splitting himself into so many people that he could be in many different places at once to hear the many different interpretations which I, also split into "lots of people", was now able to give simultaneously instead of one by one. His greed, and the attacks on verbal communication by the internal persecutors, were therefore related to each other.

39. Clearly this patient felt that splitting had destroyed his ability to think. This was the more serious for him because he no longer felt that action provided a solution for the kind of problem with which he was struggling. This state is equated by the patient with "insanity".

The patient believes he has lost his capacity for verbal thought because he has left it behind inside his former state of mind, or inside the analyst, or inside psychoanalysis. He also believes that his capacity for verbal thought has been removed from him by the analyst who is now a frightening person. Both beliefs give rise to characteristic anxieties. The belief that he has left it behind has, as we have seen, helped to make the patient feel he is insane. He thinks that he will never be able to progress unless he goes back, as it were, into his former state of mind in order to fetch it. This he dare not do because he dreads his former state of mind and fears that he would once more be imprisoned in it. The belief that the analyst has removed his capacity for verbal thought makes him afraid of employing his new-found capacity for verbal thought, lest it should arouse the hatred of the analyst and cause him to repeat the attack.

From the patient's point of view the achievement of verbal thought has been a most unhappy event. Verbal thought is so interwoven with catastrophe and the painful emotion of depression that the patient, resorting to projective identification, splits it off and pushes it into the analyst. The results are again unhappy for the patient; lack of this capacity is now felt by him to be the same thing as being insane. On the other hand, resumption of this capacity seems to him to be inseparable from depression and awareness, on a reality level this time, that he is 'insane'. This fact tends to give reality to the patient's phantasies of the catastrophic results that would accrue were he to risk re-introjection of his capacity for verbal thought.

It must not be supposed that the patient leaves his problems untouched during this phase. He will occasionally give the analyst concrete and precise information about them. The analyst's problem is the patient's dread, now quite manifest, of attempting a psychoanalytic understanding of what they mean for him, partly because the patient now understands that psychoanalysis demands from him that very verbal thought which he dreads.

So far I have dealt with the problem of communication between analyst and schizophrenic patient. I shall now consider the experience the patient has when he lives through the process of achieving sufficient mastery of language to emerge from the "prison of psychoanalysis", or state of mind in which he previously felt himself to be hopelessly enclosed. The patient is apparently unaware of any existence outside the consulting room; there is no report of any external activity. There is merely an existence away from the analyst of which nothing is known except that he is "all right" or "better" and a relationship with the analyst which the patient says is bad. The intervals between sessions are admitted and feared. He complains that he is insane, expresses his fear of hallucination and delusion, and is extremely cautious in his behaviour lest he should become insane.

The living through of the emotions belonging to this phase leads to a shift towards higher valuation of the external object at the expense of the hallucinated internal object. This depends on the analysis of the patient's hallucinations and his insistence on allotting to real objects a subordinate role. If this has been done the analyst sees before him the ego and more normal object relations in process of development. I am assuming that there has been an adequate working through of the processes of splitting and the underlying persecutory anxiety as well as of reintegration. Herbert Rosenfeld has described some of the dangers of this phase. My experiences confirm his findings. I have observed the progress from multiple splits to four and from four to two and the great anxiety as integration proceeds with the tendency to revert to violent disintegration. This is due to intolerance of the depressive position, internal persecutors, and verbal thought. If splitting has been adequately worked through the tendency to split the object and the ego at the same time is kept within bounds. Each session is then a step in ego development.

E. Realization of insanity

40. One of the penalties of attempting to clarify the complex phenomena of the schizophrenic patient's relationship with his objects is that if the attempt is successful it is delusively misleading. I would now redress the balance by approaching the phenomena I have already described from a rather different angle. I wish to take up the story at the point at which the splits are brought together, the patient escapes from his state of mind and the depressive position is ushered in. In particular I wish to draw attention to this concatenation of events when it is suffused by the illumination achieved through the development of a capacity for verbal thought. I have made it clear that this is a most important turning-point in the whole analysis. You may therefore have formed the impression that at this point the analysis enters into calm waters. It is necessary therefore that I should leave you with no illusions about this.

What takes place, if the analyst has been reasonably successful, is a realization by the patient of psychic reality; he realizes that he has hallucinations and delusions, may feel unable to take food, and have difficulty with sleep. The patient will direct powerful feelings of hatred towards the analyst. He will state categorically that he is insane and will express with intense conviction and hatred that it is the analyst who has driven him to this pass. The analyst ought to expect concern for the patient's welfare to drive the family to intervene and he must be prepared to explain an alarming situation to them. He should strive to keep at bay surgeons and shock therapists alike while concentrating on not allowing the patient for a single moment to retreat either from his realization that he is insane or from his hatred of the analyst who has succeeded, after so many years, in bringing him to an emotional realization of the facts that he has spent his whole life trying to evade. This may be the more difficult because, when the first panic begins to subside, the patient himself will begin to suggest that he feels better. Due weight must be given to this, but care must be taken to prevent its being used to delay investigation in detail of the ramifications in the analytic situation of the changes brought about in the patient's object relationships by the realization of his insanity.

F. Results

41. I am not yet prepared to offer any opinion about the prospects of treatment except to say that two of the three schizophrenics of whom I am speaking are now earning their living. I believe that if the course I have indicated above is followed there is reason to anticipate that the schizophrenic may achieve his own form of adjustment to reality which may be no less worthy of the title of 'cure' because it is not of the same kind as that which is achieved by less disordered patients. I repeat that I do not think that any cure, however limited, will be achieved if, at the point I have tried to describe to you, the analyst attempts to reassure the patient and so undoes all the good work that has led to the latter's being able to realize the severity of his condition. At this point an opportunity, which must not be lost, has been created for exploring with the patient what it means to do analytic or any other kind of work when insane.

The experiences I have described to you compel me to conclude that at the onset of the infantile depressive position, elements of verbal thought increase in intensity and depth. In consequence the pains of psychic reality are exacerbated by it and the patient who regresses to the paranoid-schizoid position will, as he does so, turn destructively on his embryonic capacity for verbal *thought* as one of the elements which have led to his pain.

4

The development of schizophrenic thought

42. In this paper, which must be regarded as a preliminary announcement, I do three things:

(i) I discuss the point at which the psychotic personality diverges from the non-psychotic; (ii) I examine the nature of that divergence; and (iii) I consider the consequences of it. Experience at the Congress at Geneva showed that the attempt to give clinical illustrations in a paper as compressed as this produced far more obscurity than illumination. This version is accordingly restricted to theoretical description.

The conclusions I arrive at were forged in analytic contact with schizophrenic patients and have been tested by me in practice. That I arrived at some degree of clarification, I owe mainly to three pieces of work. As they occupy a key position in this paper I shall remind you of them.

First: Freud's description, which I referred to in my paper at the London Congress of 1953 [chapter 3], of the mental apparatus called into activity by the demands of the reality principle and in particular of that part of it which is concerned with conscious awareness of sense impressions. Second: Freud's tentative suggestion, in *Civilization and Its Discontents* [1930a], of the importance of the conflict between life and death instincts. The point was taken up and developed by Melanie Klein, but Freud seemed to recede from it. Melanie Klein believes that this conflict persists throughout life, and this view I believe to be of great importance to an understanding of the schizophrenic. Third: Melanie Klein's description of the phantasied sadistic attacks that the infant makes on the breast during the paranoid-schizoid phase, and her discovery of Projective Identification. Projective Identification is a splitting off by the patient of a part of his personality and a projection of it into the object where it becomes installed, sometimes as a persecutor, leaving the psyche from which it has been split off correspondingly impoverished.

Schizophrenic disturbance springs from an interaction between (i) the environment, and (ii) the personality. In this paper I ignore the environment and focus attention on four essential features of schizophrenic personality. First is a preponderance of destructive impulses so great that even the impulses to love are suffused by them and turned to sadism. Second is a hatred of reality which, as Freud pointed out, is extended to all aspects of the psyche that make for awareness of it. I add hatred of internal reality and all that makes for awareness of it. Third, derived from these two, is an unremitting dread of imminent annihilation. Fourth is a precipitate and premature formation of object relations, foremost amongst which is the transference, whose thinness is in marked contrast to the tenacity with which it is maintained. The prematurity, thinness, and tenacity are pathognomic and are alike derived from dread of annihilation by the death instincts. The schizophrenic is preoccupied with the conflict, never finally resolved, between destructiveness on the one hand and sadism on the other.

Transference

The relationship with the analyst is premature, precipitate, and intensely dependent. When the patient broadens it under pressure of his life or death instincts, two concurrent streams of phenomena become manifest. First, projective identification, with the analyst as object, becomes over-active with the resulting painful confusional states such as Rosenfeld has described. Second, the mental and other activities by which the dominant impulse, be it life instincts or death instincts, strives to express itself, are at once subjected to mutilation by the temporarily subordinated impulse. Driven by the wish to escape the confusional states and harassed by the mutilations, the patient strives to restore the restricted relationship; the transference is again invested with its characteristic featurelessness. Whether the patient walks straight past me into the consulting room as if scarcely aware of my presence, or whether he displays an effusive, mirthless bonhomie, the restricted relationship is unmistakable. Restriction and expansion alternate throughout the analysis.

The divergence

43. To sum up; ignoring the effect of the external environment, the schizophrenic personality depends on the existence in the patient of four features; (i) a conflict that is never decided between life and death instincts; (ii) a preponderance of destructive impulses; (iii) hatred of external and internal reality; (iv) a tenuous but tenacious object relationship. This peculiar endowment makes it certain that the schizophrenic patient's progression through the paranoid-schizoid and depressive positions is markedly different from that of the non-psychotic personality. This difference hinges on the fact that this combination of characteristics leads to a massive resort to projective identification. It is therefore to projective identification that I now turn, *but my examination of it is restricted to its deployment by the schizophrenic against all that apparatus of awareness that Freud described as being called into activity by the demands of the reality principle.*

Divergence of psychotic from non-psychotic personality

44. I spoke of Melanie Klein's picture of the paranoid-schizoid position and the important part played in it by the infant's phantasies of sadistic attacks on the breast. Identical attacks are directed against the apparatus of perception from the beginning of life. This part of his personality is cut up, split into minute fragments, and then, using the projective identification, expelled from the personality. Having thus rid himself of the apparatus of conscious awareness of internal and external reality, the patient achieves a state which is felt to be neither alive nor dead.

This apparatus of conscious awareness is intimately connected with verbal thought and all that provides, at the early stage of which I speak, the foundations of its inchoation. Projective identification of conscious awareness and the associated inchoation of verbal thought is the central factor in the differentiation of the psychotic from the non-psychotic personality. I believe it takes place at the outset of the patient's life. These sadistic attacks on the ego and on the foundations of inchoate verbal thought, and the projective identification of the fragments, make certain that from this point on there is an ever-widening divergence between the psychotic and non-psychotic parts of the personality until at last the gulf is felt to be unbridgeable.

Fate of the expelled fragments

45. In so far as the destruction is successful, the patient experiences a failure in his capacity for perception. All his sense impressions appear to have suffered mutilation of a kind which would be appropriate had they been attacked as the breast is felt to be attacked in the sadistic phantasies of the infant. The patient feels imprisoned in the state of mind he has achieved and unable to escape from it because he feels he lacks the apparatus of awareness of reality, which is both the key to escape and the freedom itself to which he would escape. This sense of imprisonment is intensified by the menacing presence of the expelled fragments within whose planetary movements he is contained. The nature of this imprisonment will become clearer with the discussion of the fate of these expelled fragments, to which I now turn.

In the patient's phantasy the expelled particles of ego lead to an independent and uncontrolled existence outside the personality, but either containing or contained by external objects, where they exercise their functions as if the ordeal to which they have been subjected has served only to increase their number and to provoke their hostility to the psyche that ejected them. In consequence the patient feels himself to be surrounded by bizarre objects whose nature I shall now describe.

The particles

46. Each particle is felt to consist of a real external object which is encapsulated in a piece of personality that has engulfed it. The character of this complete particle will depend partly on the character of the real object, say a gramophone, and partly on the character of the particle of personality that engulfs it. If the piece of the personality is concerned with sight, the gramophone when played is felt to be watching the patient; if with hearing, then the gramophone when played is felt to be listening to the patient. The object, angered at being engulfed, swells up, so to speak, and suffuses and controls the piece of personality that engulfs it: to that extent the particle is felt to have become a thing. Since these particles are used by the patient as if they were prototypes of ideas – later to become words – this suffusion of the piece of personality by the contained but controlling object leads the patient to feel that words are the actual things they name, and so to the confusions (described by Segal) that arise because the patient equates but does not symbolize.

Consequences for the patient

47. The patient now moves, not in a world of dreams, but in a world of objects which are ordinarily the furniture of dreams. These objects, primitive yet complex, partake of qualities which in the non-psychotic are peculiar to matter, anal objects, senses, ideas, superego, and the remaining qualities of personality. One result is that the patient strives to use real objects as ideas, and is baffled when they obey the laws of natural science – not those of mental functioning.

Associated with projective identification is the psychotic personality's inability to introject. If he wishes to take in an interpretation, or bring back these objects I have been describing, he does so by projective identification reversed, and by the same route. This situation was neatly summed up by the patient who said he used his intestine as a brain. When I said he had swallowed something, he replied, "The intestine doesn't swallow." Dr Segal has described in her paper, which I had the good fortune to see before the Congress, some of the patient's vicissitudes in the depressive position (Segal, 1956); I would now add that, thanks to this employment of projective identification, he cannot synthesize his objects: he can only agglomerate and compress them. Further, whether he feels he has had something put into him, or whether he feels he has introjected it, he feels the ingress as an assault, and a retaliation by the object for his violent intrusion into it.

Repression

48. It will be clear that where the non-psychotic personality, or part of the personality employs repression, the psychotic has employed projective identification. Therefore there is no repression, and what should be his unconscious is replaced by the world of dream furniture in which I have described him as moving.

Verbal thought

49. The inception of verbal thought which I described as appertaining to the depressive position is gravely disturbed because it is that which synthesizes and articulates impressions and thus is essential to awareness of internal and external reality; for that reason it is subject to continuing attacks such as I have described.

Further, excessive projective identification in the paranoid-schizoid position prevented smooth introjection and assimilation of sense impressions and consequently the establishment of the firm base of good objects on which the inception of verbal thought depends.

An attempt to think involves bringing back to control, and therefore to his personality, the expelled particles and their accretions. Projective identification is therefore reversed and the concomitant agglomeration and compression lead to highly compact speech, the construction of which is more appropriate to music than the articulation of words as used for non-psychotic communication.

Moreover, since, as we have seen, these particles share the qualities of things, the patient can feel he is being split by their re-entry. Again, since these particles include pieces of conscious awareness of sense impressions, the senses are felt to become painfully compressed and acute to an intolerable degree. The patient can be seen to be in the grip of extremely painful, tactile, auditory, or visual hallucinations. Depression and anxiety being subject to the same mechanism are similarly intensified till the patient is compelled to deal with these emotions in the way that Segal has described.

Conclusion

50. Experience of these theories in practice has convinced me that the treatment of the psychotic personality will not be successful until the patient's destructive attacks on his ego, and his substitution of projective identification for repression and introjection, have been worked through. I further consider that even in the severe neurotic there is a psychotic personality that has to be dealt with in the same way before success is achieved.

5

The differentiation of the psychotic from the non-psychotic personalities

51. The theme of this paper is that the differentiation of the psychotic from the non-psychotic personalities depends on a minute splitting of all that part of the personality that is concerned with awareness of internal and external reality, and the expulsion of these fragments so that they enter into or engulf their objects. I shall describe this process in some detail and shall then discuss its consequences and how they affect treatment.

The conclusions were arrived at in analytic contact with schizophrenic patients and have been tested by me in practice. I ask your attention for them because they have led to developments in my patients which are analytically significant and not to be confused, either with the remissions familiar to psychiatrists, or with that class of improvement that it is impossible to relate to the interpretations given or to any coherent body of psychoanalytic theory. I believe that the improvements I have seen deserve psychoanalytic investigation.

52. I owe my clarification of the obscurity that pervades the whole of a psychotic analysis mainly to three pieces of work. As they are crucial for understanding what follows I shall remind you of them. First: Freud's description (1911b), to which I referred in my paper to the London Congress of 1953 [chapter 3], of the mental apparatus called into activity by the demands of the reality principle and in particular of that part of it which is concerned with the consciousness attached to the sense-organs. Second: Melanie Klein's (1928) description of the phantasied sadistic attacks that the infant makes on the breast during the paranoid-schizoid phase. Third: her discovery of projective identification (Klein, 1946).

By this mechanism the patient splits off a part of his personality and projects it into the object where it becomes installed, sometimes as a persecutor, leaving the psyche, from which it has been split off, correspondingly impoverished.

53. Lest it be supposed that I attribute the development of schizophrenia exclusively to certain mechanisms apart from the personality that employs them, I shall enumerate now what I think are the preconditions for the mechanisms on which I wish to focus your attention. There is the environment, which I shall not discuss at this time, and the personality which must display four essential features. These are: a preponderance of destructive impulses so great that even the impulse to love is suffused by them and turned to sadism; a hatred of reality, internal and external, which is extended to all that makes for awareness of it; a dread of imminent annihilation (Klein, 1946), and finally a premature and precipitate formation of object relations, foremost amongst which is the transference, whose thinness is in marked contrast with the tenacity with which they are maintained. The prematurity, thinness and tenacity are pathognomonic and have an important derivation in the conflict, never decided in the schizophrenic, between the life and death instincts.

54. Before I consider the mechanisms that spring from these characteristics I must dispose briefly of a few points that concern the transference. The relationship with the analyst is premature, precipitate, and intensely dependent; when (under pressure of his life and death instincts) the patient broadens the contact, two concurrent streams of phenomena become manifest.

First, splitting of his personality and projection of the fragments into the analyst (i.e. projective identification) becomes overactive, with consequent confusional states such as Rosenfeld (1952) has described. Second, the mental and other activities by which the dominant impulse, be it of life or death instincts, strives to express itself, are at once subjected to mutilation by the temporarily subordinated impulse. Harassed by the mutilations and striving to escape the confusional states, the patient returns to the restricted relationship. Oscillation between the attempt to broaden the contact and the attempt to restrict it continues throughout the analysis.

55. To return now to the characteristics I listed as intrinsic to the schizophrenic personality; these constitute an endowment that makes it certain that the possessor of it will progress through the paranoid-schizoid and depressive positions in a manner markedly different from that of one not so endowed. The difference hinges on the fact that this combination of qualities leads to minute fragmentation of the personality (particularly of the apparatus of awareness of reality which Freud described as coming into operation at the behest of the reality principle) and excessive projection of these fragments of personality into external objects.

I described some aspects of these theories in my paper to the International Congress of 1953 [chapter 3] when I spoke of the association of the depressive position with the development of verbal thought and the significance of this association for awareness of internal and external reality. In this paper I am taking up the same story at a much earlier stage, namely at the outset of the patient's life. I am dealing with phenomena in the paranoid-schizoid position which are associated, ultimately, with the inchoation of verbal thought. How this should be so will, I hope, presently emerge.

56. The theories of Freud and Melanie Klein to which I referred earlier must now be considered in more detail. Quoting his formulation in 'The Loss of Reality in Neurosis and Psychosis' (1924e) – Freud defines one of the features distinguishing the neuroses from the psychoses as: "in the former the ego, in virtue of its allegiance to reality, suppresses a part of the id (the life of instinct), whereas in the psychoses the same ego in the service of the id, withdraws itself from a part of reality".

I assume that when Freud speaks of the allegiance of the ego to reality he is speaking of the developments he described as taking place with the institution of the reality principle. He said, "the new demands made a succession of adaptations necessary in the mental apparatus, which, on account of insufficient knowledge, we can only detail very cursorily". He then lists: the heightened, significance of the sense organs directed towards the outer world and of the consciousness attached to them; attention, which he calls a special function, which had to search the outer world in order that its data might be already familiar if an urgent inner need should arise; a system of notation whose task was to deposit the results of this periodical activity of consciousness which he describes as a part of that which we call memory; judgement which had to decide whether a particular idea was true or false; the employment of motor discharge in appropriate alteration of reality and not simply in unburdening the mental apparatus of accretions of stimuli; and finally, thought which he says made it possible to tolerate the frustration which is an inevitable accompaniment of action by virtue of its quality as an experimental way of acting. As will be seen, I very much extend the function and importance of thought, but otherwise accept the classification of ego function, which Freud put forward as putative, as giving concreteness to a part of the personality with which this paper is concerned. It accords well with clinical experience and illuminates events which I would have found infinitely more obscure without it.

I make two modifications in Freud's description to bring it into closer relation with the facts; I do not think, at least as touches those patients likely to be met with in analytic practice, that the ego is ever wholly withdrawn from reality. I would say that its contact with reality is masked by the dominance, in the patient's mind and behaviour, of an omnipotent phantasy that is intended to destroy either reality or the awareness of it, and thus to achieve a state that is neither life nor death. Since contact with reality is never entirely lost, the phenomena which we are accustomed to associate with the neuroses are never absent and serve to complicate the analysis, when sufficient progress has been made, by their presence amidst psychotic material. On this fact – that the ego retains contact with reality – depends the existence of a non-psychotic personality parallel with, but obscured by, the psychotic personality.

57. My second modification is that the withdrawal from reality is an illusion, not a fact, and arises from the deployment of projective identification against the mental apparatus listed by Freud. Such is the dominance of this phantasy it is evident that it is no phantasy, but a fact to the patient, who acts as if his perceptual apparatus could be split into minute fragments and projected into his objects.

As a result of these modifications we reach the conclusion that patients ill enough, say, to be certified as psychotic, contain in their psyche a part of the personality prey to the various neurotic mechanisms with which psychoanalysis has made us familiar, and a psychotic part of the personality, which is so far dominant that the non-psychotic part of the personality, with which it exists in negative juxtaposition, is obscured.

One concomitant of the hatred of reality that Freud remarked is the psychotic infant's phantasies of sadistic attacks on the breast which Melanie Klein described as a part of the paranoid-schizoid phase.[1] I wish to emphasize that in this phase the psychotic splits his objects, and contemporaneously all that part of his personality, which would make him aware of the reality he hates, into exceedingly minute fragments, for it is this that contributes materially to the psychotic's feelings that he cannot restore his objects or his ego. As a result of these splitting attacks, all those features of the personality which should one day provide the foundation for intuitive understanding of himself and others are jeopardized at the outset. All the functions which Freud described as being, at a later stage, a developmental response to the reality principle – that is to say consciousness of sense impressions, attention, memory, judgement, thought – have brought against them, in such inchoate forms as they may possess at the outset of life, the sadistic splitting eviscerating attacks that lead to their being minutely fragmented and then expelled from the personality to penetrate, or encyst, the objects. In the patient's phantasy the expelled particles of ego lead an independent and uncontrolled existence, either contained by or containing the external objects; they continue to exercise their functions as if the ordeal to which they have been subjected had served only to increase their number and provoke their hostility to the psyche that ejected them. In consequence the patient feels himself to be surrounded by bizarre objects whose nature I now describe.

58. Each particle is felt to consist of a real object which is encapsulated in a piece of personality that has engulfed it. The nature of this complete particle will depend partly on the character of the real object, say a gramophone, and partly on the character of the particle of personality that engulfs it. If the piece of personality is concerned with sight, the gramophone when played is felt to be watching the patient; if with hearing, then the gramophone when played is felt to be listening to the patient. The object, angered at being engulfed, swells up, so to speak, and suffuses and controls the piece of personality that engulfs it: to that extent the particle of personality has become a thing. Since these particles are what the patient depends on for use as the prototypes of ideas – later to form the matrix from which words should spring – this suffusion of the piece of personality by the contained but controlling object leads the patient to feel that

[1] 'Notes on Some Schizoid Mechanisms' (Klein, 1946).

words are the actual things they name and so adds to the confusions, described by Segal, that arise because the patient equates, but does not symbolize. The fact that the patient uses these bizarre objects for achieving thought leads now to a fresh problem. If we consider that one of the patient's objects in using splitting and projective identification is to rid himself of awareness of reality, it is clear that he could achieve the maximum of severance from reality with the greatest economy of effort if he could launch these destructive attacks on the link, whatever it is, that connects sense impressions with consciousness. In my paper to the 1953 International Congress I showed that awareness of psychic reality depended on the development of a capacity for verbal thought the foundation of which was linked with the depressive position. It is impossible to go into this now; I refer you to Melanie Klein's 1930 paper on 'The Importance of Symbol-formation in the Development of the Ego' and to the paper given to the British Psychological Society (1955) by H. Segal.[1] In this, Segal demonstrates the importance of symbol formation and explores its relationship to verbal thought and the reparative drives normally associated with the depressive position. I am concerned with an earlier stage in the same story. It is my belief that the mischief that becomes much more apparent in the depressive position has in fact been initiated in the paranoid-schizoid phase when the foundations for primitive thought should be laid, but are not, because of the overaction of splitting and projective identification.

59. Freud attributes to thought the function of providing a means of restraint of action. But he goes on to say, "It is probable that thinking was originally unconscious, in so far as it rose above mere ideation and turned to the relations between the object-impressions, and that it became endowed with further qualities which were perceptible to consciousness only through its connection with the memory traces of words" (1911b). My experiences have led me to suppose that some kind of thought, related to what we should call ideographs and sight rather than to words and hearing, exists at the outset. This thought depends on a capacity for balanced introjection and projection of objects and, *a fortiori*, on awareness of them. This is within the

---

[1]Paper on Symbol Formation read to the Medical Section of the British Psychological Society.

capacity of the non-psychotic part of the personality, partly because of the splitting and ejection of the apparatus of awareness I have already described, and partly for the following reasons.

Thanks to the operations of the non-psychotic part of the personality, the patient is aware that introjection is leading to the formation of the unconscious thought of which Freud speaks as "turned to the relations between object-impressions" I believe that it is this unconscious thought which Freud describes as turned to the relations between the object impressions which is responsible for the "consciousness attached to" the sense impressions. I am fortified in this belief by his statement twelve years later in the paper *The Ego and the Id* (1923b). In this he says, "that the question 'How does a thing become conscious?' could be put more advantageously thus: 'How does a thing become preconscious?' And the answer would be: 'By coming into connection with the verbal images that correspond to it'."

In my 1953 paper I said that verbal thought is bound up with awareness of psychic reality; this I also believe to be true of the early pre-verbal thought of which I am now speaking. In view of what I have already said of the psychotic's attacks on the whole mental apparatus responsible for consciousness of external and internal reality, it is to be expected that the deployment of projective identification would be particularly severe against the thought, of whatever kind, that turned to the relations between object-impressions; for if this link could be severed (or better still never forged) then at least consciousness of reality would be destroyed even though reality itself could not be. But in fact the work of destruction is already half done; the material from which thought is forged, in the non-psychotic by balanced introjection and projection, is not available to the psychotic part of the personality because the displacement of projection and introjection by projective identification has left him with only the bizarre objects I have described.

60. In fact, not only is primitive thought attacked because it links sense-impressions of reality with consciousness, but thanks to the psychotic's over-endowment with destructiveness the splitting processes are extended to the links within the thought processes themselves. As Freud's phrase regarding thought being turned to the relations between object-impressions implies, this primitive matrix of ideographs from which thought springs contains within itself links between one ideograph and another. All these are now attacked till finally two objects cannot be brought together in a way which leaves each object with its intrinsic qualities intact and yet able, by their conjunction, to produce a new mental object. Consequently the formation of symbols, which depends for its therapeutic effect on the ability to bring together two objects so that their resemblance is made manifest, yet their difference left unimpaired, now becomes difficult. At a still later stage the result of these splitting attacks is seen in the denial of articulation as a principle for the combining of words. This last does not mean that objects cannot be brought together; as I shall show later when speaking of agglomeration, that is by no means true. Further, since that-which-links has been not only minutely fragmented but also projected out into objects to join the other bizarre objects, the patient feels surrounded by minute links which, being impregnated now with cruelty, link objects together cruelly.

To conclude my description of the fragmentation of the ego and its expulsion into and about its objects, I shall say that I believe the processes I have described to be the central factor, in so far as such a factor can be isolated without distortion, in the differentiation of the psychotic from the non-psychotic part of the personality. It takes place at the outset of the patient's life: the sadistic attacks on the ego and on the matrix of thought, together with projective identification of the fragments, make it certain that from this point on there is an ever-widening divergence between the psychotic and non-psychotic parts of the personality until at last the gulf between them is felt to be unbridgeable.

61. The consequences for the patient are that he now moves not in a world of dreams, but in a world of objects which are ordinarily the furniture of dreams. His sense impressions appear to have suffered mutilation of a kind which would be appropriate had they been attacked as the breast is felt to be attacked in the sadistic phantasies of the infant (Klein, 1928). The patient feels imprisoned in the state of mind he has achieved, and unable to escape from it because he feels he lacks the apparatus of awareness of reality which is both the key to escape and the freedom to which he would escape. The sense of imprisonment is intensified by the menacing presence of the expelled fragments within whose planetary movements he is contained. These objects, primitive yet complex, partake of qualities which in the non-psychotic personality are peculiar to matter, anal objects, senses, ideas and superego.

62. The diversity of such objects, dependent as it is on the sense by which they are suffused, prevents more than the cursory indication of their mode of genesis that I have given. The reaction of these objects to material for ideographic thought leads the patient to confound real objects with primitive ideas, and therefore to confusion, when they obey the laws of natural science and not those of mental functioning. If he wishes to bring back any of these objects in an attempt at restitution of the ego (and in analysis he feels impelled to make the attempt) he has to bring them back by projective identification in reverse and by the route by which they were expelled. Whether he feels he has had one of these objects put into him by the analyst or whether he feels he had taken it in, he feels the ingress as an assault. The extreme degree to which he has carried the splitting of objects and ego alike makes any attempt at synthesis hazardous. Furthermore, as he has rid himself of that-which-joins – his capacity for articulation – the methods available for synthesis are felt to be macilent; he can compress but cannot join, he can fuse but cannot articulate. The capacity to join is felt, as a result of its ejection, to have become, like all other expelled particles, infinitely worse than they were when ejected. Any joining that takes place is done with a vengeance, that is to say in a manner expressly contrary to the wishes of the patient at the moment. In the course of the analysis this process of compression or agglomeration loses some of its malignancy and then fresh problems arise.

63. I must now draw your attention to a matter that demands a paper to itself and therefore cannot be more than mentioned here. It is implicit in my description that the psychotic personality or part of the personality has used splitting and projective identification as a substitute for repression. Where the non-psychotic part of the personality resorts to repression as a means of cutting off certain trends in the mind both from consciousness and from other forms of manifestation and activity, the psychotic part of the personality has attempted to rid itself of the apparatus on which the psyche depends to carry out the repressions; the unconscious would seem to be replaced by the world of dream furniture.

64. I shall now attempt a description of an actual session; it is a clinical experience based on these theories rather than the description of an experience on which the theories are based, but I hope I shall be able to indicate the material from previous sessions which led me to interpret as I did.

The patient at the time of this session, of which I describe a small part, had been coming to me for six years. He had once been as late as *forty-five* minutes, but had never missed a session; the sessions were never continued over time. On this morning he arrived a quarter of an hour late and lay on the couch. He spent some time turning from one side to another, ostensibly making himself comfortable. At length he said, "I don't suppose I shall do anything today. I ought to have rung up my mother." He paused and then said "No; I thought it would be like this." A more prolonged pause followed; then, "Nothing but filthy things and smells", he said. "I think I've lost my sight". Some twenty-five minutes of our time had now passed, and at this point I made an interpretation, but before I repeat it I must discuss some previous material which will, I hope, make my intervention comprehensible.

When the patient was manoeuvring on the couch I was watching something with which I was familiar. Five years earlier he had explained that his doctor advised an operation for hernia and it was to be assumed that the discomfort caused by the hernia compelled these adjustments. It was, however, evident that more was involved than the hernia and rational activity to increase his physical comfort. I had sometimes asked him what these movements were, and to these questions his reply had been, "Nothing". Once he had said, "I don't know". I had felt that "Nothing" was a thinly veiled invitation to me to mind my own business as well as a denial of something very bad. I continued, over the weeks and years, to watch his movements. A handkerchief was disposed near his right pocket; he arched his back – surely a sexual gesture here? A lighter fell out of his pocket. Should he pick it up? Yes. No. perhaps not. Well, yes. It was retrieved from the floor and placed by the handkerchief. Immediately a shower of coins spilled over the couch on to the floor. The patient lay still and waited. Perhaps, his gesture seemed to suggest, he had been unwise to bring back the lighter. It had seemed to lead to the shower of coins. He waited, cautiously, furtively. And finally he made the remark I have reported. It reminded me of his descriptions, not given in any one session but produced over many months, of the tortuous manoeuvres through which he had to go before he went to the lavatory, or went down to breakfast, or telephoned to his mother. I was quite used to recalling many of the free associations which might easily be appropriate to the behaviour he displayed on this as on many other mornings. But these were now my associations, and once when I had tried to make use of such material in an interpretation that is exactly the reply lie had made. One interpretation I remembered which had met with some success. I had pointed out that he felt much the same about these movements as he had about a dream he had told me – he had no ideas about the dream and he had no ideas about the movements. "Yes", he had agreed, "that's so". "And yet", I replied, "you once had an idea about it; you thought it was the hernia". "That's nothing", he replied, and had then paused, almost slyly I thought, to see if I had grasped the point. So, "Nothing is really a hernia", I said. "No idea", he replied, "only a hernia." I had been left feeling that his "no idea" was very like the "no ideas" about the dreams or the movements, but for that session at least I could get no further. In this respect the movements and the dreams were very fair instances of mutilated attempts at co-operation, and this too was something to which I had drawn his attention.

65. It may have occurred to you, as it often had to me, that I was watching a series of miniature dramatic presentations, preparations for a baby's bath or feed, or a change of nappies, or a sexual seduction. More often it would be correct to say that the presentation was a conglomeration of bits out of a number of such scenes, and it was this impression that led me finally to suppose that I was watching an ideomotor activity, that is to say a means of expressing an idea without naming it. From this it was a short step to think of it as the kind of motor activity which Freud had described as characteristic of the supremacy of the pleasure principle. For, in so far as I was watching psychotic phenomena, the patient could not be acting in response to awareness of external reality; he was exhibiting the kind of motor discharge which Freud said, "had served to unburden the mental apparatus of accretions of stimuli, and in carrying out this task had sent innervations into the interior of the body (mien expressions of affect)." It was this impression which returned to me when the patient said, "I don't expect I shall do anything today." It was a remark that could refer to the likelihood of his producing any material for interpretation or, equally, to the likelihood that I would produce any interpretations. "I ought to have rung up my mother" could mean that his failure to do so was being visited upon him by the punishment of not being able to do any analysis. It also meant that his mother would have known what to do about it – she could get associations out of him or interpretations out of me; something depended on what his mother meant to him, but on this point I was really in the dark. She had come in to the analysis as a simple working-class woman who had to go to work for the family; this view was entertained with the same degree of conviction that stamped his statements that the family were extremely wealthy. I was vouchsafed glimpses of her as a woman with such multitudinous social engagements that scant time was left her to satisfy the needs either of the patient, who was her eldest son, her eldest daughter, two years older than the patient, or the remainder of the family. She had been spoken of, if anything so inarticulate could be described as speech, as devoid of common sense or culture, though in the habit of visiting art galleries of international fame. I was left to infer that the bringing up of her children was ignorant and painstaking in the extreme.

I may say that at the time of which I write I knew little more of his real mother than would be known by a person who had rid himself of his ego in the way I have described as typical of the psychotic personality. Nevertheless I had these impressions, and others which I omit, and on them I based my interpretations. The patient's responses to these interpretations were outright rejection as either quite inadmissible because wrong, or accurate but improperly arrived at in that I must have been using his mind (really his capacity for contact with reality) without his permission. It will be observed that he thereby expresses a jealous denial of my insight.

66. When the patient said, after a pause, that he knew it would be like this, I felt on fairly sure ground in assuming that it was I who was unlikely to do anything in that session and that his mother was some person or thing who could have enabled him to deal with me more satisfactorily. This impression was strengthened by the next association.

If the theories I have described are correct, then, in any given situation, the patient who is ill enough, as this one was, to have achieved certification, has two main problems to solve, one appertaining to the non-psychotic part of the personality and one to the psychotic part. With this particular patient, at this particular juncture, the psychotic personality and its problems still obscured the non-psychotic personality and its problems. Nevertheless, as I hope to show, the latter were discernible in the material. The non-psychotic personality was concerned with a neurotic problem, that is to say a problem that centred on the resolution of a conflict of ideas and emotions to which the operation of the ego had given rise. But the psychotic personality was concerned with the problem of repair of the ego, and the clue to this lay in the fear that he had lost his sight. Since it was the psychotic problem that obtruded I dealt with that, taking his last association first. I told him that these filthy things and smells were what he felt he had made me do, and that he felt he had compelled me to defecate them out, including the sight he had put into me.

The patient jerked convulsively and I saw him cautiously scanning what seemed to be the air around him. I accordingly said that he felt surrounded by bad and smelly bits of himself including his eyes which he felt he had expelled from his anus. He replied: "I can't see:" I then told him he felt he had lost his sight and his ability to talk to his mother, or to me, when he had got rid of these abilities so as to avoid pain.

67. In this last interpretation I was making use of a session, many months earlier, in which the patient complained that analysis was torture, memory torture. I showed him then that when he felt pain, as evidenced in this session by the convulsive jerks, he achieved anaesthesia by getting rid of his memory and anything that could make him realize pain.

Patient. "My head is splitting; maybe my dark glasses."

Some five months previously I had worn dark glasses; the fact had, as far as I could tell, produced no reaction whatever from that day to this, but that becomes less surprising if we consider that I, wearing dark glasses, was felt by him as one of the objects to which I referred when describing the fate of the expelled particles of ego. I have explained that the psychotic personality seems to have to await the occurrence of an apt event before it feels it is in possession of an ideograph suitable for use in communication with itself or with others. Reciprocally, other events, which might be supposed to have immediate significance for the non-psychotic personality, are passed by because they are felt to be significant only as ideographs serving no immediate need. In the present instance the problem created by my wearing dark glasses was obscured in the non-psychotic part of the personality because the psychotic part of the personality was dominant: and in that part of the personality the event was merely significant as an ideograph for which it had had no immediate need. When at last the fact obtruded in analysis it had the appearance, superficially, of being perhaps some kind of delayed reaction, but such a view depends on the supposition that the association of the dark glasses was an expression of neurotic conflict in the non-psychotic part of the personality. In fact it was not a delayed expression of a conflict in the non-psychotic part of the personality but, as I shall show, the mobilization of an ideograph needed by the psychotic part of the personality for an immediate repair of an ego damaged by the excessive projective identification that I have described. Such obtrusions of fact, originally passed by in silence, must then be regarded not so much as significant because their appearance is delayed, but because they are evidence of activity in the psychotic part of the personality.

Assuming then that the dark glasses here are a verbal communication of an ideograph, it becomes necessary to determine the interpretation of the ideograph. I shall have to compress, almost I fear to the point of risking incomprehensibility, the evidence in my possession. The glasses contained a hint of the baby's bottle. They were two glasses, or bottles, thus resembling the breast. They were dark because frowning and angry. They were of glass to pay him out for trying to see through them when they were breasts. They were dark because he needs darkness to spy on the parents in intercourse. They were dark because he had taken the bottle not to get milk but to see what the parents did. They were dark because he had swallowed them, and not simply the milk they had contained. And they were dark because the clear good objects had been made black and smelly inside them. All these attributes must have been achieved through the operation of the non-psychotic part of the personality. Added to these characteristics were those that I have described as appertaining to them as part of the ego that has been expelled by projective identification, namely their hatred of him as part of himself he had rejected. Making use of these accretions of analytic experience, and still concentrating on the psychotic problem, that is to say, the need to repair the ego to meet the demands of the external situation, I said,

Analyst. Your sight has come back into you but splits your head; you feel it is very bad sight because of what you have done to it.

Patient (moving in pain as if protecting his back passage). Nothing.

Analyst. It seemed to be your back passage.

Patient. Moral strictures.

I told him that his sight, the dark glasses, were felt as a conscience that punished him, partly for getting rid of them to avoid pain, partly because he had used them to spy on me, and on his parents. I could not feel I had done justice to the compactness of the association.

It will be observed that I have not been able to offer any suggestions as to what might be stimulating these reactions in the patient. This is not surprising, for I am dealing with a psychotic problem, and since the psychotic problem as opposed to the non-psychotic problem is precisely related to the destruction of all the mental apparatus that brings awareness of stimuli from reality, the nature and even existence of such stimuli would not be discernible. However, the patient's next remark gave it.

Patient. The weekend; don't know if I can last it.

This is an instance of the way in which the patient felt he had repaired his capacity for contact and could therefore tell me what was going on around him. It was a phenomenon by now familiar to him and I did not interpret it. Instead I said,

Analyst. You feel that you have to be able to get on without me. But to do that you feel you need to be able to see what happens around you, and even to be able to contact me; to be able to contact me at a distance, as you do your mother when you ring her up; so you tried to get your ability to see and talk back again from me.

Patient. Brilliant interpretation. (With a sudden convulsion) O God!

Analyst. *You* feel you can see and understand now, but what you see is so brilliant that it causes intense pain.

Patient (clenching his fists and showing much tension and anxiety). I hate you.

Analyst. When you see, what you see – the week-end break and the things you use darkness to spy on – fills you with hate of me and admiration.

It is my belief that at this point the restoration of the ego meant that the patient was confronted with the non-psychotic problem, the resolution of neurotic conflicts. This was supported by the reactions in the following weeks, when he would display his inability to tolerate the neurotic conflicts stimulated by reality and his attempt to solve that problem by projective identification. This would be followed by attempts to use me as his ego, anxieties about his insanity, further attempts to repair his ego and return to reality and neurosis; and so the cycle would repeat itself.

68. I have described this portion of a session in detail because it can be used to illustrate a number of points without burdening the reader with a number of different examples of association and interpretation. I have regretfully had to exclude some striking and dramatic material, because to include it without including a quite overwhelming mass of description of day-to-day mundane analysis with its load of sheer incomprehensibility, error and so forth would produce an entirely misleading picture. At the same time I do not wish to leave any doubt that the approach I am describing is one which in my opinion is producing striking results. The change that took place in this patient during the weeks when I was able to demonstrate the interplay I have just described, was of a kind that I believe any analyst would accept as worth the name of psychoanalytic improvement. The patient's demeanour softened: his expression became much less tense. At the beginnings and ends of sessions he met my eyes and did not either evade me or, what with him had been a common event, focus beyond me as if I were the surface of a mirror before which he rehearsed some inner drama, a peculiarity that had often helped me to realize that I was not a real person to him. Unfortunately these phenomena are not easy to describe and I cannot dwell on the attempt; for I wish to draw attention to an improvement which I found, and still find with other patients, both surprising and baffling. As it touches the main theme of this paper I can deal with it by returning to the theoretical discussion that I interrupted to introduce my clinical example.

69. If verbal thought is that which synthesizes and articulates impressions, and is thus essential to awareness of internal and external reality, it is to be expected that it will be subjected, on and off throughout analysis, to destructive splitting and projective identification. I described the inception of verbal thought as appertaining to the depressive position; but the depression that is proper to this phase is itself something to which the psychotic personality objects and therefore the development of verbal thought comes under attack, its inchoate elements being expelled from the personality by projective identification whenever depression occurs. In her paper to the International Congress of 1955,[1] Hanna Segal described the manner in which the psyche deals with depression; I would refer you to that description as apposite to that part of the depressive position which I here include in the discussion of the development of verbal thought. But I have said that in the even earlier phase, the paranoid-schizoid position, thought processes that should be developing are in fact being destroyed. At this stage there is no question of verbal thought but only of inchoation of primitive thought of a preverbal kind. Excessive projective identification at this early stage prevents smooth introjection and assimilation of sense impressions and so denies the personality a firm base on which the inception of pre-verbal thought can proceed. Furthermore, not only is thought attacked, as itself being a link, but the factors which make for coherence in thought itself are similarly attacked so that in the end the elements of thought, the units, as it were, of which thought is made up, cannot be articulated. The growth of verbal thought is therefore compromised both by the continuing attacks I have described as typical of the depressive position, and by the fact of the long history of attacks on thought of any kind that precedes this.

The attempt to think, which is a central part of the total process of repair of the ego, involves the use of primitive pre-verbal modes

[1]['Depression in the Schizophrenic', read at the 19th International Psycho-Analytical Congress, Geneva, 24–28 July, 1955. *International Journal of Psycho-Analysis, 37* (1956): 339–343. *Ed.*]

which have suffered mutilation and projective identification. This means that the expelled particles of ego, and their accretions, have to be brought back into control and therefore into the personality. Projective identification is therefore reversed and these objects are brought back by the same route as that by which they were expelled. This was expressed by a patient who said he had to use an intestine, not a brain, to think with, and emphasized the accuracy of his description by correcting me when, on a subsequent occasion, I spoke of his having taken in something by swallowing it; the intestine does not swallow, he said. In order to bring them back, these objects have to be compressed. Owing to the hostility of the rejected function of articulation, itself now an object, the objects can only be joined inappropriately, or agglomerated. I suggested in my clinical example that the dark glasses were an instance of this kind of agglomeration of bizarre objects which were the product of projective identification of the ego. Furthermore, that owing to the patient's inability to distinguish between such objects and real objects, frequently he had to wait for appropriate events to provide him with the ideograph his impulse to communicate required, and that this case was a reciprocal of this – namely an instance of the storing of an event not on account of its neurotic significance but on account of its value as an ideograph. Now this means that this particular use of dark glasses is fairly advanced: for one thing, the storage of such an event for use as an ideograph approximates to Freud's description of a search for data, so that they might be already familiar, if an urgent inner need should arise, as a function of attention as one of the aspects of the ego. But it also shows, albeit in this instance in a somewhat rudimentary form, a skilful agglomeration which is successful in conveying meaning. Now the surprising, and even disconcerting, improvement of which I spoke touches this point of skilful agglomeration; for I have found not only that patients resorted more and more to ordinary verbal thought, thus showing an increased capacity for it and increased consideration for the analyst as an ordinary human being, but also that they seemed to become more and more skilful at this type of agglomerated rather than articulated speech. The whole point about civilized speech is that it greatly simplifies the thinker's or speaker's task. With that tool, problems can be solved because at least they can be stated, whereas without it certain questions, no matter how important, cannot even be posed. The extraordinary thing is the *tour de force* by which primitive modes of thought are used by the patient for the statement of themes of great complexity. And I find it significant that his ability to do this improves concurrently with more welcome advances. I say more welcome because I have not yet satisfied myself that it is right to ignore the content of an association because dealing with it would keep the analyst talking at infinitely greater length than the patient. What, for example, is the correct interpretation of the content of 'moral strictures'? And having decided that, what is the correct procedure? For how long is one to continue the elucidation?

The particles which have to be employed share, as we have seen, the qualities of things. The patient seems to feel this as an additional obstacle to their re-entry. As these objects which are felt to have been expelled by projective identification become infinitely worse after expulsion than they were when originally expelled, the patient feels intruded upon, assaulted, and tortured by this re-entry even if willed by himself. This is shown, in the example I gave, by the convulsive movement of the patient and by his striking reaction to the "brilliant" interpretation. But this last also shows that the senses, as part of the expelled ego, also become painfully compressed on being taken back, and this is often the explanation of the extremely painful tactile, auditory, and visual hallucinations in the grip of which he seems to labour. Depression and anxiety, being subject to the same mechanism, are similarly intensified until the patient is compelled to deal with them by projective identification, as Segal described.

CONCLUSION

70. Experience of these theories in practice has convinced me that they have a real value and lead to improvements which even psychoanalysts may feel to deserve stern testing and scrutiny. Conversely, I do not think real progress with psychotic patients is likely to take place until due weight is given to the nature of the divergence between the psychotic and non-psychotic personality, and in particular the role of projective identification in the psychotic part of the personality as a substitute for repression in the neurotic part. The patient's destructive attacks on his ego and the substitution of projective identification for repression and introjection must be worked through. Further, I consider that this holds true for the severe neurotic, in whom I believe there is a psychotic personality concealed by neurosis as the neurotic personality is screened by psychosis in the psychotic, that has to be laid bare and dealt with.

6

On hallucination

71. Descriptions of hallucinations with which I am acquainted lack the precision necessary to afford material for psychoanalytic interpretation. In this paper I describe some detailed observations of hallucination and the results that followed. I hope to persuade you that such observation of the hallucinatory processes is essential and rewarding.

The content of the paper is narrowly circumscribed and much material excluded which would be helpful to perspicuity. I must indicate two important categories of facts which suffer under this limitation. First, all the material is derived from the practical application of the theories I put forward in my paper 'Differentiation of the Psychotic from the Non-Psychotic Personalities' [chapter 5]. I am compelled to assume the reader's acquaintance with them and the acknowledgements I then made of my indebtedness to the work in this field of Melanie Klein and her co-workers. Second, I must emphasize that the clinical descriptions though disguised, come from the analysis of a patient who has been, but now is not, under certificate diagnosed as schizophrenic. Light was shed on the case by experiences with two other patients in analysis who have also been under certificate with the same diagnosis. I hope that the rest of the paper will yield the bare minimum of fact necessary for comprehension, for I shall now turn at once to the clinical descriptions.

72. The patient has arrived on time and I have asked for him to be called. As he has been with me in analysis for some years and a great deal of work has been done, I am not surprised when he appears without further ado, though such unceremonious progression has not always been the rule. As he passes into the room he glances rapidly at me; such frank scrutiny has been a development of the past six months and is still a novelty. While I close the door he goes to the foot of the couch, facing the head pillows and my chair, and stands, shoulders stooping, knees sagging, head inclined to the chair, motionless until I have passed him and am about to sit down. So closely do his movements seem to be geared with mine that the inception of my movements to sit appears to release a spring in him. As I lower myself into my seat he turns left about, slowly, evenly, as if something would be spilled, or perhaps fractured, were he to be betrayed into a precipitate movement. As I sit, the turning movement stops as if we were both parts of the same clockwork toy. The patient, now with his back to me, is arrested at a moment when his gaze is directed to the floor near that corner of the room which would be to his right and facing him if he lay on the couch. This pause endures perhaps for a second and is closed by a shudder of his head and shoulders which is so slight and so rapid that I might suppose myself mistaken. Yet it marks the end of one phase and the start of the next; the patient seats himself on the couch preparatory to lying down.

He reclines slowly, keeping his eye on the same corner of the floor, craning his head forward now and then as he falls back on to the couch as if anxious not to become unsighted. His scrutiny, as if he feared the consequences of being detected in it, is circumspect.

He is recumbent at last; a few more surreptitious glances and he is still. Then he speaks: "I feel quite empty. Although I have eaten hardly anything, it can't be that. No, it's no use; I shan't be able to do any more today." He then relapses into silence.

So far this session differs little from many others. I hardly know when I began to notice, amongst the varying forms of opening, the features to which I have drawn attention in this account. The pattern must often have been there, though overlaid, as it seemed to me at the time, by other features that required more urgent interpretation. The gradual obtrusion, through constant repetition, of a pattern of behaviour which, when I recognized it, seemed already to be familiar, was a common experience with this patient. For the present I wish to discuss one aspect only of the features that have a bearing on hallucination.

When the patient glanced at me he was taking a part of me into him. It was taken into his eyes, as I later interpreted his thought to him, as if his eyes could suck something out of me. This was then removed from me, before I sat down, and expelled, again through his eyes, so that it was deposited in the right-hand corner of the room where he could keep it under observation while he was lying on the couch. The expulsion took a moment or two to complete. The shudder I have described was the sign that the expulsion was completed. Then, and only then, was the hallucination in being. I do not suggest that all this was revealed to me through the patient's behaviour in this series of sessions. It had emerged gradually over the years until finally it was borne in on me, and the patient in due course confirmed it, that he felt his sense organs to expel as well as to receive. This I put forward as the first step in the comprehension of hallucinatory phenomena: if the patient says he sees an object it may mean that an external object has been perceived by him, or it may mean that he is ejecting an object through his eyes; if he says he hears something it may mean he is ejecting a sound – this is not the same as making a noise; if he says he feels something it may mean tactile sensation is being extruded, thrown off by his skin. An awareness of the double meaning that verbs of sense have for the psychotic sometimes makes it possible to detect an hallucinatory process before it betrays itself by more familiar signs.

To turn now to the content of the hallucination: what is it? First, I confine my attention to the object supposedly deposited in the corner of the room: I am led to it because, judging by his glances, that is what most exercises the patient's mind. Evidently it is an hostile object: its extrusion has emptied the patient: its presence threatens him and makes him fear he will be able to make no further use of the session. The nature of his inspection of it and such meaning as lies easily accessible on the surface of his disjointed phrases tell me that much.

But in addition, I have in mind the end of the previous day's session. The patient had been hostile and afraid that he would murder me. I was able to show him that he was splitting off painful feelings, mostly envy and revenge, of which he hoped to rid himself by forcing them into me. There the session ended. Melanie Klein has described how this mechanism produces problems for the patient by engendering fear of the analyst who now is a container of a bad part of himself. I was familiar with this sequence in this patient's analysis, so I was prepared to find that a session ending in this way would overflow into the next. And so it did; developments in the session I am describing showed I was correct to interpret his behaviour as an attempt to remove from me these bad aspects of himself before he attempted the main business of the session, the ingestion of cure.

73. Hallucinations and the fantasy of the senses as ejecting as well as receiving, point to the severity of the disorder from which the patient is suffering, but I must indicate a benign quality in the symptom which was certainly not present earlier. Splitting, evacuatory use of the senses, and hallucinations were all being employed in the service of an ambition to be cured, and may therefore be supposed to be creative activities. To contrast this experience with similar episodes earlier will help to illuminate both. First, the late experience has a coherence, a degree of integration, which was quite lacking in any early session. Even the disjointed sentences yield an impression without much difficulty: the bizarre automaton-like synthesis of physical movement in which patient and analyst are geared together like clockwork toys does bring two objects together even though the relationship has been denuded of life. The splitting is akin to that described by Melanie Klein as a separation of the bad breast from the good breast, of love from hate. This patient had attempted to bring objects together at least three and a half years before this. They were brought together with such violence that fission and fusion were adumbrated in terms of atomic explosions. Finally, the splitting with which I have been familiar through the whole analysis has been altering its character until, in the example I have given, it is achieved with a degree of gentleness, and a regard for psychic structure and function, which makes it doubtful whether an appellation that is justified by the historical development of the patient's analysis is any longer justified by the intrinsic nature of the activity. Freud used the terms "splitting" and "dissociation" indifferently (1893c), but it seems to me that the phenomena which I have observed in this and other severely disturbed patients are best described by the term "splitting" as it is used by Melanie Klein, leaving the term "dissociation" free to be employed where a more benign activity is being discussed. The original splitting processes evinced by this patient were violent, intended to produce minute fragmentation and deliberately aimed at effecting separations which run directly counter to any natural lines of demarcation between one part of the psyche, or one function of the psyche, and another. Dissociation, on the other hand, appears to be gentler and to have respect for natural lines of demarcation between whole objects, and indeed to follow those lines of demarcation to effect the separation; the patient who dissociates is capable of depression. Dissociation also appears to me to betray dependence on the pre-existence of elementary verbal thought, as indeed Freud's statement[1] that, "it is the common popular idea of the organs and of the body in general that is at work in the hysterical paralyses" would seem to indicate. Where I wish to stress the developmental aspect of the activity in the history of the patient's analysis I shall continue to use the term splitting: where I wish to speak of a benign process related to the non-psychotic part of the personality I shall speak of dissociation.

I hope it is now clear that I am speaking of a psychotic patient who has achieved a stage of development in which creative impulses are discernible and can even be detected as motives in mental mechanisms which at the beginning of his analysis appeared to be wholly subservient to wishes to destroy.

I did not on this occasion give the patient the explanations I have given here, for, as I have said, he was by this time familiar with the fact that he was not sure whether any given sensation was a sign that something was being taken in by him or a sign that something had been, or was being, expelled by him. It may give an idea of some of the difficulties of interpretation if I recount an episode from one of the early sessions in which the nature of the hallucinatory experience was becoming more evident. I had drawn the patient's attention to the fact that when he said, with every evidence of persecutory anxiety, "Tears are coming to my eyes", he meant that these tears were coming into his eyes from outside and were going to blind him. He thereupon sat up and stared at the opposite wall with much the same demeanour and bearing that he exhibited in the course of the expulsion of an object into the right-hand corner of the room that I have been describing. When, as it appeared to me, the evacuation was complete, he said, "A man told me it was good to be depressed." I was pretty sure that I was the man and that that is what he had heard me say, but I felt I lacked any supporting evidence that would make an interpretation on those lines relevant, and said, You are seeing that man in front of you now, I think." He replied, "It's all gone dark. I can't see.

[1]Freud (1893c), p. 170. [This is not quoted absolutely accurately. Freud wrote: ". . . what is in question in hysterical paralysis, just as in anaesthesia, etc., is the everyday, popular conception of the organs and of the body in general." *Ed.*]

I'm shut in." This response may appear to be as puzzling as it did to me, until I realized that the patient felt, when psychotic mechanisms were in the forefront of his mental activity, that the same mechanisms and modes of thought were being employed by me. Thanks to familiarity with this fact, I was able to realize that the patient thought I must have seen the man who was visible to him. As I have explained elsewhere, the bizarre objects with which the psychotic part of the personality feels itself to be surrounded when projective identification is over-active, are always compounded of a variety of elements of which one is a part of the personality of the patient himself. If, therefore, I had seen the man, a part of the patient's personality which was mingled with this object, had been sucked into me through my eyes. It will be realized that I am describing in some detail the clinical manifestation of the confusional states which have been described by Melanie Klein and confirmed by Herbert Rosenfeld. I therefore told him that he felt that a part of himself had been greedily swallowed up by my eyes, which had taken in not only the man he saw, but also a bit of himself.

To return to the session which I am using as the main source of my clinical material for this paper: I resume my description from the point where I had interpreted the hallucinatory activity as an attempt to deal with the dangerous parts of his personality. I have said that the patient relapsed into silence after his disjointed sentences. While I gave my interpretation he made jerky convulsive movements which were confined mostly to the upper part of his body. Each syllable that I uttered seemed to be felt by him as a stabbing thrust from me. I pointed this out and said that he felt a very bad thing was being violently intruded into him, partly by me, who he thought was trying to get rid of the object he had left inside me, and partly by himself in spite of the precaution he had taken by hardly eating anything. His greed remained, though he no longer wished to be greedy, because it was now felt to be independent of any control by himself.

I did not explain my reference to greed because I assumed that the patient was by this time familiar, through work which we had previously done, with the fact that he often used his eyes as organs of ingestion so that his greed could be satisfied, though his object strove to preserve itself by denying him physical contact. In this instance my assumption proved correct, but in fact I have often found that such assumptions, which if successful enable me to preserve the interpretation from being overburdened with detail, have proved to be beyond the patient's grasp until his capacity for integration is developed.

The convulsive movements stopped and he said, "I have painted a picture." His subsequent silence meant that the material for my next interpretation was already in my possession.

74. The lineaments of the picture that he has painted must be sought in the totality of material of which my interpretation so far has illuminated only one aspect, namely that which I adumbrated as centring on the bad object which he had withdrawn from me and immediately deposited in the right-hand corner of the room. My task, therefore, was to consider all the events of the session up to this point, as if it were a palimpsest in which I must detect another pattern whose outline was confused with that which I had already revealed in my interpretation. Before I passed on to a consideration of this pattern, I interpreted to the patient an aspect of this situation to which I draw your attention. It is that the patient is playing a dominant role, and expressing, with an unusual degree of urgency and force, a belief in his capacity to communicate matters, which he feels to be worthwhile, to a person whom he thinks likely to be receptive of them. But, I said, I was in addition a part of the picture which he had painted when he made himself and myself into two automata in a reciprocal but lifeless relationship. He replied, "The wireless next door kept me awake last night."

I knew that strong persecutory feelings were associated by him with all electrical apparatus, and I said he felt attacked by the electricity which he felt was like the life and sex which he had removed from the two objects which he had pushed out of himself when he painted his picture. He said, "Quite right" and then remarked that he did not know what would happen after the session, which in fact ended at this point.

This session, like some others which achieved a similar degree of integration, was called by the patient a 'good' session, and to some extent this may be accepted as a gratifying confirmation of a judgement I was myself disposed to make. But I had noticed that such sessions were followed with great consistency by 'bad' sessions, that is, sessions in which the patient seemed to return to an apparently uncooperative state of mind and produced material which I, as likely as not, found it almost impossible to interpret. His preoccupation with what would occur after the session was partly due to his own realization of this. He disliked the prospect of losing what he now recognized as an agreeable state of mind, namely, that which accompanied his awareness of co-operation. Work on this had revealed a number of contributory causes, such as: hatred and envy of analyst or patient, or the collaboration of both, for a successful creative achievement; a method of expiating guilt at benefiting; or expiation of guilt at having engaged in what, being a friendly co-operation, was to the patient a sexual act. In the session I have described, this last point might be expected to apply with peculiar force and cogency, especially in view of the implication in my interpretation that a sexual bond, though denied, was to be supposed to exist.

In fact the session following did have many of the features of the so-called 'bad' session, though my reason for reporting it is for the light it shed on our problems – not because of the lack of it. I find the description of such a session very difficult, because it is not possible to make notes, however soon after a session, of long passages of verbalization whose meaning, if any, eluded me. I am prepared to vouch for a reasonable degree of accuracy in my report of behaviour that I was able to interpret.

The patient came in, gave me a swift glance, waited till I reached my chair, and then lay down without further ado. He said tonelessly: "I don't know how much I shall be able to do today. As a matter of fact I got on quite well yesterday." At this point I felt his attention began to wander and he faltered in his speech. This kind of opening was quite familiar as a prelude to the bad session. He went on: "I am definitely anxious. Slightly. Still I suppose that does not matter." Rapidly becoming more incoherent, he continued, "I asked for some coffee. She seemed upset. It may have been my voice. but it was definitely good coffee too. I don't know why I shouldn't like it. When I passed the mews I thought the walls bulged outwards. I went back later but it was all right." There was more that I cannot attempt to reconstruct. He continued to speak hesitatingly, with minor pauses, for some five or more minutes. On the whole the sample I have given is fairly representative of the material, except that the reference to the coffee and the mews had by this stage in the analysis a good many associations for the patient and me, but the subsequent material had no associative value that I knew of, whatever it might mean to him.

75. As I have said, this kind of behaviour was familiar to me. It had been the rule in the early stages of analysis and was common after 'good' sessions, but I must say more of this now to clarify the nature of the problem confronting me in this session. Although it is not apparent in the account I have given, this patient was capable of coherent verbal expression. Within the last year he had on one occasion shown me that he was capable of making a psychoanalytic review of some emotional experience he had been through with good insight into his state of mind and good understanding of the analytic work done in the previous years of analysis. It had been in response to an interpretation which he seemed to take as a slight on his understanding, but it had shown that he had in fact learned much and could use it. Nothing could be in greater contrast than the state of mind revealed in that outburst and the state of mind which he usually presented and with which he was confronting me in the session I now describe. It seemed as if all the interpretations I had ever given needed to be given all over again, but it was equally obvious that these interpretations would tell him nothing new. Indeed, his response to the interpretation I did give him showed that my suspicion was correct. I pointed out that he was showing me how 'much' he could do, but without regard to the quality. He replied that he had placed his gramophone on the seat, which was his way of indicating that my interpretation combined the characteristics of a recording with which he was familiar and a defecation. I had reason, very shortly after that, to suppose that this response was far more than a mere criticism.

I was unwilling to repeat interpretations that I felt reasonably sure he could make for himself, but nevertheless there were borderline instances where I felt repetition was called for. The effect of these interpretations was not encouraging to further efforts of the same kind. I felt I had exhausted my supply of explanations and was more exercised with the possible causes of the patient's return to a pattern of behaviour which seemed to disprove the efficacy of any analytic approach to his problems. Something must have happened, but what? I drew his attention to the fact that he was having what he often called a 'bad' session and that there must be a reason. He seemed to accept the fact but offered no explanation, nor could I detect any in his material. The one reason that did not occur to me but which, in the light of later events, might have led me to some illumination of the material, was the possibility that he had had a dream. He had begun occasionally to report dreams to me. It was a comparatively recent development, some three or four months only, but in the absence of associations I had not felt able to make much headway beyond a few somewhat obvious suggestions such as that he felt it was something important to tell me, or that I would be the kind of person who understood them.

76. I cannot say now what it was in the session that first made me realize that the patient was hallucinated. It may have been that he was so manipulating the analysis and myself that I felt I was no longer an independent object, but was being treated by him as an hallucination. My suspicion was that when he said he had placed his gramophone on the seat, he was denying me life and independent existence in the analytic chair and treating my interpretations as auditory hallucinations. I did not immediately interpret this, but said that it appeared that he was reactivating a state of mind which, we must assume, had now become important to him to preserve as a good object. His response to this was to move his head and eyes as if my words were visible objects which were passing over his head to become impacted on the opposite wall. This behaviour was familiar from an early stage, and indeed I had seen it in other patients. Rodriguez reports similar behaviour in a psychotic child.[1] On previous occasions I had interpreted his behaviour to mean that he saw my words as things and was following them with his eyes. He had shown relief, almost amounting to amusement, and he appeared to agree that my words were seen as evacuated objects like bits of faeces. It had seemed to me then that the hallucination had a reassuring quality in that my interpretations, felt as persecutory objects, were seen to be passing harmlessly overhead. I said that he was again seeing objects passing overhead and reminded him of the previous occasion. This time he became anxious, and he said, "I feel quite empty. Better to close my eyes." He remained silent and very anxious and then said, somewhat apologetically I thought. "I have to use my ears. I seem to hear things all wrong." This association brought to my mind that he was not observing a direct relationship between me and the opposite wall, as I had supposed to be the case on earlier occasions. My interpretation was being taken in by his ears, but in a way which he

[1][In all likelihood the work Bion mentions here is Rodriguez (1968). *Ed.*]

felt to be "all wrong" – that is to say, cruelly and destructively. If so, the interpretations were being taken in and transformed by his ears and ejected by his eyes. This seemed so extraordinary that it was a moment or two before the explanation flashed upon me. I gave it in the following interpretation: "You", I said to him, "are feeling that your ears are chewing up and destroying all that I say to you. You are so anxious to get rid of it that you at once expel the pieces out of your eyes." I reminded him that when he had wished greedily to take something in, he did so through his eyes because his eyes could reach a long way to things he could not possibly touch with his mouth. I went on, "You are now using your eyes for the opposite reason – that is to say, to throw these broken up bits of interpretation as far away from yourself as you possibly can." He seemed extremely frightened, yet there was relief in his voice when he agreed. I drew his attention to his fear. He replied that he felt too weak to go on, "I am fading out." I suggested that he was afraid of me because he felt he was destroying me as well as my interpretations, and was also afraid because he could not get enough interpretations to cure him. This interpretation enabled him to go on with his associations; they were similar to those at the beginning of the session, yet there was a difference. He said that he had seen a painting in D; it had a penis in it. He complained that he had ruined a painting by making it pretty instead of ugly. He then said, "All sounds turn into things I see around me." I interpreted that he was again turning my interpretations into sounds and then evacuating them through his eyes, so that he now saw them as objects surrounding him. He replied, "Then everything around me is made by me. This is megalomania." After a pause he said, "I like your interpretation very much." In parenthesis, I must add that from this time onward I was able to recognize how very common it was for the patient, when he received an interpretation which for some reason was unwelcome, to give evidence of becoming hallucinated. He would strain forward on the couch as if looking at something in a far corner of the room. It became clear that these were frequent repetitions of the mechanism I have been describing. I shall suggest later some of the implications of this substitute for denial.

77. At this point his associations became less coherent. Unfortunately, I cannot report this material with any accuracy for reasons which I hope will be apparent. The associations seemed to consist of parts of sentences, disjointed references to what I assumed to be actual events, and a certain amount of material which had a meaning for me because it had appeared in other sessions. For an appreciable time my attention dwelt on this parade of associations to the exclusion of a peculiar accompaniment of running commentary on how he was feeling. As this obtruded, I became aware of a pattern which went like this: association, association, association, "definitely a bit anxious", association, association, "yes, slightly depressed", associations, "a bit anxious now", and so on. His behaviour was striking, but the session came to an end without my being able to formulate any clear idea of what was going on. I said that we did not know why all his analytic intuition and understanding had disappeared. He said "Yes" commiseratingly, and if one word can be made to express, "and I think that your intuition must have gone too", then his "Yes" did so on this occasion.

He started the next session in the matter-of-fact tone that he employed on the rare occasions when he spoke rationally and coherently. "I had a peculiar dream", he said, "it was a day or two ago." His voice became depressed during the course of this short communication, and by the end of it I felt that all trace of the matter-of-fact tone had gone. "You were in it", he added. It was clear that I was not going to hear any more about this dream, at any rate for the present, and that there were going to be no associations to it. I was not unduly disturbed by this because I had already been led to some conclusions about the nature of psychotic dreams. I had noticed that much work was needed before a psychotic patient reported a dream at all, and that when he did so he seemed to feel that he had said all that was necessary in reporting the fact that he had dreamt. I felt that I was expected to say something. I was not clear why the patient called his experience a dream, and in what way he distinguished it from other experiences which, though variously described by him to me, seemed to be hallucinations. I came to the conclusion that the patient meant that it was something that happened to him at night, when he was in bed. and probably when he was asleep. I felt that the 'dreams' shared so many characteristics of the hallucination that it was possible that actual experiences of hallucination in the consulting room might serve to throw light on the psychotic dream. It is a short step from what I have already said about hallucinations to suppose that when a psychotic patient speaks of having a dream, he thinks that his perceptual apparatus is engaged in expelling something, and that the dream is an evacuation from his mind strictly analogous to an evacuation from his bowels. A patient cannot report a dream until much analytic work has been done, and he cannot have done that analytic work without feeling that if he, as it were, passes a dream, he must at some time have taken that dream in. In short, to the psychotic a dream is an evacuation of material that has been taken in during waking hours. Much development must take place before the psychotic dream becomes sufficiently coherent to be communicable at all. Before that, I doubt whether its connexion with objects perceived is ever made. After that, I think it always is. Bearing this in mind, an approach to understanding the patient's dream becomes simpler. There is still a point: why does the patient say he had a peculiar dream? I hoped the session would throw light on this. In the meantime I said that this dream, together with the 'good' session, had been the cause which we had not found for reactivation of the state of mind in the 'bad' session. He replied, "I was mad." He had described these states of mind before, when hallucinations, splitting, projective identification and confusion were dominant, as "mad" or "insane". I made no observation on this, but used the term 'mad' myself whenever it served as a rapid method of referring to this complex state. I did so now. "You seem to feel", I said, "that you are mad when you are denying my interpretations by taking them in and getting rid of them at once. You must have felt that they have something to do with the peculiar dream. Why are you moving like that?"

My question was prompted by a series of convulsive twitchings of his chest. He said he did not know. "My thoughts go too quickly."

78. Whenever the patient had exhibited this kind of action, at least in the latter stages of his analysis, I had been reminded of Freud's description of motor activity, before the establishment of the reality principle, as not directed to alteration of the environment but to an unburdening of "the mental apparatus of accretions of stimuli." I said it was his way of showing his feelings. "Like smiling", he replied. His movements then ceased, and he began a series of associations which seemed to have the same characteristics as those I described as occurring at the latter end of the previous session. Still wondering why the dream should be regarded by the patient as peculiar, I listened to his disjointed associations with the running commentary to me of "anxious", "slightly anxious", and "depressed". After some time I thought I discerned a pattern. It was as if his stream of associations were by way of being a prolonged evacuation; some were merely disjointed phrases, others far more articulate. Although I could not be sure, I thought that his report of anxiety was associated with the more fragmented material, his report of depression with such parts as tended to be articulated wholes. I therefore said, "Your dream has frightened and upset you because when I came into it you felt I was a real person whom your mind had swallowed up and was losing while you slept. It made you think that during your analysis you must have been greedily destroying a real person and not just a thing." He at once began to talk quite rationally about a visit that he planned to make to see his brother. I drew his attention to the change in his behaviour since I had made the interpretation about his dream. He replied, "What dream?" And then, as if to cover up his bewilderment, said, "Oh yes: I think I must have forgotten", but in fact I did not have the impression he had recalled the dream. A little later he said he felt he had made some progress, but felt very depressed, he did not know why.

Work during the next fortnight convinced me that my suspicions about his dream, and the interpretations I based on them, were substantially correct. I was confirmed in my impression that the appearance of whole objects in dreams and elsewhere, is at one and the same moment a sign of progress and a forerunner of depression which may reach a dangerous intensity if its source is not elucidated. The 'peculiarity' of the dream to the psychotic is not its irrationality, incoherence, and fragmentation, but its revelation of objects which are felt by the patient to be whole objects, and therefore fit and proper reason for the powerful feelings of guilt and depression which Melanie Klein has associated with the onset of the depressive position. Their presence is felt to be evidence that real and valued objects have been destroyed. However, the immediate oscillation to fragmentation does not, as I have shown in my account of the stream of associations with a running commentary on the patient's feelings, afford any true relief, because it merely substitutes persecutory anxiety for the dread depression.

There are two dangerous features in the situation I am describing. Rosenfeld has pointed out how a patient who brings fragments together to make a whole object can be so disturbed by the cohesion of the fragments that an immediate explosive fragmentation follows. I supported his findings in my paper, 'Notes on the Theory of Schizophrenia' [chapter 3], and would now bring forward the events I then described for comparison with this less explosive yet dangerous alternation I am now describing. The danger here lies in the possibility of suicide, on the one hand or, on the other, a return to the paranoid-schizoid position that is characterized by a secondary fragmentation which is imposed on the already severe primary fragmentation that Melanie Klein has described as characteristic of the paranoid-schizoid position. It seems as if the patient, regressing from the depressive position, turns with increased hatred and anxiety against the fragments that have shown their power to coalesce, and splits them with great thoroughness; as a result we have a danger of a fragmentation so minute that reparation of the ego becomes impossible, and the prospects of the patient correspondingly hopeless.

I regard this phase of advance to, and retreat from, the depressive position as critical, not least because the danger of suicide is liable to obscure the significance of the retreat to the paranoid-schizoid position, and in particular the fact that secondary splitting is an inherent factor in the retreat and one which, if not detected and interpreted, is liable not merely to jeopardize promising developments of the analysis, but also to reverse the whole process and usher in a deterioration from which no recovery is possible.

79. Understanding of the material demands reference to certain collateral phenomena. During the period when this work that I have been describing was done, the patient was complaining that he could not distinguish between what was real and what was unreal, that he did not know whether something was an hallucination or not. In my paper on the 'Differentiation of the Psychotic from the Non-psychotic Personalities' [chapter 5], I described one of the consequences of the excessive use of projective identification as a state in which the patient felt he was surrounded by bizarre objects compounded partly of real objects and partly of fragments of the personality – and in particular those aspects of the personality listed putatively by Freud as being in the course of normal development called into being under the dominance of the reality principle. Amongst these aspects of the personality was the patient's capacity for judgement. The patient's complaint that he could not distinguish the real from the unreal was one of the consequences of this expulsion from his psyche, by the mechanism of projective identification, of his capacity for judgement. From the theory I then propounded it would be natural to suppose that amongst these bizarre objects it should be possible to trace something analogous to a capacity for judgement. From my experience I am persuaded that these particular bizarre objects are to be found in what ordinarily are described as the patient's 'delusions'. In his paper 'Constructions in Analysis' (1937d), Freud suggests that delusions may be the, "equivalents of the constructions which we build up in the course of an analytic treatment-attempts at explanation and cure . . .", though he points out that under the conditions of a psychosis they are bound to be ineffectual. It appeared to me, during this period of the analysis, that the patient's delusions had this aspect, and that some of his delusions were attempts at employing bizarre objects in the service of therapeutic intuition. If so, it may afford a definition of the relationship, between delusion and hallucination.

80. The hallucinatory experiences which I have been describing seem to approximate more closely to what Freud described as hysterical hallucinations than the psychotic hallucinations which were exclusively in evidence in the earlier phases of the analysis. I would say that the development of this difference was directly related to an increase in the patient's capacity to tolerate depression.

A differentiation of two types of hallucination – hysterical and psychotic – could be referred to a difference in content. The hysterical hallucination contains whole objects and is associated with depression; the psychotic hallucination contains elements analogous to part-objects. Both types are to be found in the psychotic patient.

I conclude this paper by drawing attention to certain features of it on which I have done work that cannot be communicated at this juncture.

First, the patient's fear of committing murder owes much of its intensity to his belief that he has already been guilty of it. The reasons for this belief emerge in associations of which I have given one example in the charade-like episode, when he was coupled with myself, so that both appeared as lifeless automatons. It will be remembered that there he was guilty of removing a life which then becomes a persecutory object, the radio that embodies electricity, sex, and life itself. The episode shows how guilt is evaded by resort to persecution by the life that has been destroyed.

Second, this fear of making a murderous attack is intensified by the patient's awareness of the extent to which he is dominated by a state of mind and feeling appropriate to that phase of development which Freud described as under the sway of the pleasure principle. He suggested that in that phase the patient's actions are not directed towards a change in the environment, but are intended rather to unburden the psychic apparatus of accretions of stimuli and therefore correspond to muscular movements of the kind involved in changes of mien and expression.

Let us suppose that in this state of mind the patient feels an impulse to express feelings of love towards a girl whom he regards as a prospective mate: furthermore, that he feels obstructed in this aim by the presence of feelings of impotence together with feelings of hatred and envy towards the sexual parents who are thought by him to possess, and to deny him the use of, the potent breast or penis that makes the possessor potent in the expression of love. In this state he is dominated by feelings of impotence, envy, and a hatred which is further strengthened by a sense of frustration and inability to tolerate the frustration. Over all is the sense of obstructed love. At once the need becomes imperative, in the service of expression of the feelings of love for his object, to disburden his psyche of destructive hate and envy. The lack of any impulse to alter the environment, together with the wish for speed that is associated with the inability to tolerate frustration, contribute to forcing a resort to muscular action of the kind characteristic of the phase of dominance by the pleasure principle; for experience has shown the patient that action of that kind achieves its purpose far more swiftly than action directed to alteration of the environment. The unburdening of the psyche by hallucination, that is by the use of the sensory apparatus in reverse, is reinforced by muscular action which may best be understood as being an extremely complex analogue of a scowl; the musculature does not simply change the expression to one of murderous hate, but gives effect to an actual murderous assault. The resultant act must, therefore, be understood as an ideo-motor activity, and is felt by the patient to appertain to that class of phenomena that I have described as creating bizarre objects. He does not feel he has altered his environment, but he does feel that he is now free to love his object without any conflicting feelings of impotence, hatred or envy. Such relief is short-lived. This description is an approximation to the state of mind of which the patient is dreadfully aware in the non-psychotic part of his personality; it contributes to his fear of any progress that might lead him to form loving attachments which would give rise to desires to express his love, and from that to intolerance of the frustration preserved by the existence of his destructive impulses, and from that to being overwhelmed by the psychotic part of his personality – in which only he can find mechanisms that hold promise of instantaneous solution of the problems presented by the existence of unwanted emotions. The danger which the patient fears is, therefore, one he has good reason to fear. It can be stated in analytic terms as follows:

He wishes to love, but feeling incapable of frustration he resorts to a murderous assault, or a token assault, as a method of disburdening his psyche of the unwanted emotions. The assault is but the outward expression of an explosive projective identification by virtue of which his murderous hatred, together with bits of his personality, is scattered far and wide into the real objects, members of society included, by which he is surrounded. He now feels free to be loving, but is surrounded by bizarre objects each compounded of real people and things, destructive hatred, and murderous conscience. The picture is further complicated because, although it is true to say the patient feels free to love, at least in intention, the violence of the explosion also leaves him denuded of his feelings of love.

81. From all that I have said it may now be seen that in the event of the patient making an actual assault, a complex situation has arisen, and that this situation can for simplicity of description be resolved into the following elements:

(a) The patient's resort to an omnipotent fantasy as a means towards loving his object.

(b) An external manifestation, which in fact, though not by the patient's intent, affects the environment and incidentally gives the analyst his material on which he bases his interpretations.

(c) In extreme cases, a reaction of society to the external manifestation, which is itself complex and compounded, amongst other elements, of psychotic reactions typical of unconscious collusion in receiving the projective identifications of one of its members.

(d) The resort to projective identification as a substitute for repression[1] implies a weakness of a capacity for denial, and this is shown by the resort to destructive attacks upon the perceptual apparatus, and by the use of perceptual apparatus. of which he is in fact unable to

---

[1]Referred to in 'Differentiation of the Psychotic from the Non-Psychotic Personalities', first presented on 6 October 1955 [chapter 5].

rid himself, for expulsion of unwanted stimuli as they are received. The attempt to rid himself of his perceptual system leads to compensatory hypertrophy of sense impressions, e.g. Lord Adrian's distant perception.[1]

(e) The danger that, in the course of the analysis, the patient will become incurable through an unanalysed retreat from the depressive position to the paranoid-schizoid position, in the course of which secondary splitting will be imposed upon the primary splitting intrinsic to his original experience of the paranoid-schizoid position; the danger lies in the minute fragmentation which results from this renewal of splitting and the impossibility thereafter of effecting any reparation.

(f) The relation of depression to the appearance of what the patient feels to be whole objects in material expelled from his personality.

(g) The analyst's need to appreciate that the presence of hallucinations is much more frequent than is realized, and depends upon the fact that, the senses being two-way, an object may be to the patient an excretion, or, as we should say, an hallucination, rather than something existing independently of himself A striking example of this is presented when the patient sees double with one eye.

(h) The relation of over-action of expulsion to megalomania.

82. This summary list may serve to indicate the possibilities for further research which are opened up by attempting that close and detailed observation of hallucinations for which I hope I have made a case.

---

[1] [A reference to the classical theory of sensory coding derived from Lord Adrian's (1934) early concepts of sensory coding. Lord Edgar Douglas Adrian (1889–1977) received the Nobel Prize for Physiology in 1932. *Ed.*]

7

On arrogance

83. In this paper I propose to deal with the appearance, in the material of a certain class of patient, of references to curiosity, arrogance and stupidity which are so dispersed and separated from each other that their relatedness may escape detection. I shall suggest that their appearance should be taken by the analyst as evidence that he is dealing with a psychological disaster. The meaning with which I wish to invest the term 'arrogance' may be indicated by supposing that in the personality where life instincts predominate, pride becomes self-respect, where death instincts predominate, pride becomes arrogance.

Their separation from each other and the lack of evidence of any relatedness is evidence that a disaster has occurred. To make clear the connection between these references, I shall rehearse the Oedipus myth from a point of view which makes the sexual crime a peripheral element of a story in which the central crime is the arrogance of Oedipus in vowing to lay bare the truth at no matter what cost.

84. This shift of emphasis brings the following elements into the centre of the story: the sphinx, who asks a riddle and destroys herself when it is answered; the blind Tiresias, who possesses knowledge and deplores the resolve of the king to search for it; the oracle that provokes the search which the prophet deplores; and again the king who, his search concluded, suffers blindness and exile. This is the story of which the elements are discernible amongst the ruins of the psyche to which the scattered references to curiosity, arrogance, and stupidity have pointed the way.

I said that these references are significant in a certain class of patient; the class to which I refer is one in which psychotic mechanisms are active and have to be analytically uncovered before a stable adjustment can be achieved. In practice, analysis of such a patient may seem to follow the patterns with which we are familiar in the treatment of the neuroses, but with the important difference that improvement in the patient's condition does not appear to be commensurate with the analytic work that is done. To recapitulate, the analyst who is treating an apparently neurotic patient must regard a negative therapeutic response together with the appearance of scattered, unrelated references to curiosity, arrogance and stupidity, as evidence that he is in the presence of a psychological catastrophe with which he will have to deal.

85. It may be supposed that an approach to the problem is provided by the emergence in the analysis of one of these references, and this is in fact the case. It is important that reference to any of these three qualities should be treated by the analyst as a significant event demanding investigation and provoking more than usually stubborn resistances. Unfortunately the problem is complicated by a fact which must be already evident – the analytic procedure itself is precisely a manifestation of the curiosity which is felt to be an intrinsic component of the disaster. As a consequence, the very act of analysing the patient makes the analyst an accessory in precipitating regression and turning the analysis itself into a piece of acting out. From the point of view of successful analysis, this is a development that should be avoided. Yet I have not been able to see how this can be done. The alternative course is to accept the acting out and regression as inevitable, and if possible to turn it to good account. This, I believe, can be done, but it involves detailed interpretation of events that are taking place in the session. These events are active displays of the mechanisms of splitting, projective identification, and the related subsidiary phenomena of confusional states, depersonalization and hallucination, which have been described by Melanie Klein, Segal, and Rosenfeld as part of the analysis of psychotic patients.

86. In this phase of the analysis, the transference is peculiar in that (in addition to the features to which I have drawn attention in previous papers) it is to the analyst as analyst. Features of this are his appearance, and that of the patient in so far as he is identified with the analyst as, by turns, blind, stupid, suicidal, curious, and arrogant, but I shall have more to say later about the qualities of arrogance. I must emphasize that at this stage the patient would appear to have no problems other than the existence of the analyst himself; furthermore, that the spectacle presented is one, to borrow Freud's analogy, similar to that of the archaeologist who discovers in his field-work the evidences, not so much of a primitive civilization, as of a primitive catastrophe. In analytic terms that hope must be that the investigations which are being carried out will issue in the reconstitution of the ego. This aim is, however, obscured because this analytic procedure has become an acting out of destructive attacks launched against the ego, wherever it is discerned; that is to say, the ego whether it appears manifest in the patient or the analyst. These attacks closely resemble the description given by Melanie Klein of the infant's fantasied attacks on the breast.

87. If we now turn to consider what there is in reality that makes it so hateful to the patient that he must destroy the ego which brings him into contact with it, it would be natural to suppose that it is the sexually orientated Oedipus situation, and indeed I have found much to substantiate this view. When reconstitution of the ego has proceeded sufficiently to bring the Oedipus situation into sight, it is quite common to find that it precipitates further attacks on the ego. But there is evidence that some other element is playing an important part in provoking destructive attacks on the ego and its consequent disintegration. The key to this lies in the references to arrogance which I promised to explore further.

Briefly, it appears that overwhelming emotions are associated with the assumption by the patient or analyst of the qualities required to pursue the truth, and in particular a capacity to tolerate the stresses associated with the introjection of another person's projective identifications. Put into other terms, the implicit aim of psychoanalysis to pursue the truth at no matter what cost is felt to be synonymous with a claim to a capacity for containing the discarded, split-off aspects of other personalities while retaining a balanced outlook. This would appear to be the immediate signal for outbreaks of envy and hatred.

88. I propose now to devote the remainder of this paper to description of the clinical aspect of the material which I have so far approached theoretically. The patient in question did not at any time behave in a way which in my view would warrant a diagnosis of psychosis; he had, however, displayed the features I have mentioned, namely, scattered references to curiosity, arrogance, and stupidity together with what I felt was an inadequate therapeutic response. At the period with which I deal, the significance of these features had become clear and I had been able to give him some insight into their relatedness and the increasing frequency with which they appeared in the forefront of his material. He described his behaviour in the sessions as mad or insane, and he showed anxiety at his inability to behave in a way which his experience of analysis had shown him to be helpful in furthering analytic progress. For my part I was impressed by the fact that for several sessions at a time he seemed to be devoid of the insight and judgement which I knew from previous experience that he possessed. Furthermore, the material was almost entirely of the kind with which I was familiar in the analysis of psychotic patients. That is to say, projective identification was extremely active, and the patient's states of confusion and depersonalization easy to detect and frequently in evidence. For a matter of some months sessions were taken up entirely with psychotic mechanisms to an extent which made me wonder how it was that the patient was apparently continuing his extra-analytic life without, as far as I knew, any material change for the worse.

89. I shall not describe this stage further, as it does not differ from previous accounts of work with the psychotic patient. I wish to concentrate on that aspect of the analysis which relates to a particular form of internal object.

In its simplest form this material appeared in sessions when the patient's associations lacked coherence and consisted of 'sentences' which were remarkably deficient in one or the other aspect of the grammar of conversational English. Thus, a significant object might be mentioned, but there would be no pronoun or verb, or a significant verbal form would appear such as "going skating", but there would be no mention of who was supposed to be doing this or where, and so on in an apparently inexhaustible number of variations. The establishment of an analytically potent relationship by means of verbal communication thus seemed to be impossible. Analyst and patient together formed a frustrated couple. This in itself was not new, and on one occasion, during a relatively lucid session, the patient himself observed that the method of communication was so mutilated that creative work was impossible, and he despaired of the possibility that any cure would come about. He was already quite familiar with the sexual anxiety inherent in such conduct, so it seemed reasonable to suppose that some progress would follow, and it was the more surprising that this did not in fact happen; the anxiety of the patient increased. I was eventually forced to assume, on theoretical grounds, that progress had taken place and that there was a change in his behaviour which I was failing to observe. With this assumption in mind I attempted to cast about for some revealing clue which would indicate what this change might be. In the meantime the sessions continued much as before. I remained at a loss until one day, in a lucid moment, the patient said he wondered that I could stand it. This gave me a clue: at least I now knew that there was something I was able to stand which he apparently could not. He realized already that he felt he was being obstructed in his aim to establish a creative contact with me, and that this obstructive force was sometimes in him, sometimes in me, and sometimes occupied an unknown location. Furthermore, the obstruction was effected by some means other than mutilation or verbal communications. The patient had already made it clear that the obstructing forces or object were out of his control.

90. The next step forward occurred when the patient said that I was the obstructing force, and that my outstanding characteristic was "that I could not stand it". I now worked on the assumption that the persecuting object that could not permit any creative relationship was one that "could not stand it", but I was still not clear what "it" was. It was tempting to assume that "it" was any creative relationship which was made intolerable to the persecuting object through envy and hate of the creative couple. Unfortunately this did not lead any further because it was an aspect of the material which had already been made clear without producing any advance. Therefore the problem of what "it" was still awaited solution.

Before I discuss this problem further, I must mention a feature of the material which had led up to this point, because it contributes to an understanding of the next step. During the whole of the period I have been describing, references to curiosity, arrogance, and stupidity became more frequent and more obviously related to each other. The stupidity was purposeful, and arrogance – not always called by that name – was sometimes an accusation, sometimes a temptation, and sometimes a crime. The cumulative effect of these references was to persuade me that their relatedness depended upon their association with the obstructive object. Curiosity and stupidity waxed or waned together; that is to say, if curiosity increased, so did the stupidity. I therefore felt some gain in knowledge of the character of the obstructive force. What it was that the object could not stand became clearer in some sessions where it appeared that in so far as I, as analyst, was insisting on verbal communication as a method of making the patient's problems explicit, I was felt to be directly attacking his methods of communication. From this it became clear that when I was identified with the obstructive force, what I could not stand was the patient's methods of communication. In this phase my employment of verbal communication was felt by the patient to be a mutilating attack on *his* methods of communication. From this point onwards, it was only a matter of time to demonstrate that the patient's link with me was his ability to employ the mechanism of projective identification. That is to say, his relationship with me and his ability to profit by the association lay in the opportunity to split off parts of his psyche and project them into me.

On this depended a variety of procedures which were felt to ensure emotionally rewarding experiences such as, to mention two, the ability to put bad feelings in me and leave them there long enough for them to be modified by their sojourn in my psyche, and the ability to put good parts of himself into me, thereby feeling that he was dealing with an ideal object as a result. Associated with these experiences was a sense of being in contact with me, which I am inclined to believe is a primitive form of communication that provides a foundation on which, ultimately, verbal communication depends. From his feelings about me when I was identified with the obstructive object, I was able to deduce that the obstructive object was curious about him, but could not stand being the receptacle for parts of his personality and accordingly made destructive and mutilating attacks, largely through varieties of stupidity, upon his capacity for projective identification. I, therefore, concluded that the catastrophe stemmed from the mutilating attacks made upon this extremely primitive species of link between the patient and analyst.

Conclusion

91. In some patients the denial to the patient of a normal employment of projective identification precipitates a disaster through the destruction of an important link. Inherent in this disaster is the establishment of a primitive superego which denies the use of projective identification. The clue to this disaster is provided by the emergence of widely separated references to curiosity, arrogance, and stupidity.

8

Attacks on linking

92. In a previous paper [chapter 5] I have had occasion, in talking of the psychotic part of the personality, to speak of the destructive attacks which the patient makes on anything which is felt to have the function of linking one object with another. It is my intention in this paper to show the significance of this form of destructive attack in the production of some symptoms met with in borderline psychosis.

The prototype for all the links of which I wish to speak is the primitive breast or penis. The paper presupposes familiarity with Melanie Klein's descriptions of the infant's fantasies of sadistic attacks upon the breast (Klein, 1935); of the infant's splitting of its objects; of projective identification – which is the name she gives to the mechanism by which parts of the personality are split off and projected into external objects – and finally, her views on early stages of Oedipus complex (Klein, 1928). I shall discuss phantasied attacks on the breast as the prototype of all attacks on objects that serve as a link, and projective identification as the mechanism employed by the psyche to dispose of the ego fragments produced by its destructiveness.

I shall first describe clinical manifestations in an order dictated not by the chronology of their appearance in the consulting room, but by the need for making the exposition of my thesis as clear as I can. I shall follow this with material selected to demonstrate the order which these mechanisms assume when their relationship to each other is determined by the dynamics of the analytic situation. I shall conclude with theoretical observations on the material presented. The examples are drawn from the analysis of two patients and are taken from an advanced stage of their analyses. To preserve anonymity I shall not distinguish between the patients, and shall introduce distortions of fact which I hope do not impair the accuracy of the analytic description.

Observation of the patient's disposition to attack the link between two objects is simplified because the analyst has to establish a link with the patient and does this by verbal communication and his equipment of psychoanalytic experience. Upon this the creative relationship depends and we should therefore be able to see attacks being made upon it.

I am not concerned with typical resistance to interpretations, but with expanding references [in chapter 5] to the destructive attacks on verbal thought itself.

Clinical examples

93. The following examples describe occasions which afforded me an opportunity to give the patient an interpretation (which at that point he could understand) of conduct designed to destroy whatever it was that linked two objects together.

(i) I gave the patient an interpretation making explicit his feelings of affection and his expression of them to his mother for her ability to cope with a refractory child. He attempted to express his agreement with me, but although he needed to say only a few words his expression of them was interrupted by a very pronounced stammer which had the effect of spreading out his remark over a period of as much as a minute and a half. The actual sounds emitted bore resemblance to gasping for breath; gaspings were interspersed with gurgling sounds as if he were immersed in water. I drew his attention to these sounds and he agreed that they were peculiar, and suggesting the descriptions I have just given.

(ii) The patient complained that he could not sleep. Showing signs of fear, lie said, "It can't go on like this". Disjointed remarks gave the impression that he felt superficially that some catastrophe would occur, perhaps akin to insanity, if he could not get more sleep. Referring to material in the previous session I suggested that he feared he would dream if he were to sleep. He denied this and said he could not think because he was wet. I reminded him of his use of the term "wet" as an expression of contempt for somebody he regarded as feeble and sentimental. He disagreed and indicated that the state to which he referred was the exact opposite. From what I knew of this patient I felt that his correction at this point was valid, and that somehow the wetness referred to an expression of hatred and envy such as he associated with urinary attacks on an object. I therefore said that in addition to the superficial fear which he had expressed, he was afraid of sleep because for him it was the same thing as the oozing away of his mind itself. Further associations showed that he felt that good interpretations from me were so consistently and minutely split up by him that they became mental urine which then seeped uncontrollably away. Sleep was therefore inseparable from unconsciousness, which was itself identical with a state of mindlessness which could not be repaired. He said, "I am dry now". I replied that he felt he was awake and capable of thought, but that this good state was only precariously maintained.

(iii) In this session the patient had produced material stimulated by the preceding week-end break. His awareness of such external stimuli had become demonstrable at a comparatively recent stage of the analysis. Previously it had been a matter for conjecture how much he was capable of appreciating reality. I knew that he had contact with reality because he came for analysis by himself, but that fact could hardly be deduced from his behaviour in the sessions. When I interpreted some associations as evidence that he felt he had been and still was witnessing an intercourse between two people, he reacted as if he had received a violent blow. I was not then able to say just where he had experienced the assault and even in retrospect I have no clear impression. It would seem logical to suppose that the shock had been administered by my interpretation and that therefore the blow came from without, but my impression is that he felt it as delivered from within; the patient often experienced what he described as a stabbing attack from inside. He sat up and stared intently into space. I said that he seemed to be seeing something. He replied that he could not see what he saw. I was able from previous experience to interpret that he felt he was 'seeing' an invisible object, and subsequent experience convinced me that in the two patients on whose analysis I am depending for material for this paper, events occurred in which the patient experienced invisible-visual hallucinations. I shall give my reasons later for supposing that in this and the previous example similar mechanisms were at work.

(iv) In the first twenty minutes of the session the patient made three isolated remarks which had no significance for me. He then said that it seemed that a girl he had met was understanding. This was followed at once by a violent, convulsive movement which he affected to ignore. It appeared to be identical with the kind of stabbing attack I mentioned in the last example. I tried to draw his attention to the movement, but he had ignored my intervention as he had ignored the attack. He then said that the room was filled with a blue haze. A little later he remarked that the haze had gone, but said he was depressed. I interpreted that he felt understood by me. This was an agreeable experience, but the pleasant feeling of being understood had been instantly destroyed and ejected. I reminded him that we had recently witnessed his use of the word "blue" as a compact description of vituperative sexual conversation. If my interpretation was correct, and subsequent events suggested that it was, it meant that the experience of being understood had been split up, converted into particles of sexual abuse and ejected. Up to this point I felt that the interpretation approximated closely to his experience. Later interpretations, that the disappearance of the haze was due to reintrojection and conversion into depression, seemed to have less reality for the patient, although later events were compatible with its being correct.

(v) This session, like the one in my last example, began with three or four statements of fact, such as that it was hot; that his train was crowded; and that it was Wednesday – this occupied thirty minutes. An impression that he was trying to retain contact with reality was confirmed when he followed up by saying that he feared a breakdown. A little later he said I would not understand him. I interpreted that he felt I was bad and would not take in what he wanted to put into me. I interpreted in these terms deliberately because he had shown in the previous session that he felt that my interpretations were an attempt to eject feelings that he wished to deposit in me. His response to my interpretation was to say that he felt there were two probability clouds in the room. I interpreted that he was trying to get rid of the feeling that my badness was a fact. I said it meant that he needed to know whether I was really bad or whether I was some bad thing which had come from inside him. Although the point was not at that moment of central significance, I thought the patient was attempting to decide whether he was hallucinated or not. This recurrent anxiety in his analysis was associated with his fear that envy and hatred of a capacity for understanding was leading him to take in a good, understanding object in order to destroy and eject it – a procedure which had often led to persecution by the destroyed and ejected object. Whether my refusal to understand was a reality or an hallucination was important only because it determined what painful experiences were to be expected next.

(vi) Half the session passed in silence; the patient then announced that a piece of iron had fallen on the floor. Thereafter he made a series of convulsive movements in silence as if he felt he was being physically assaulted from within. I said he could not establish contact with me because of his fear of what was going on inside him. He confirmed this by saying that he felt he was being murdered. He did not know what he would do without the analysis as it made him better. I said that he felt so envious of himself and of me for being able to work together to make him feel better that he took the pair of us into him as a dead piece of iron and a dead floor that came together not to give him life but to murder him. He became very anxious and said he could not go on. I said that he felt he could not go on because he was either dead, or alive and so envious that he had to stop good analysis. There was a marked decrease of anxiety, but the remainder of the session was taken up by isolated statements of fact which again seemed to be an attempt to preserve contact with external reality as a method of denial of his phantasies.

Features common to the above illustrations

94. These episodes have been chosen by me because the dominant theme in each was the destructive attack on a link. In the first, the attack was expressed in a stammer which was designed to prevent the patient from using language as a bond between him and me. In the second, sleep was felt by him to be identical with projective identification that proceeded unaffected by any possible attempt at control by him. Sleep for him meant that his mind, minutely fragmented, flowed out in an attacking stream of particles.

The examples I give here throw light on schizophrenic dreaming. The psychotic patient appears to have no dreams, or at least not to report any, until comparatively late in the analysis. My impression now is that this apparently dreamless period is a phenomenon analogous to the invisible-visual hallucination. That is to say, the dreams consist of material so minutely fragmented that they are devoid of any visual component. When dreams are experienced which the patient can report because visual objects have been experienced by him in the course of the dream, he seems to regard these objects as bearing much the same relationship to the invisible objects of the previous phase as faeces seem, to him, to bear to urine. The objects appearing in experiences which we call dreams are regarded by the patient as solid and are, as such, contrasted with the contents of the dreams which were a continuum of minute, invisible fragments.

At the time of the session the main theme was not an attack on the link but the consequences of such an attack, previously made, in leaving him bereft of a state of mind necessary for the establishment of a satisfying relationship between him and his bed. Though it did not appear in the session I report, uncontrollable projective identification, which was what sleep meant to him, was thought to be a destructive attack on the state of mind of the coupling parents. There was therefore a double anxiety: one arising from his fear that he was being rendered mindless, the other from his fear that he was unable to control his hostile attacks, his mind providing the ammunition, on the state of mind that was the link between the parental pair. Sleep and sleeplessness were alike unacceptable.

In the third example, in which I described visual hallucinations of invisible objects, we witness one form in which the actual attack on the sexual pair is delivered. My interpretation, as far as I could judge, was felt by him as if it were his own visual sense of a parental intercourse; this visual impression is minutely fragmented and ejected at once in particles so minute that they are the invisible components of a continuum. The total procedure has served the purpose of forestalling an experience of feelings of envy for the parental state of mind by the instantaneous expression of envy in a destructive act. I shall have more to say of this implicit hatred of emotion and the need to avoid awareness of it.

In my fourth example – the report of the understanding girl and the haze – my understanding and his agreeable state of mind have been felt as a link between us which could give rise to a creative act. The link had been regarded with hate and transformed into a hostile and destructive sexuality rendering the patient–analyst couple sterile.

In my fifth example, of the two probability clouds, a capacity for understanding is the link which is being attacked, but the interest lies in the fact that the object making the destructive attacks is alien to the patient. Furthermore, the destroyer is making an attack on projective identification which is felt by the patient to be a method of communication. In so far as my supposed attack on his methods of communication is felt as possibly secondary to his envious attacks on me, he does not dissociate himself from feelings of guilt and responsibility. A further point is the appearance of judgement, which Freud regards as an essential feature of the dominance of the reality principle, among the ejected parts of the patient's personality. The fact that there were two probability clouds remained unexplained at the time, but in subsequent sessions I had material which led me to suppose that what had originally been an attempt to separate good from bad survived in the existence of two objects, but they were now similar in that each was a mixture of good and bad. Taking into consideration material from later sessions, I can draw conclusions which were not possible at the time; his capacity for judgement, which had been split up and destroyed with the rest of his ego and then ejected, was felt by him to be similar to other bizarre objects of the kind which I have described in my paper, 'Differentiation of the Psychotic from the Non-psychotic Personalities' [chapter 5]. These ejected particles were feared because of the treatment he had accorded them. He felt that the alienated judgement – the probability clouds – indicated that I was probably bad. His suspicion that the probability clouds were persecutory and hostile led him to doubt the value of the guidance they afforded him. They might supply him with a correct assessment or a deliberately false one, such as that a fact was an hallucination or vice versa; or would give rise to what, from a psychiatric point of view, we would call delusions. The probability clouds themselves had some qualities of a primitive breast and were felt to be enigmatic and intimidating.

In my sixth illustration, the report that a piece of iron had fallen on the floor, I had no occasion for interpreting an aspect of the material with which the patient had by this time become familiar. (I should perhaps say that experience had taught me that there were times when I assumed the patient's familiarity with some aspect of a situation with which we were dealing, only to discover that, in spite of the work that had been done upon it, he had forgotten it.) The familiar point that I did not interpret, but which is significant for the understanding of this episode, is that the patient's envy of the parental couple had been evaded by his substitution of himself and myself for the parents. The evasion failed, for the envy and hatred were now directed against him and me. The couple engaged in a creative act are felt to be sharing an enviable, emotional experience; he, being identified also with the excluded party, has a painful, emotional experience as well. On many occasions the patient, partly through experiences of the kind which I describe in this episode, and partly for reasons on which I shall enlarge later, had a hatred of emotion, and therefore, by a short extension, of life itself. This hatred contributes to the murderous attack on that which links the pair, on the pair itself, and on the object generated by the pair. In the episode I am describing, the patient is suffering the consequences of his early attacks on the state of mind that forms the link between the creative pair and his identification with both the hateful and creative states of mind.

In this, and the preceding illustration, there are elements that suggest the formation of a hostile persecutory object, or agglomeration of objects, which expresses its hostility in a manner of great importance in producing the predominance of psychotic mechanisms in a patient; the characteristics with which I have already invested the agglomeration of persecutory objects have the quality of a primitive, and even murderous, superego.

Curiosity, arrogance, and stupidity

95. In my paper 'On Arrogance' [chapter 7] I suggested that Freud's analogy of an archaeological investigation with a psychoanalysis is helpful if it is considered that we are exposing evidence not so much of a primitive civilization as of a primitive disaster. The value of the analogy is lessened because in the analysis we are confronted not so much with a static situation that permits leisurely study, but with a catastrophe that remains at one and the same moment actively vital and yet incapable of resolution into quiescence. This lack of progress in any direction must be attributed in part to the destruction of a capacity for curiosity and the consequent inability to learn, but before I go into this I must say something about a matter that plays hardly any part in the illustrations I have given.

Attacks on the link originate in what Melanie Klein (1948) calls the paranoid-schizoid phase. This period is dominated by part-object relationships. If it is borne in mind that the patient has a part-object relationship with himself as well as with objects not himself, it contributes to the understanding of phrases such as "it seems" which are commonly employed by the deeply disturbed patient on occasions when a less disturbed patient might say "I think" or "I believe". When he says "it seems" he is often referring to a feeling – an "it seems" feeling – which is a part of his psyche and yet is not observed as part of a whole object. The conception of the part-object as analogous to an anatomical structure, encouraged by the patient's employment of concrete images as units of thought, is misleading because the part-object relationship is not with the anatomical structures only but with function, not with anatomy but with physiology, not with the breast but with feeding, poisoning, loving, hating. This contributes to the impression of a disaster that is dynamic and not static. The problem that has to be solved on this early yet superficial level, must be stated in adult terms by the question, "What is something?" – not the question, "Why is something?", because "why" has, through guilt, been split off. Problems, the solution of which depends upon an awareness of causation, cannot therefore be stated, let alone solved. This produces a situation in which the patient appears to have no problems except those posed by the existence of analyst and patient. His preoccupation is with what is this or that function of which he is aware, though unable to grasp the totality of which the function is a part. It follows that there is never any question why the patient or the analyst is there, or why something is said or done or felt, nor can there be any question of attempting to alter the causes of some state of mind. Since "what?" can never be answered without "how?" or "why?", further difficulties arise. I shall leave this on one side to consider the mechanisms employed by the infant to solve the problem "what?", when it is felt in relation to a part-object relationship with a function.

Denial of normal degrees of projective identification

96. I employ the term 'link' because I wish to discuss the patient's relationship with a function rather than with the object that subserves a function; my concern is not only with the breast or penis or verbal thought, but with their function of providing the link between two objects.

In her 'Notes on Some Schizoid Mechanisms' (1946) Melanie Klein speaks of the importance of an excessive employment of splitting and projective identification in the production of a very disturbed personality. She also speaks of "the introjection of the good object, first of all the mother's breast" as a "precondition for normal development". I shall suppose that there is a normal degree of projective identification, without defining the limits within which normality lies, and that associated with introjective identification this is the foundation on which normal development rests.

This impression derives partly from a feature in a patient's analysis which was difficult to interpret because it did not appear to be sufficiently obtrusive at any one moment for an interpretation to be supported by convincing evidence. Throughout the analysis the patient resorted to projective identification with a persistence suggesting it was a mechanism of which he had never been able sufficiently to avail himself; the analysis afforded him an opportunity for the exercise of a mechanism of which he had been cheated. I did not have to rely on this impression alone: there were sessions which led me to suppose that the patient felt there was some object that denied him the use of projective identification. In the illustrations I have given, particularly in the first (the stammer) and the fourth (the understanding girl and the blue haze) there are elements which indicate that the patient felt the parts of his personality that he wished to repose in me were refused entry by me, but there had been associations prior to this which led me to this view.

When the patient strove to rid himself of fears of death which were felt to be too powerful for his personality to contain, he split off his fears and put them into me, the idea apparently being that if they were allowed to repose there long enough they would undergo modification by my psyche and could then be safely reintrojected. On the occasion I have in mind the patient had felt, probably for reasons similar to those I give in my fifth illustration (the probability clouds), that I evacuated them so quickly that the feelings were not modified, but had become more painful.

Associations from a period in the analysis earlier than that from which these illustrations have been drawn, showed an increasing intensity of emotions in the patient. This originated in what he felt was my refusal to accept parts of his personality. Consequently he strove to force them into me with increased desperation and violence. His behaviour, isolated from the context of the analysis, might have appeared to be an expression of primary aggression: the more violent his phantasies of projective identification, the more frightened he became of me. There were sessions in which such behaviour expressed unprovoked aggression, but I quote this series because it shows the patient in a different light – his violence a reaction to what he felt was my hostile defensiveness. The analytic situation built up in my mind a sense of witnessing an extremely early scene. I felt that the patient had experienced in infancy a mother who dutifully responded to the infant's emotional displays. The dutiful response had in it an element of impatient, "I don't know what's the matter with the child." My deduction was that, in order to understand what the child wanted, the mother should have treated the infant's *cry* as more than a demand for her presence. From the infant's point of view she should have taken into her, and thus experienced, the fear that the child was dying. It was this fear that the child could not contain. He strove to split it off together with the part of the personality in which it lay and project it into the mother. An understanding mother is able to experience the feeling of dread, that this baby was striving to deal with by projective identification, and yet retain a balanced outlook. This patient had had to deal with a mother who could not tolerate experiencing such feelings and reacted either by denying them ingress, or alternatively by becoming a prey to the anxiety which resulted from introjection of the infant's feelings. The latter reaction must, I think, have been rare denial was dominant.

To some this reconstruction will appear to be unduly fanciful; to me it does not seem forced and is the reply to any who may object that too much stress is placed on the transference to the exclusion of a proper elucidation of early memories.

In the analysis a complex situation may be observed. The patient feels he is being allowed an opportunity of which he had hitherto been cheated; the poignancy of his deprivation is thereby rendered the more acute and so are the feelings of resentment at the deprivation. Gratitude for the opportunity coexists with hostility to the analyst as the person who will not understand and refuses the patient the use of the only method of communication by which he feels he can make himself understood. Thus the link between patient and analyst, or infant and breast, is the mechanism of projective identification. The destructive attacks upon this link originate in a source external to the patient or infant, namely the analyst or breast. The result is excessive projective identification by the patient and a deterioration of his developmental processes.

I do not put forward this experience as the cause of the patient's disturbance; that finds its main source in the inborn disposition of the infant as I described it in 'Differentiation of the Psychotic from the Non-psychotic Personalities' [chapter 5]. I regard it as a central feature of the environmental factor in the production of the psychotic personality.

Before I discuss this consequence for the patient's development, I must refer to the inborn characteristics and the part that they play in producing attacks by the infant on all that links him to the breast, namely, primary aggression and envy. The seriousness of these attacks is enhanced if the mother displays the kind of unreceptiveness which I have described, and is diminished, but not abolished, if the mother can introject the infant's feelings and remain balanced (Klein, 1957); the seriousness remains because the psychotic infant is overwhelmed with hatred and envy of the mother's ability to retain a comfortable state of mind although experiencing the infant's feelings. This was clearly brought out by a patient who insisted that I must go through it with him, but was filled with hate when he felt I was able to do so without a breakdown. Here we have another aspect of destructive attacks upon the link, the link being the capacity of the analyst to introject the patient's projective identifications. Attacks on the link, therefore, are synonymous with attacks on the analyst's, and originally the mother's, peace of mind. The capacity to introject is transformed by the patient's envy and hate into greed devouring the patient's psyche; similarly, peace of mind becomes hostile indifference. At this point analytic problems arise through the patient's employment (to destroy the peace of mind that is so much envied) of acting out, delinquent acts and threats of suicide.

Consequences

97. To review the main features so far: the origin of the disturbance is twofold. On the one hand there is the patient's inborn disposition to excessive destructiveness, hatred, and envy: on the other the environment which, at its worst, denies to the patient the use of the mechanisms of splitting and projective identification. On some occasions the destructive attacks on the link between patient and environment, or between different aspects of the patient's personality, have their origin in the patient; on others, in the mother, although in the latter instance and in psychotic patients, it can never be in the mother alone. The disturbances commence with life itself. The problem that confronts the patient is: What are the objects of which he is aware? These objects, whether internal or external, are in fact part-objects and predominantly, though not exclusively, what we should call functions and not morphological structures. This is obscured because the patient's thinking is conducted by means of concrete objects and therefore tends to produce, in the sophisticated mind of the analyst, an impression that the patient's concern is with the nature of the concrete object. The nature of the functions which excite the patient's curiosity he explores by projective identification. His own feelings, too powerful to be contained within his personality, are amongst these functions. Projective identification makes it possible for him to investigate his own feelings in a personality powerful enough to contain them. Denial of the use of this mechanism, either by the refusal of the mother to serve as a repository for the infant's feelings, or by the hatred and envy of the patient who cannot allow the mother to exercise this function, leads to a destruction of the link between infant and breast, and consequently to a severe disorder of the impulse to be curious on which all learning depends. The way is therefore prepared for a severe arrest of development. Furthermore, thanks to a denial of the main method open to the infant for dealing with his too powerful emotions, the conduct of emotional life, in any case a severe problem, becomes intolerable. Feelings of hatred are thereupon directed against all emotions including hate itself, and against external reality which stimulates them. It is a short step from hatred of the emotions to hatred of life itself. In 'Differentiation of the Psychotic from the Non-psychotic Personalities' I stated that this hatred results in a resort to projective identification of all the perceptual apparatus including the embryonic thought which forms a link between sense impressions and consciousness. The tendency to excessive projective identification when death instincts predominate is thus reinforced.

Superego

98. The early development of the superego is affected by this kind of mental functioning in a way I must now describe. As I have said, the link between infant and breast depends upon projective identification and a capacity to introject projective identifications. Failure to introject makes the external object appear intrinsically hostile to curiosity and to the method, namely projective identification, by which the infant seeks to satisfy it. Should the breast be felt as fundamentally understanding, it has been transformed by the infant's envy and hate into an object whose devouring greed has as its aim the introjection of the infant's projective identifications in order to destroy them. This can show in the patient's belief that the analyst strives, by understanding the patient, to drive him insane. The result is an object which, when installed in the patient, exercises the function of a severe and ego-destructive superego. This description is not accurate applied to any object in the paranoid-schizoid position because it supposes a whole-object. The threat that such a whole-object impends contributes to the inability, described by Melanie Klein and others (Klein, 1946, 1948; Rosenfeld, 1952; Segal, 1950), of the psychotic patient to face the depressive position and the developments attendant on it. In the paranoid-schizoid phase the bizarre objects composed partially of elements of a persecutory super-ego which I described in 'Differentiation of the Psychotic from the Non-psychotic Personalities' are predominant.

Arrested development

The disturbance of the impulse of curiosity on which all learning depends, and the denial of the mechanism by which it seeks expression, makes normal development impossible. Another feature obtrudes if the course of the analysis is favourable; problems which in sophisticated language are posed by the question "Why?" cannot be formulated. The patient appears to have no appreciation of causation and will complain of painful states of mind while persisting in courses of action calculated to produce them. Therefore when the appropriate material presents itself the patient must be shown that he has no interest in why he feels as he does. Elucidation of the limited scope of his curiosity issues in the development of a wider range and an incipient preoccupation with causes. This leads to some modification of conduct which otherwise prolongs his distress.

Conclusions

99. The main conclusions of this paper relate to that state of mind in which the patient's psyche contains an internal object which is opposed to, and destructive of, all links whatsoever from the most primitive (which I have suggested is a normal degree of projective identification) to the most sophisticated forms of verbal communication and the arts.

In this state of mind emotion is hated; it is felt to be too powerful to be contained by the immature psyche, it is felt to link objects and it gives reality to objects which are not self and therefore inimical to primary narcissism.

The internal object which in its origin was an external breast that refused to introject, harbour, and so modify the baneful force of emotion, is felt, paradoxically, to intensify, relative to the strength of the ego, the emotions against which it initiates the attacks. These attacks on the linking function of emotion lead to an over-prominence in the psychotic part of the personality of links which appear to be logical, almost mathematical, but never emotionally reasonable. Consequently the links surviving are perverse, cruel, and sterile.

The external object which is internalized, its nature, and the effect when so established on the methods of communication within the psyche and with the environment, are left for further elaboration later.

9

A theory of thinking

100. In this paper I am primarily concerned to present a theoretical system. Its resemblance to a philosophical theory depends on the fact that philosophers have concerned themselves with the same subject matter; it differs from philosophical theory in that it is intended, like all psychoanalytic theories, for use. It is devised with the intention that practising psychoanalysts should restate the hypotheses of which it is composed in terms of empirically verifiable data.

In this respect it bears the same relationship to similar statements of philosophy as the statements of applied mathematics bear to pure mathematics.

The derived hypotheses that are intended to admit of empirical test, and to a lesser extent the theoretical system itself, bear the same relationship to the observed facts in a psychoanalysis, as statements of applied mathematics, say about a mathematical circle, bear to a statement about a circle drawn upon paper.

This theoretical system is intended to be applicable in a significant number of cases; psychoanalysts should therefore experience realizations that approximate to the Theory.

I attach no diagnostic importance to the Theory though I think it may be applicable whenever a disorder of thought is believed to exist. Its diagnostic significance will depend upon the pattern formed by the constant conjunction of a number of theories of which this theory would be one.

It may help to explain the Theory if I discuss the background of emotional experience from which it has been abstracted: I shall do this in general terms without attempting scientific rigour.

101. It is convenient to regard thinking as dependent on the successful outcome of two main mental developments. The first is the development of thoughts; they require an apparatus to cope with them. The second development therefore, is of this apparatus that I shall provisionally call thinking. I repeat – thinking has to be called into existence to cope with thoughts.

It will be noted that this differs from any theory of thought as a product of thinking, in that thinking is a development forced on the psyche by the pressure of thoughts – not the other way round. Psychopathological developments may be associated with either phase or both; they may be related to a breakdown in the development of thoughts, or a breakdown in the development of the apparatus for 'thinking' or dealing with thoughts, or both.

'Thoughts' may be classified, according to the nature of their developmental history, as pre-conceptions, conceptions or thoughts, and finally concepts; concepts are named and are therefore fixed conceptions or thoughts. The conception is initiated by the conjunction of a pre-conception with a realization. The pre-conception may be regarded as the analogue in psychoanalysis of Kant's concept of "empty thoughts". Psychoanalytically the theory that the infant has an inborn disposition corresponding to an expectation of a breast may be used to supply a model. When the preconception is brought into contact with a realization that approximates to it, the mental outcome is a conception. Put in another way, the pre-conception (the inborn expectation of a breast, the a priori knowledge of a breast, the "empty thought") when the infant is brought into contact with the breast itself, mates with awareness of the realization and is synchronous with the development of a conception. This model will serve for the theory that every junction of a preconception with its realization produces a conception. Conceptions therefore will be expected to be constantly conjoined with an emotional experience of satisfaction.

I shall limit the term 'thought' to the mating of a preconception with a frustration. The model I propose is that of an infant whose expectation of a breast is mated with a realization of no breast available for satisfaction. This mating is experienced as a no-breast, or 'absent' breast inside. The next step depends on the infant's capacity for frustration: in particular it depends on whether the decision is to evade frustration or to modify it.

If the capacity for toleration of frustration is sufficient, the 'no-breast' inside becomes a thought, and an apparatus for 'thinking it' develops. This initiates the state, described by Freud in his 'Two Principles of Mental Functioning' (1911b), in which dominance by the reality principle is synchronous with the development of an ability to think, and so to bridge the gulf of frustration between the moment when a want is felt and the moment when action appropriate to satisfying the want culminates in its satisfaction. A capacity for tolerating frustration thus enables the psyche to develop thought as a means by which the frustration that is tolerated is itself made more tolerable.

If the capacity for toleration of frustration is inadequate, the bad internal 'no-breast' that a personality capable of maturity ultimately recognizes as a thought, confronts the psyche with the need to decide between evasion of frustration or of its modification.

Incapacity for tolerating frustration tips the scale in the direction of evasion of frustration. The result is a significant departure from the events that Freud describes as characteristic of thought in the phase of dominance of the reality principle. What should be a thought, a product of the juxtaposition of pre-conception and negative realization, becomes a bad object, indistinguishable from a thing-in-itself, fit only for evacuation. Consequently the development of an apparatus for thinking is disturbed, and instead there takes place a hypertrophic development of the apparatus of projective identification. The model I propose for this development is a psyche that operates on the principle that evacuation of a bad breast is synonymous with obtaining sustenance from a good breast. The end result is that all thoughts are treated as if they were indistinguishable from bad internal objects; the appropriate machinery is felt not to be an apparatus for thinking the thoughts, but an apparatus for ridding the psyche of accumulations of bad internal objects. The crux lies in the decision between modification or evasion of frustration.

102. Mathematical elements, namely straight lines, points, circles and something corresponding to what later becomes known by the names of numbers, derive from realizations of two-ness as in breast and infant, two eyes, two feet and so on.

If intolerance of frustration is not too great modification becomes the governing aim. Development of mathematical elements, or mathematical objects as Aristotle calls them, is analogous to the development of conceptions.

If intolerance of frustration is dominant, steps are taken to evade perception of the realization by destructive attacks. In so far as pre-conception and realization are mated mathematical conceptions are formed but they are treated as if indistinguishable from things-in-themselves and are evacuated at high speed as missiles to annihilate space. In so far as space and time are perceived as identical with a bad object that is destroyed, that is to say a no-breast, the realization that should be mated with the pre-conception is not available to complete the conditions necessary for the formation of a conception. The dominance of projective identification confuses the distinction between the self and the external object. This contributes to the absence of any perception of two-ness since such an awareness depends on the recognition of a distinction between subject and object.

The relationship with time was graphically brought home to me by a patient who said over and over again that he was wasting time – and continued to waste it. The patient's aim is to destroy time by wasting it. The consequences are illustrated in the description in *Alice's Adventures in Wonderland* of the Mad Hatter's tea-party – it is always four o'clock.

Inability to tolerate frustration can obstruct the development of thoughts and a capacity to think, though a capacity to think would diminish the sense of frustration intrinsic to appreciation of the gap between a wish and its fulfilment. Conceptions, that is to say the outcome of a mating between a pre-conception and its realization, repeat in a more complex form the history of pre-conception. A conception does not necessarily meet a realization that approximates sufficiently closely to satisfy. If frustration can be tolerated the mating of conception and realizations whether negative or positive initiates procedures necessary for learning by experience. If intolerance of frustration is not so great as to activate the mechanisms of evasion, and yet is too great to bear dominance of the reality principle, the personality develops omnipotence as a substitute for the mating of the pre-conception or conception, with the negative realization. This involves the assumption of omniscience as a substitute for learning from experience by aid of thoughts and thinking. There is therefore no psychic activity to discriminate between true and false. Omniscience substitutes for the discrimination between true and false a dictatorial affirmation that one thing is morally right and the other wrong. The assumption of omniscience that denies reality ensures that the morality thus engendered is a function of psychosis. Discrimination between true and false is a function of the non-psychotic part of the personality and its factors. There is thus potentially a conflict between assertion of truth and assertion of moral ascendancy; the extremism of the one infects the other.

103. Some pre-conceptions relate to expectations of the self. The pre-conceptual apparatus is adequate to realizations that fall in the narrow range of circumstances suitable for the survival of the infant. One circumstance that affects survival is the personality of the infant itself. Ordinarily the personality of the infant, like other elements in the environment, is managed by the mother. If mother and child are adjusted to each other projective identification plays a role in the management through the operation of a rudimentary and fragile reality sense; usually an omnipotent phantasy, it operates realistically. This, I am inclined to believe, is its normal condition. When Melanie Klein (1946, p. 102) speaks of "excessive projective identification", I think the term *excessive* should be understood to apply not only to the frequency with which projective identification is employed, but to excess of belief in omnipotence. As a realistic activity it shows itself as behaviour reasonably calculated to arouse in the mother feelings of which the infant wishes to be rid; if the infant feels it is dying it can arouse fears in the mother that it is dying. A well-balanced mother can accept these and respond therapeutically: that is to say in a manner that makes the infant feel it is receiving its frightened personality back again but in a form that it can tolerate – the fears are manageable by the infant personality. If the mother cannot tolerate these projections, the infant is reduced to continued projective identification carried out with increasing force and frequency. The increased force seems to denude the projection of its penumbra of meaning. Reintrojection is effected with similar force and frequency. Deducing the patient's feelings from his behaviour in the consulting room, and using the deductions to form a model, the infant of my model does not behave in a way I ordinarily expect of an adult who is thinking: it behaves as if it felt an internal object with the characteristics of a greedy vagina-like 'breast' has been built-up, stripping of its goodness all that the infant receives or gives, leaving only degenerate objects. This internal object starves its host of all understanding that is made available. In analysis such a patient seems unable to gain from his environment and therefore from his analyst. The consequences for the development of a capacity for thinking are serious; I shall describe only one – namely precocious development of consciousness. (By consciousness I mean, in this context, what Freud described as a "sense-organ for the perception of psychic qualities".[1]

104. I have described previously (at a Scientific Meeting of the British Psychoanalytical Society) the use of a concept of alpha-function[2] as a working tool in the analysis of disturbances of thought. It seemed convenient to suppose an alpha-function to convert sense data into alpha-elements, and thus provide the psyche with the material for dream thoughts and hence the capacity to wake up or go to sleep, to be conscious or unconscious. According to this theory consciousness depends on alpha-function, and it is a logical necessity to suppose that such a function exists if we are to assume that the self is able to be conscious of itself in the sense of knowing itself from experience of itself. Yet the failure to establish between infant and mother a relationship in which normal projective identification is possible, precludes the development of an alpha-function and therefore of a differentiation of elements into conscious and unconscious.

The difficulty is avoided by restricting the term 'consciousness' to the meaning conferred on it by Freud's definition. Using the term in this restricted sense it is possible to suppose that this consciousness produces "sense-data" of the self but that there is no alpha-function to convert them into alpha-elements and therefore permit of a capacity for being conscious or unconscious of the self. The infant personality by itself is unable to make use of the sense-data, but has to evacuate these elements into the mother, relying on her to do whatever has to be done to convert them into a form suitable for employment by the infant as alpha-elements.

The limited consciousness defined by Freud (that I am using to define a rudimentary infant consciousness) is not associated with an unconscious. All impressions of the self are of equal value; all are conscious. The mother's capacity for reverie is the receptor organ for the infant's harvest of self-sensation gained by its conscious.

---

[1]["But what part is there left to be played in our scheme by consciousness, which was once so omnipotent and hid all else from view? *Only that of a sense-organ for the perception of psychical qualities"* (Freud, 1900a, p. 615). *Ed.*]

[2][See *Learning from Experience* (1962): Volume IV, p. 270. *Ed.*]

A rudimentary conscious could not perform the tasks that we ordinarily regard as the province of consciousness, and it would be misleading to attempt to withdraw the term 'conscious' from the sphere of ordinary usage where it is applied to mental functions of great importance in rational thinking. For the present I make the distinction only to show what happens if there is a breakdown of interplay through projective identification between the rudimentary consciousness and maternal reverie.

Normal development follows if the relationship between infant and breast permits the infant to project a feeling that it is dying into the mother and to reintroject it after its sojourn in the breast has made it tolerable to the infant psyche. If the projection is not accepted by the mother the infant feels that its feeling that it is dying is stripped of such meaning as it has. It therefore reintrojects not a fear of dying made tolerable, but a nameless dread.

The tasks that the breakdown in the mother's capacity for reverie have left unfinished are imposed on the rudimentary consciousness; they are all in different degrees related to the function of correlation.

The rudimentary consciousness cannot carry the burden placed on it. The establishment internally of a projective-identification-rejecting object means that instead of an understanding object the infant has a wilfully misunderstanding object – with which it is identified. Further, its psychic qualities are perceived by a precocious and fragile consciousness.

105. The apparatus available to the psyche may be regarded as fourfold:

1. *Thinking*, associated with modification and evasion.
2. *Projective identification*, associated with evasion by evacuation and not to be confused with normal projective identification (para 100 on "realistic" projective identification).
3. *Omniscience* (on the principle of *tout savoir tout condamner*).
4. *Communication*.

Examination of the apparatus I have listed under these four heads shows that it is designed to deal with thoughts, in the broad sense of the term; that is, including all objects I have described as conceptions, thoughts, dream thoughts, alpha-elements and beta-elements, as if they were objects that had to be dealt with (a) because they in some form contained or expressed a problem, and (b) because they were themselves felt to be undesirable excrescences of the psyche and required attention – elimination by some means or other – for that reason.

106. As expressions of a problem it is evident they require an apparatus designed to play the same part in bridging the gap between cognizance and appreciation of lack, and action designed to modify the lack as is played by alpha-function in bridging the gap between sense-data and appreciation of sense-data. (In this context I include the perception of psychic qualities as requiring the same treatment as sense-data.) In other words, just as sense-data have to be modified and worked on by alpha-function to make them available for dream thoughts etc., so the thoughts have to be worked on to make them available for translation into action.

Translation into action involves publication, communication and common sense. So far I have avoided discussion of these aspects of thinking although they are implied in the discussion, and one at least was openly adumbrated; I refer to correlation.

Publication in its origin may be regarded as little more than one function of thoughts, namely making sense-data available to consciousness. I wish to reserve the term for operations that are necessary to make private awareness (that is, awareness that is private to the individual) public. The problems involved may be regarded as technical and emotional. The emotional problems are associated with the fact that the human individual is a political animal and cannot find fulfilment outside a group and cannot satisfy any emotional drive without expression of its social component. His impulses, and I mean all impulses and not merely his sexual ones, are at the same time narcissistic. The problem is the resolution of the conflict between narcissism and social-ism. The technical problem is that concerned with expression of thought or conception in language, or its counterpart in signs.

This brings me to communication. In its origin communication is effected by realistic projective identification. The primitive infant procedure undergoes various vicissitudes including, as we have seen, debasement through hypertrophy of omnipotent phantasy. It may develop, if the relationship with the breast is good, into a capacity for toleration by the self of its own psychic qualities, and so pave the way for alpha-function and normal thought. But it does also develop as a part of the social capacity of the individual. This development, of great importance in group dynamics, has received virtually no attention; its absence would make even scientific communication impossible. Yet its presence may arouse feelings of persecution in the receptors of the communication. The need to diminish feelings of persecution contributes to the drive to abstraction in the formulation of scientific communications. The function of the elements of communication, words and signs, is to convey either by single substantives or in verbal groupings, that certain phenomena are constantly conjoined in the pattern of their relatedness.

An important function of communication is to achieve correlation. While communication is still a private function, conceptions, thoughts and their verbalization are necessary to facilitate the conjunction of one set of sense-data with another. If the conjoined data harmonize, a sense of truth is experienced and it is desirable that this sense should be given expression in a statement analogous to a truth-functional-statement. The failure to bring about this conjunction of sense-data, and therefore of a common-sense view, induces a mental state of debility in the patient as if starvation of truth was somehow analogous to alimentary starvation. The truth of a statement does not imply that there is a realization approximating to the true statement.

We may now consider further the relationship of rudimentary consciousness to psychic quality. The emotions fulfil a similar function for the psyche to that of the senses in relation to objects in space and time. That is to say the counterpart of the common-sense view in private knowledge is the common emotional view; a sense of truth is experienced if the view of an object which is hated can be conjoined to a view of the same object when it is loved, and the conjunction confirms that the object experienced by different emotions is the same object. A correlation is established.

107. A similar correlation, made possible by bringing conscious and unconscious to bear on the phenomena of the consulting room, gives to psychoanalytic objects a reality that is quite unmistakeable even though their very existence has been disputed.

10

Commentary

The distortions in "The Imaginary Twin" of the patient's past are designed to prevent him or anyone who knew him from thinking it referred to him. Such aims underestimate the power of rumour and suspicion.

If the distortions are judged effective, the narrative must be regarded as fiction. If the narrative were a work of art it might be reasonable to regard it as more nearly representative of truth than any literal transcription; but this psychoanalyst is not an artist. Expectations that the record represents what actually took place must be dismissed as vain.

The first paragraph is evocative; the reader is invited to appreciate the serious nature of the illness of the patient, the state of mind of one who has been advised to consider a severe brain operation, the pessimism and despair of one who has had so many years of unsuccessful treatment. The reader is prepared for the triumph of psychoanalysis in contrast with the patient's previous misfortunes under psychotherapy.

Paragraphs **2** and **3** are factually inaccurate;[1] the statements in the two paragraphs are representations of facts to which the realization did approximate closely. I thought this was true then; I think it is true now. What importance should be ascribed to these statements, one in the paper, made within months of the experience; the other in this book, made twenty years after?

It is usual to think that a report written within an hour or so of the events it is supposed to describe has a special 'built-in' validity and superiority over the account written many months or even years

[1]Numbers in bold refer to numbered paragraphs in preceding pages.

later. I shall suppose simply that they are two different accounts of the same event without any implication that one is superior to the other. A technique is needed which will reveal the nature of the contrasting stories and of the contrasting elements in them. Historians are familiar with the uses of 'contemporary' history and history written sufficiently long after the event for 'passions to have cooled' and perspective to have matured. A psychoanalyst will require some more precise definition of the realities behind these distinguishing formulations.

The need for discretion means that certain facts are replaced by falsifications intended to make no material difference to the account of the emotional tensions which were part of the patient's environment. I have now no doubt that this idea is quite fallacious, for the substitution is made in accordance with certain pre-conceptions derived from the experience of psychoanalysing the patient. The emotional background from which this account derives must include my ideas of what he told me, my interpretations, and my interpretations of the results of the encounter. When I wrote this I believed I was giving a factual account of the patient's behaviour together with a factual account of my interpretations – based partly on my beliefs about the meaning of psychoanalytic theory – followed by a factual account of the consequences of the interpretations. It seems to me now that it is more nearly accurate to regard this and all other articles written by me (for those are the articles of which I have most intimate knowledge) as consisting of statements of varying quality. For example, in paragraph **5** the statement is a verbal formulation of a visual image. Reading it now after seventeen years, I am able to receive a visual impression which up to a point reminds me of something that cannot be sensuously grasped – depression. The phrase "monosyllabic listlessness", coming in the context of the rest of the paragraph, makes me suppose now that the patient was depressed, but it is not the same to say he was depressed, as to describe him as being listless and monosyllabic. This is the crux of the situation; for the more unobstructed the relationship that the psychoanalyst has with his patient, the more subtle it is. It is an ineffable experience. The psychoanalyst's interpretation must be of a state of mind which it is the more difficult to describe in sensuous terms the more he aspires to be accurate.

In the psychoanalysis itself it is not so difficult to formulate an interpretation as it is here. To start with, the patient knows, because he is present, what the psychoanalyst is talking about. The same qualities inhere in the psychoanalyst's interpretation as in the association. Therefore the communication between the psychoanalyst and the patient has not the same difficulties as those existing in the written communication between psychoanalyst and reader.

The experience of the patient's communication and the psychoanalyst's interpretation is ineffable and essential. The communication of this quality plays a vital part in any interpretation given to the psychotic patient. The patient's reaction to the interpretation often depends more on this quality of the interpretation than on its verbal meaning. Thanks to the nature of the psychotic transference, the fate of the verbal meaning hangs on the patient's reaction to the tone of the interpretation.

Now the sensuous image, C category in the Grid,[1] gives body to the description in paragraph **5**. If I tried to formulate it in more precise terms as the scientist can with his mathematical formulae, the communication degenerates into verbal jugglery. Yet more precise formulation is required if the reader is to have an accurate idea of the association that had to be interpreted. How is the communication between the psychoanalyst reading and the psychoanalyst writing to be made at least as effective as the communication between analyst and analysand? What has to be communicated is real enough; yet every psychoanalyst knows the frustration of trying to make clear, even to another psychoanalyst, an experience which sounds unconvincing as soon as it is formulated. We may have to reconcile ourselves to the idea that such communication is impossible at the present stage of psychoanalysis. Transformations of the psychoanalytic experience into formulations which effect communication between psychoanalyst and reader, remains an activity to be pursued. Some may wish to transform it into group terms, some into mathematical, scientific or artistic terms. Some may be satisfied to perfect interpretations in the context of the psychoanalytic session. No psychoanalyst will be content to leave things as they are.

A special instance of the problem of communication between the psychoanalyst writing and the psychoanalyst reading, of which I have been reminded by preparing these papers for publication, arises when the writer and the reader is the same man. Here, one might sup-

[1] [See p. vii, this volume. *Ed.*]

pose, are the perfect conditions for communication. Yet in the days when I used to write elaborate notes on my sessions with patients, I found that I was no more successful when the interval between writing and reading was relatively short than I do now when the interval is measured in years. At first I thought I could easily understand notes dashed off at speed, a squiggle here, an exclamation mark there, sometimes an interpolated conjecture or comment on my own feelings on what was happening. I will not say they were meaningless when I came to read them, but they did not convey the meaning I hoped to find. They resembled nothing so much as a sleepy note that I sometimes tried to make to pin down what I felt to be an important dream for study in the morning. The squiggles remained: the dream had gone. I found I could not make better interpretive use of them than of squiggles I made on the spot while fully awake. So it is with this paper here. I am not unappreciative of the account; If it were some other psychoanalyst's report I would think it quite good. But as it is, I do not recognize the patient or myself.

This sort of experience led me to try a number of experiments in note taking, including some, perhaps the most convincing, which were intentionally subjective reports on my feelings about the day's work. A card index served to find references to patients so that I might scrutinize the material quickly if I should wish to be reminded of his or her psychoanalytic history. This I thought helpful – once or twice. I have the same feeling now, for example, on reading paragraphs **8–11**, but I am not sure in what way this was a helpful experience then, or is helpful now. Finally I abandoned note taking altogether, but that was not till some years after the first paper was written. My reasons for doing so cannot be simply or comprehensively stated. One reason, relevant in this immediate context, was my growing awareness that the most evocative notes were those in which I came nearest to a representation of a sensory image; say an event visually recalled (for example see **5**). The evocation however was not of the past but of interpretations wise after the event. In short the value of the notes lay not in their supposed formulation of a record of the past but in their formulation of a sensory image evocative of the future. The notes did not make it possible to remain conscious of the past but to evoke expectations of the future. Using the Grid I have tentatively constructed for this purpose, the statements made in my notes are better categorized as C4 than as C3.

In the Grid these two categories appear close together. It is common in everyday life to hear of two people whose views are said to be "poles apart"; it is but one expression of mental 'distance'. The visual image of the Grid suggests that these categories are neighbours and are we then to assume there is some corresponding 'closeness' in the relationship of the *objects represented* by the Grid? In the context of this discussion I am arguing that the actual value of the formulation categorized as C3 is in fact 'far from' the real value represented by C¢. Would the Grid be more nearly representative of the realizations it is intended to categorize if these categories were differently spaced on the paper? The notes I am discussing can be said to belong to categories which are similar or close in that, if they purport to be records of the past, their object is to evoke memories presumed to be unconscious because they have been forgotten or suppressed or repressed: if they are to evoke ideas about the future, they are to evoke prophecies or conjectures about what has not yet happened. The distance between the two, measured not in space but in time, might be infinitely small or infinitely large. Again, if my note tells me 'what happened' in yesterday's session and makes me think of what is shortly going to happen in today's, can the 'distance' between these two ideas be measured by the time that has elapsed between the two sessions? Perhaps it would be better not to think of it as distance in space or time between the ideas, but rather in terms of difference relative to some scale with an entirely different genetic background from that of physical space or physical time. For further consideration – in what useful sense can it be said that the mind 'travels' from earth to the nearest quasar with the 'speed of thought'?

For psychoanalysts these are not ideas but practical questions; consider the importance of the analyst's or patient's ability to grasp an idea very 'slowly' or very 'fast'. A patient may see the meaning of an interpretation so quickly that the analyst is surprised to find a moment later that the patient has apparently no understanding of what has been said to him. The speed of his thought makes him able to closure the statement being discussed before he has had time to understand it. The terms in which I am describing this are all modelled on sensuous experience of a sensible background. The model serves to illuminate many phenomena in psychoanalysis, but the light that these models shed (this one included) is fitful and their inadequacy is easily apparent. The analyst needs models which are quickly constructed, widely applicable, robust. Those we use now are short-winded; they serve well enough up to a point, but that point is quickly reached and from it the analyst can see nothing but darkness beyond. That, in my opinion, is what is wrong with these papers on which I am commenting. I comment on them because their defect is not peculiar to these papers but to the method of which they are typical. The problem is to transform formulations such as 'time', 'distance', 'space', so that the re-formulation is not so abstract that it becomes verbal jugglery and not so impacted with meaning that growth is obstructed.

The analyst's note on a session may be far from a record of what took place, yet near to anticipation of a future development. Scientific training seems to suppose that capacity for anticipation is a desirable attribute and worth developing. It appears important for the analyst to be able to predict his patient's attempt at suicide, or conversely, his probable improvement. Let us examine this supposition more closely.

If it is supposed that the analyst must anticipate his patient's suicide, it means no more than that the analyst should be able to entertain as wide a spectrum of thought and feeling, pleasant or unpleasant, as is possible. The idea that his patient might commit suicide is only one particular instance of the painful thoughts which the analyst must be capable of sustaining; otherwise he will be deflected from doing the work he exists to do and which no one else can do, namely to analyse. If analysing the impulse to suicide cannot change the patient's impulse, prevention, say by hospitalization, will certainly not do so. Others have to fulfil different roles in such a contingency; they may believe that the analyst should fulfil these other tasks, but their beliefs may have disagreeable consequences for the analyst in a position to know that his function is to psychoanalyse. He is under pressure, isolated and vulnerable, subjected to the temptation to abandon his role and assume one which, however unfitted he may be for it, conforms to the accepted conventions and preconceptions of the group. If he does so, the analysis is hopelessly compromised: the patient loses his analyst and gains a doubtfully valuable auxiliary.

The above arguments apply with equal cogency to the supposition that the patient might become a psychoanalyst – a supposition which the analyst should be able to consider.[1] If he can entertain a spectrum of possibilities, from the suicide of his patient to his survival as a robust and stable personality, the analyst should be able to analyse each as it appears in the context of the analysis. The rock on which the analysis comes to shipwreck is the obtrusion of the memories and desires of the psychoanalyst; of this point I shall have occasion to speak later.

At **12** a retrospective glance at the analysis begins. It is not my intention to question the accuracy of the description, but to use it to illustrate my present view. The account as it stands could be a description of either memory or evolution; they need to be distinguished.

As the report of a memory it purports to describe my 'memory' of what I now call an 'evolution', namely, the coming together, by a sudden precipitating intuition, of a mass of apparently unrelated incoherent phenomena which are thereby given coherence and meaning not previously possessed. This I distinguish from the reports of the story told by the homosexual brother-in-law. That element, and others like it, I class as 'memories' together with recollections somewhat deliberately and painstakingly recalled, as for example when a patient pieces together a dream he thinks he has had. In contrast is a dream which is recalled suddenly, as if in a single whole. Or perhaps similarly lost as a single whole. This experience resembles the phenomenon of transformation of the paranoid-schizoid position to the depressive position. I have in the past drawn attention to a striking description of the experience given by H. Poincaré in his *Science and Method* (1914).

The event described in **13** would do very well as an illustration of an 'evolution'. From the material the patient produces, there emerges, like the pattern from a kaleidoscope, a configuration which seems to belong not only to the situation unfolding, but to a number of others not previously seen to be connected and which it has not been designed to connect. I do not now regard the pattern of the 'imaginary twin' as of any central importance, though I have found it illuminating for some aspects of the analysis of an only child. It is then very often a particular fact of the more general pattern of splitting. The patient of whom I wrote was not an only child, but circumstances

[1]For important comments touching training analysis see D. Meltzer on 'The Relation of Anal Masturbation to Projective Identification' (1966).

led him to feel so. At the outset of his career, any psychoanalyst must find his own way and come upon well-known and well-established theories through experiences of his own realizations. It is clear that the realization which approximates to a theory he has learned will be unique, and may therefore appear to be so different from the theoretical formulation that he cannot recognize the bearing of the one upon the other. By contrast he will force a theory to fit a realization because it is difficult for an inexperienced analyst to tolerate doubt and uncertainty which he imagines that a more experienced analyst – probably his own – would not have.

There can be no harm in errors of this kind: 'original discoveries' of the already well-known, and 'confirmation' where none would be found if clinical flair were mature. It becomes fatal to good analysis if premature application of a theory becomes a habit which places a screen between the psychoanalyst and the exercise of his intuition on fresh and therefore unknown material.

The dream reported in **15** was, I think, as nearly in the patient's words as is possible. I assumed that it was correctly reported by the patient, correctly remembered by me, and correctly transcribed. There is no doubt that this convenient assumption is false. It remains none-the-less convenient and most analysts, including myself, will continue to use it for most occasions. It is not always convenient and the modern trends in psychoanalytic practice will make these assumptions misleading unless they are used with circumspection. Failure to recognize the point at which an assumption, known to be false but convenient, becomes inconvenient as well as false, leads to deflections of psychoanalytic practice into an impasse where pessimism reigns. I make this dream and the reports in **16–20** the subject of critical comment not because I have changed my views on the value of what I reported then, but because I require a jumping-off point for the exposition of something else now.

As I 'remember' it, the dream was reported by the patient in vivid terms. The report given in **15** recalled the episode, when I read it, in such 'complete' fashion that I regard it as having 'evolved' in the course of the actual reading. This is in contrast with my experience on re-reading **16**.

I 'remembered' that in my opinion my interpretation was a good one – 'correct', as I would then have said, and I 'remember' that the experience of dream and interpretation had the same convincing quality of reality at the time. The description in **16** cannot 'evolve' anything now as the description in **15** can. I do not attribute this to the inferior quality of **16** but to a difference in kind in the nature of the two formulations. I find myself unable to be impressed either with the truth or falsity of the interpretation. With **15** I experience an 'evolution' of emotional experience now; with **16,** I experience nothing but a sense of manipulation of theories.

As I participated in the reported experience, I know there was no deliberate or conscious falsification. I also know that the formulation of **16** was as good as taking pains could make it. Even making allowance for personal defects in powers of description, the real problem arises in the lack of apparatus for recording the only part of an analytic session that is worthy of record. Occasionally, as in **15**, something can be recorded adequately enough to lead to an evolution when the reader is the analyst. Psychoanalytic literature has meaning for one or two readers of a particular article at most; it must be the dreariest and most unrewarding scientific literature for the others.

If this dreariness adequately represented the realization, no great harm would follow: psychoanalysis would disappear, with other pseudo-sciences. To anyone who has experienced the reality of psychoanalysis, the possibility of such an outcome of faulty communication is tragic.

The formulations of **17** differ in kind from those of **15** or **16**. They are descriptions of events in terms which are themselves theoretical formulations of psychoanalytic intuitions. They are therefore removed from the world of emotional experience in a way in which the dream description of **15** is not, although, as we have already seen, the description in **15** is a description of a description of something alleged by the patient to have happened while he slept. As a practising analyst, I tolerate for the present the misgivings to which such an insecure foundation gives rise. I think the insecurity should be noticed but disregarded till it becomes relevant. The difference in kind between **15** and **16**, and then again **17** and **19–20** is no longer tolerable because the nature of the work today does not permit lack of discrimination between realizations which are so different from each other. The verbal formulation of the dream in **15** is relatively tolerable; it can be regarded as category C3. The descriptions in **16–20** cannot be so regarded. They lack the immediacy which gives body to the description in **15**. Similarly, except to a few analysts, the formulations of **17** become theoretical statements of psychoanalytic intuitions which are vulnerable because they lack 'body' on the one hand and scientific rigour on the other.

I tolerate the formulations of **17–18** because I do not see my way to producing anything better, but their value is debatable. What they communicate may not be worth communicating; conversely, what was, in the psychoanalytic experience, worth communicating may not in fact have been communicated.

The position with regard to **18–20** is more complex. I cannot now say to what extent the account given represents fairly what took place. I know that in intention it does, but psychoanalytic experience shows how misleading such an impression can be. Furthermore, I have since learned that no amount of psychoanalysis can insure the analyst against distortion of his material, though his distortions may become less crude than they were before he was analysed.

The account **18–20** is therefore subject to unconscious distortion of the kind present in psychoanalysis. Moreover the account is written with conscious aim to 'illustrate' what I thought I had learned from the analytic experience. The need to 'illustrate' the theme means that an attempt is made to represent the experience in terms of sensuous experience – C category terms. Description in such terms avoids the danger of manipulation of jargon, but it introduces dangers which are as great though different. First, the terms cannot represent the psychoanalytic experience which they purport to describe, but only a sensuous experience of physical fact supposedly analogous to the mental experience. The account **18–20** is a transformation[1] of an emotional experience into a verbal formulation of a sensuous experience (**19**). This is perhaps the most direct representation in the whole account **18–20**.

In ordinary extra-analytic experience, rigorous scrutiny would be irrelevant; possibly it would be irrelevant in most psychoanalytic experience. It is irrelevant to the man in this paper, but not in the analyses of patients whose sense of reality is disturbed. It is essential to understand the nature of the analyst's formulations of his experience of reality to obtain a grasp of the nature of the patient's formulations of his experience of reality, and thus compare the two.

---

[1]See *Transformations* [Volume V].

The descriptions in the last paragraph of **19,** or the whole of **20,** do not make clear how much the reader is to suppose that the account is a direct intuition of what was taking place, and how much a report of selected facts. The analyst must discern the underlying pattern by a process of discrimination and selection. If the account given is a selection made to demonstrate the correctness of the original selection, it is clearly worthless. Only if the original experience is a genuine evolution of a psychoanalytic realization, i.e. a precipitation of coherence by a "selected fact", does the writer's conscious discrimination and selection become legitimate as a method of representation.

In the passages discussed, there is a further complication because I had deliberately to falsify the facts to make identification of the patient impossible. This I achieved but at the cost of an account which I now consider worthless. It fails to represent the realization I wanted to depict and it fails to explain the interpretations given.

This leads to the dilemma of psychoanalytic communication as it is at present. The report of a session (that is, the psychoanalytic realization) must be a literal and incomprehensible jumble, or it must be an artistic representation. The former need not detain us: the latter, assuming the requisite degree of artistic capacity in the analyst, implies a transformation during which selection and ordering of the material takes place. The interpretation given the patient is a formulation intended to display an underlying pattern. It therefore is itself similar to the mathematical formula as described by Poincaré (1914, p. 30). It is also similar to some aspects of a painting, sculpture or musical composition. At their best these formulations make us aware of a coherence and order where, without them, incoherence and disorder would reign.

In practice, the psychoanalyst does not possess the conditions, even if he has the attributes, for artistic creation – unless we suppose that a capacity for conversational expression can be sublimed into a minor ephemeral art. He can however give an interpretation, and the patient experiences the realization to which the interpretation purports to approximate. When it comes to psychoanalytic communication, the reader does not have the advantage of the patient. He depends on a verbal transformation of the psychoanalytic experience which has been formulated by the same person as the one who has made the interpretation in the terms he chooses to report.

There is nothing new in the criticism of lack of objectivity in psychoanalysis, and I am not proposing to waste time on it. I wish to consider a few of the defects which are loosely combined under this general head, in particular what the difference is supposed to be between the penultimate and ultimate paragraphs of **20**. To me the supposed report of what occurred is simply a not very good C3 formulation. That is to say, in order to convey to the reader an impression of the psychoanalytic experience (which cannot in fact be seen or smelled or heard, for one is not listening to what the *patient* thinks he is saying), a description is given in terms of what *can* be sensuously experienced. No wonder psychoanalytic interpretations give rise to scepticism.

Although no one doubts the reality of, say anxiety, it cannot be sensuously apprehended. In psychoanalytic practice, we are not concerned with crude examples even of anxiety; two analysts might disagree over a patient pouring out intense overt hostility to the analyst. He could be supposed by one to be driven by anxiety, and by the other to be showing persecutory fear. The more experienced and sensitive the analyst, the more readily he experiences the non-sensuous phenomena unfolding before him. He should therefore be able to communicate something that is at present ineffable. There should be a significant difference between the formulation of what is alleged to have happened and the formulation purporting to be an interpretation. What is the significant difference between what was expressed in the analytic session and the interpretation of it given by the analyst?

Psychoanalytic discussion often takes the form of comparing what the patient has said with the interpretations which were, or might have been, given. In addition to the objection that the psychoanalytic communication is two versions of the same observation, the psychoanalytic discussion demonstrates the futility of comparing association with interpretation. Associations are infinite in number and so are interpretations; it is therefore idle to discuss matching the one to the other. This is particularly the case since the report on the associations of the patient is a transformation, and the transformation introduces a distortion which cannot be allowed for. The distortion due to the personality of the psychoanalyst does not remain constant between the association he reports and the interpretation he gives of his reported association. A student will sometimes report an interpretation which told the patient almost nothing more than the association has already stated. In such a case, analysts consider the interpretation defective. There are occasions when the interpretation may be almost verbally identical with the association, yet, because the analyst is lending his authority to confirmation of the patient's statement, the interpretation produces significant change. It is therefore clear that nothing can be learned by a comparison of association and interpretation, but may be learned by a comparison of the nature of the interpretation with the nature of the association.

In **22** part of a dream is reported. There are two words, "rage" and "terror", which, if it is assumed that they are correctly used, represent and communicate psychic reality. The context in which they are used is a verbal transformation of a visual image. Together with the terms "rage" and "terror" they evoke a powerful impression even now when I do not remember with any certainty the occasion reported. In this respect it is different from the reported interpretation which makes no impact; I do not doubt that it represents what I said at the time. Its lack of impact is not surprising because the interpretation is formulated in F6 terms. That is, the formulation is sophisticated and is intended to be the mental counterpart of action. It is intended as a psychoanalytic action. Like all F, G, H categories, it tends to come over as a meaningless manipulation of technical terms. This is precisely the danger to be anticipated with all sophisticated formulations. It is brought out by the report in **31**; the interpretations leave a sense of meaningless verbal manipulations. They lack permanence or durability; in this respect they differ from aesthetic statements.

At the time of the interpretation, this problem does not arise because analyst and analysand are able to compare the interpretation with the facts it purports to interpret. The reader cannot do this and no amount of description, however skilful, and no interpretation, however apposite, can make up for the reader's lack of the experience to which they relate.

If the psychoanalytic situation is accurately intuited – I prefer this term to 'observed' or 'heard' or 'seen' as it does not carry the penumbra of sensuous association – the analyst finds that ordinary conversational English is surprisingly adequate for the formulation of his interpretation. Further, the emotional situation serves to make the interpretation comprehensible to the analysand – although resistances require some modification of this latter statement as too optimistic.

As a result, interpretations which, when read, appear unlikely to effect a useful purpose, are in practice efficacious. Since it is important to understand the process of psychoanalytic growth, the failure to communicate the non-sensuous experience on which the interpretation is based is a major misfortune of analytic practice at its present stage of development. I suspect it also contributes to the somewhat futile controversy about psychoanalytic theories; the argument should illuminate *what* theory has been applied to *what* realization. In fact, it does not do so because no one has discovered a method by which this vital relationship between interpretation and the realization can be communicated. Even in **15** I was not able to make the relationship clear; still less in **23–24.**

Account **26** reports considerable psychoanalytic mobility. The patient is able to move from one psychological state to another with some freedom. I do not now remember him to have felt 'better', or to have used any terms which expressed some idea of 'cure' or 'disease'. This was in conformity with his pessimistic and sceptical attitude, but did not give any impression that depression was central. He seemed, even while he was speaking of referring his students to medical men, never to be consciously concerned with himself as a patient requiring cure. He must have been the first patient to make me wonder whether the idea of cure was not introducing an irrelevant criterion in psychoanalysis. This point will be considered again later. For the present I would draw attention to the contrast presented to psychoanalytic mobility by the moral rigidity noted at the opening of **27**. I shall have more to say of this later.

At the end of **29** and the beginning of **31**, I describe the problem produced by a growth of intuition. I did not then know how common this experience is. In the paper, 'Differentiation of the Psychotic from the Non-Psychotic Personalities' [chapter 5], there is an illustration of an increase of intuition and the danger it represents for the individual's growth. The theme is developed more fully in 'Catastrophic Change'[1] in which I explain that it is part of a widespread

[1]*Bulletin of the British Psychoanalytical Society*, No. 5, 1966. [See earlier, this volume. This was republished, with very few changes, as Chapter 12 in *Attention and Interpretation*, which is also in this volume. *Ed.*]

configuration. I shall leave that topic to discuss the use of terms such as 'widespread', 'superficial', used in the second paragraph of **30**, and others drawn from realizations of physical space.

Freud's model for the mind, illustrated by diagram,[1] is based on a realization of physical space; the linear representation helps to strengthen an impression which has not so far appeared to create any difficulties. It has facilitated understanding and discovery; but these models are inadequate for the investigation of patients whose orientation in space and time is faulty. If such faults are to be understood, the model used to investigate them must be one to which the realization approximates more closely than it does to the model used by the patient. If a patient behaves as if he is unaware of the passage of time and the analyst regards the passage of time and the failure to observe it as important, he needs to know how the difference of attitude has arisen. Of what is the analyst aware and how does he come to be aware of it? Does 'time' 'pass'? If it does not, then it is absurd to expect the patient to be aware of its 'passage'. Most people accept that there is a realization which is adequately represented by the formulation, 'time is passing'; but a psychotic patient may not be aware of that realization and may not behave as if the formulation 'time is passing' represents a realization of any significance. Would he accept the significance of the realization if it were represented by a formulation to which the realization approximated more closely? As it stands, the statement, 'time is passing' is made up of words derived from sensuous experience and is a verbal formulation in category C terms. Briefly, to grasp the nature of the patient's departure from 'normal' it is necessary to have an idea of 'normal', which is not itself a departure from normal. Analysts frequently speak of 'early' and 'late' phases of mental life. The discussion of episodes in the analysis as reactivations or reminiscences, of breast experiences, implies an awareness of a dimension of time and suggests that some element which obtrudes has a history. Sometimes this may be expressed as having a 'place' in time or a 'place' in space – 'superficial' or 'deep'.

I have accepted this convention, but a problem arises when the analyst finds, as I have done, reason to question the usefulness of an interpretation based on acceptance of the convention. The complex-

[1][Bion may have been referring to the diagram on p. 24 of *The Ego and the Id* (1923b). *Ed.*]

ity of the problem is increased when it becomes clear with certain patients that measurements of time and space are based on psychic reality – not physical space or time; both measurements are possible only to the patient capable of tolerating frustration because both are derived from measures of frustration. If the patient cannot tolerate frustration, he prevents the development of any apparatus which measures it. Thus, if he is so many years or so many minutes from his objective, he annihilates space or time which measure his frustration. The development of more sophisticated usages of this capacity, such as measurement of time or space, is thus prejudiced. A state is produced in which the patient is unwilling to admit awareness of distance or time. Ordinarily this does not matter, but when I came to consider the nature of memory and desire, I realized that they were the 'past' and 'future' of the same impulse. This led to the awareness of a need to readjust ideas over too extensive an area for the mental comfort of the analyst. His experience is, in this respect, paralleled by the patient (see **32**).

Progress in psychoanalysis is inseparable from a need to tolerate the painful concomitants of mental growth of which the immediate revelation of further problems requiring solution is not the least. The importance of this will become clearer with time; even analysts seem to be unaware of the expanding nature of their universe, partly because it is difficult to be aware of movement when the participant is closely engaged with detail, partly because the implications of psychoanalysis cannot be grasped at this early stage in its history. If my suspicion that this is so is found by experience to be correct, the difficulties of the patient, adumbrated in **32**, are significant for both analysand and analyst when growth is taking place. For the analyst, the problem presents itself for solution not only by the analysand but by the analyst as part of his own growth. He may develop contemporaneously with his patient, or independently, or not at all. In the latter case, the future of his practice or of himself is no part of analysis though it may be a part of the sociology of the practice of psychoanalysis. The psychoanalytic problem is illustrated by the difficulties to be faced on re-publication of 'Notes on the Theory of Schizophrenia' [chapter 3]. As I judge now, the description given is a sound representation of the clinical realizations which it purports to describe. It represents fairly the experience from which they are derived; it points adequately to future recurrences. In terms of Grid categories (which

I had not at that time elaborated) they are C3 elements intended to represent psychoanalytic realizations, C1 statements defining experiences of the psychoanalyst, and D4 formulations pointing to future contingencies. Yet continuing experience of psychoanalysis makes dissatisfaction with the paper inevitable. So it must be with any experience accompanied by growth; the valuable experience becomes outdated. The problem is to decide whether an experience which is illuminating can be communicated to another analyst, and if so whether the communication is worth making or receiving; to this there can be no answer other than that obtained by making the attempt. Unfortunately, the time required for making the communication, for gaining experience which seems worth communication, and for receiving communications made by others, is so great that doubts of the value of the venture become intimidating. Neither can reliance be placed on hostile criticism, as the ineffable nature of psychoanalysis makes it unlikely that so-called impartial criticism has any value beyond serving as an indication of the climate of opinion in which the analyst works. This may be summed up by saying that the analyst's work is lonely work, that the only companion he has is his patient, and his patient is by definition unreliable.

Nevertheless the patient comes for analysis and no one can compel him to do this. There is therefore reason to suppose that even in the most hostile patient there is an impulse to co-operate. It is therefore of importance to know what significance is to be attached to this impulse. The nature of the problem is apparent when the patient is suicidal, or anxious to do as much injury as he can to the analyst, or to those who have his welfare at heart. The time, money and effort involved in psychoanalysis make it a useful weapon for the patient who has such an aim. If the analysand harbours such aims, it is evident that the analyst must be clear in his mind about *his* aims for being an analyst. An ambition to help the patient is inadequate, quickly grasped by him and swept into his system of attack. If the analyst has formulated any other aim he is no better off – the patient can detect and demolish it. In **35** I have used commonly accepted terms to formulate a diagnosis (F1 in Grid categories). They have a backward-looking value and probably convey a meaning to the reader. The problem of schizophrenic thought and language includes the problem of the language that the analyst is to employ in discussing it.

None of the terms used in **35** represents the state of mind of the destructive patient I want to portray. Yet the description is a representation to which some psychoanalytic experiences approximate. What then am I to think when I meet with these terms when used by others or, as in this instance, by myself? Looking back on it, it may be that all drug addicts, schizophrenics and obsessional patients should be suspect on the grounds that their destructive impulses approximate in varying degrees to the extreme I have described. A more useful supposition is that the analyst should regard the terms used in **35**, and others like them, as binding constant conjunctions, leaving the analyst to determine what the constantly conjoined elements are. In the instance postulated the significance for the analyst is not the nature of the constantly conjoined elements, but their intensity. This is true when envy, hate, sex, love are encountered. For the practising analyst the terms used in **34** are almost useless and I would now use them with circumspection. The patients in whom the difficulties described occur are important for the degree to which destructive ambitions are active. If the analyst could assess 'degree' it would be as important as his ability to assess quality. The realizations of psychoanalysis are not however such that terms like quality and quantity can be used without considering their sensuous background. The measurement of frustration (to which I refer in a forthcoming book[1]) may offer an approach to the solution of this problem. The models which an analyst is compelled to use at the present stage of psychoanalytic development, contribute to the difficulties of assessing quantity. A model is not the same size as the realization; it derives its value partly from that very fact. It is communicatively valuable to refer to a patient's greed for 'the breast'; but the his problem may arise not from his greed for 'the breast', but from his greed for what he considers the world is able to yield him.

This alteration in scale from 'breast' to 'world' can be an unobserved but outstanding feature of the communication as it is received by the patient, though of minor importance to the analyst who makes it. The reduction in scale may make the model illuminating in every respect except one – as a measure of quantity.

---

[1][*Attention and Interpretation* (especially chaps. 2 and 12) – see later, this volume. *Ed.*]

I do not propose any alteration of my formulations in **36** and **37**. They do not satisfy me, but any changes now would be made without the support of current experience. They have most value if the reader will regard them as verbal formulations of C category elements. To me they are not reports on what took place – they are verbal representations of visual images which portray an emotional state of the writer at the time of writing. As stimulants to thought in the reader, they could be useful to certain types of reader; therefore I re-publish them; I do not wish to minimize the importance of formulations which, in their time, served to represent experiences that contributed to the development of the patient and myself. If they had this merit once, they may possess it still.

The last paragraph of **38** is a formulation which represents a realization that is recurrent. Together with **39** it contains elements of a configuration which is common in the mental sphere of groups and individuals. The recurrence of the configuration, though on each occasion associated with known psychoanalytic theories, leads one to feel there must be an underlying group to which all the configurations and associated theories belong. The instance cited is one example of a relationship (which I have discussed more fully since[1]) between container and contained denoted by the sign ♀♂. The sexual model implied serves to direct the observer's attention to a constantly recurring pattern; the diversity of the elements in its composition being indicated by being 'in a group', 'in a person', 'in analysis', 'acting out', 'in a statement, word or expression', and so forth. It has been objected that, for example, 'acting out' is merely a verbal peculiarity of an English translation. I am not, however, referring to verbal expressions but to a *configuration* which may appear in a verbal formulation or in a realization, in a visual image or an emotional experience in one language but not in another; in one patient's conscious but not in another's; sometimes conscious, sometimes not; sometimes in thought, sometimes in action. The important element is that the configuration should be recognized whenever it appears. When emotional experiences betray the pattern, it may have a peculiar significance, but for the present I want to stress only the importance of recognizing the configuration wherever it appears. These words I write are supposed to 'contain' a meaning, but the verbal expression can be so formalized, so rigid, so

[1][Chapter 27 of *Learning from Experience*. See Volume IV. *Ed.*]

filled with already existing ideas that the idea I want to express can have all the life squeezed out of it. On the other hand, the meaning I wish to express may have such force and vitality, relative to the verbal formulation in which I would strive to contain it, that it destroys the verbal container. The result then is not a compact communication but an incoherence; or, to take another instance, a disrupted group or society, or a group leader manqué. Psychoanalysis itself provides an outstanding example of such a force, idea or individual in tension with its container, verbal formulation, or society.

The whole of **39** (which I have suggested is most conveniently dealt with as a C category element) brings into focus a problem which is of interest for the future of psychoanalysis. I have regarded C category elements as being the stuff from which the scientific use of models derives. One advantage of the model is that it does not commit the analyst to the formal rigidity of a theory, but presents him with a tool which he can discard when it has served its purpose. This may be soon, or only after a considerable lapse of time and after many experiences of the usefulness of the model. The use of models in the physical sciences is easily understood to be valuable because the material which has to be dealt with has a sensuous background, or at least derives at a few removes from such a background. The sensuous component, which is by definition an aspect of C category elements to which those elements owe their expository value, is precisely the quality which lays the psychoanalytic model open to misunderstanding: it reproduces an aspect of the original experience, the realization about which the communication is made, in a new medium. The model should display the invariants depicted in the new medium which are supposed to be discerned in the realization, but the psychoanalytic realization is not discerned by any of the physical senses known to the biologist. Freud, in his seventh chapter of *The Interpretation of Dreams*, speaks of consciousness as the sense organ of psychic reality. It is not necessary to be an analyst to be persuaded of the realization approximating to the term 'anxiety'. Anxiety does not smell, it has no shape, colour, or other sensuous attribute. This is true of every psychoanalytic realization. The matters with which we deal are real beyond question, but have to be described in terms that from their nature introduce distortion.

The matters discussed in **39** require a model. There is no satisfactory psychoanalytic model; the nearest approach to the functions of a model is made by the patient when he speaks of the hole, the cavity left in the skin when a blackhead is removed. This model did not help him to solve his problem, or he would not have come for analysis. The patient's problem is not the therapeutic measures required for a skin complaint; it is his feeling that his 'mental boundary' has lost an important part of itself through his destructive attack on it. He is now attacked by the 'hole' which is the part of his mental skin which was residual after he had wrought his destruction. As a model, the statement I have just formulated is inferior in sensuously phrased visual imagery to what the patient said. What then is the matter with his model that he failed to come to a solution? What is the matter with *mine*? Is it that it is implausible and imprecise? In practice the defect of my model can be overcome because the matter to which reference is being made is, at the time of discussion, being experienced by both analyst and patient and all that is necessary is that the words employed should disclose an experience available to both, *while* it is available to both. But when, as at this moment when I write and the reader reads, there is no emotional experience to which appeal can be made, and the 'disclosure' which I as writer wish to make is of an event that has not yet taken place – of an experience which in my opinion the analyst reading this will be likely to have – the failure of the communication is fundamental, not incidental. The problem for which the psychoanalytic model is needed is similar to the problem which the mathematician solves when mathematics enables him to handle a problem in the absence of the objects. In the domain of the physical sciences, when the original problem does not permit the necessary experimentation and manipulation, a model can be built which will do away with the obstructive features while retaining the essentials of the problem unaltered – invariant.

In the problem adumbrated in **39**, a model is required because the two 'original realizations' do not exist: one, because it took place in circumstances which no longer exist, and, in so far as it exists at all, it only 'exists' in memory; the other, because it has not yet happened and, in so far as it exists at all, it only 'exists' in phantasy. Both 'originals' are therefore not available for direct investigation. Is there some form of model which can do for the psychoanalyst what models will do for the physical scientist? If such a mechanism were available it could be used to take the place of the formulation in **39**. I think it would do away with misunderstandings which the present formulation invites. As it stands, it is a conglomerate of a number of different kinds of formulation, visual images, theories, statements which purport to be representations of factual events. Allowing for the fact that a more capable writer could correct some of these errors, I do not think that the capacity to write well is the issue. There needs to be a recognized formulation which is understood by all analysts to display the invariants in an event which is unconscious because obscured by memory, although it *has* happened, and an event which is manifest because disclosed by desire though it has not happened. Memory and desire may be regarded as past and future 'senses' of the same 'thing' (analogous to the mathematical concept of 'sense' and applying indifferently to time or space). Making use of sense in this way a formulation $\overleftarrow{\text{desire}}$ would have the same value as $\overrightarrow{\text{memory}}$, the former referring to an event that had happened and the latter referring to an event that had not happened, and therefore not usually described as being 'remembered'. A patient who could be described in terms of conversational English as 'remembering' something that had *not* happened would resemble a patient who was described as hallucinated. Conversely, the patient who did *not* remember what *had* happened, through the operation of $\overleftarrow{\text{desire}}$, or *remembered* what had *not* happened, through the operation of the same agency, should likewise be recognized as belonging to the same underlying group of 'hallucinosis'.

The concept of 'sense' which I have introduced has not been recognized in psychoanalytic practice, and the analyst's armoury has been correspondingly deficient in observations of omnipotence and omniscience. It is quite common for psychoanalytic students to observe patients whose references to God betray the operation of 'memories' of the father. The term 'God' is seen to indicate the scale by which the magnitude, wisdom and strength of the father is to be measured. If the psychoanalyst preserved an open mind to the mental phenomena unfolding in the psychoanalytic experience he would be free to appreciate the significance of 'sense' as I have described it above. As a consequence he would not be restricted to interpretations of God as displaying a distorted view of the father, but would be able to assess evidence, should it present itself, for supposing that the analysand was incapable of direct experience of God, and that experience of God had not occurred because it was made impossible by the existence of $\overleftarrow{\text{desires}}$ and $\overrightarrow{\text{memories}}$.

The experiences sketched out in **39** indicate the degree to which $\overrightarrow{\text{memory}}$ and $\overleftarrow{\text{desire}}$ obstruct the patient's relationship to an absent breast or penis on a level of mind, or at a time of life, when such an object would be so important as to evoke feelings analogous to what would in an adult be religious awe. This could be represented by desire. Taking the evidence in its other aspect, the sense memory, its significance would be its disclosure, to the extent to which the patient's relationship with God was disturbed by sensuously desired models (or C category elements) which prevented an ineffable experience by their concreteness and therefore unsuitability to represent the realization. In religious terms, this experience would seem to be represented by statements that the erring race or individual allowed itself to be beguiled by graven images, idols, religious statuary, or, in psychoanalysis, the idealized analyst. Interpretations should be given based on the recognition of desire, but not that they should be derived and given from recognition of the sense memory. The need for such appreciation and interpretation is far reaching. It would extend psychoanalytic theory to cover the views of mystics from the *Bhagavad Gita* to the present. The psychoanalyst accepts the reality of reverence and awe, and the possibility of a disturbance in the individual which makes atonement, and therefore an expression of reverence and awe, impossible. The central postulate is that atonement with ultimate reality, or O as I have called it to avoid involvement with an existing association, is essential to harmonious mental growth. It follows that interpretation involves elucidation of evidence touching atonement, and not evidence only of the continuing operation of immature relationship with a father. The introduction of 'sense' or 'direction' involves extensions of existing psychoanalytic theory. Disturbance in capacity for atonement is associated with megalomanic attitudes.

The patient discussed in **39** had an attitude to the persecuting holes which ultimately showed features we find in a religious attitude to idols. The analyst must contrast the attitude disclosed in the psychoanalytic experience with the attitude to his father, or his analyst, or the God that he is prepared to revere. In short the individual has, and retains, what religious people call a belief in God however much he denies it or claims to have become emancipated. The final relationship is permanent, though its formulation is subject to constant reformulation. Failure to recognize this vertex makes a balanced view of individual or group impossible and lies at the root of the supposition that there is a 'negative therapeutic reaction'. I shall discuss its bearing on the analysand's realization of insanity.

In **40** the analysand shows anxiety and hostility to what he calls schizophrenia and his capacity to be aware of it. The psychotic patient is subject to powerful emotions and is able to arouse them in others – so at least it appears until the situation is examined more closely. The analysis of such a patient soon reveals a complex 'situation' rather than a complex patient. There is a field of emotional force in which the individuals seem to lose their boundaries as individuals and become 'areas' around and through which emotions play at will. Analyst and patient cannot exempt themselves from the emotional field. The analyst must be capable of more detachment than others because he cannot be an analyst *and* dissociate himself from the state of mind he is supposed to analyse. The analysand cannot dissociate himself from the state of mind he needs to have analysed; that is easier to understand if it is regarded as the state of mind of a group rather than of an individual but transcending the boundaries we usually regard as proper to groups or individuals.

The analyst who undertakes the psycho-analysis of a schizophrenic undergoes an experience for which he must improvise and adapt the mental apparatus he requires. He has one great advantage in his relationship with his analysand which he lacks in his relationship with his colleagues and others outside the experience – the analysand has the experience available to his intuition if he will permit the analyst to draw his attention to it. Those excluded from the analysis cannot gain from the analyst's formulations, because they are formulations dependent on the presence of the experiences being formulated. They are thus in the position analogous to one whose mathematical ability has not reached a point where it can deal with the problem of objects when the objects are not there. His position *vis-à-vis* the problem is similar to that of the man who has to experiment with the original object without the aid of an intervening model which he can manipulate. There is no brother with whom to work out problems of the relationship with a father. Or, as the religious man would say, there is nothing which can intercede for the individual with God. The lack of a counterpart to the model, the direct manipulation of the original, denies the analyst one of the tools required for his job, and contributes to the state of perpetual acting-out. This last is evidence that the analyst is not – and cannot behave as if he were – dealing with models (verbal or otherwise) of his problem, but with the original itself. Analysis of the psychotic personality thus has a quality which makes it so different from the that of the non-psychotic personality. Conversely, the relationship with external reality undergoes a transformation parallel to the relationship with psychic reality which lacks an intervening (or 'interceding') model. There is no 'personality' intervening between the analyst and the 'unconscious'.

To sum up: the 'originals' are beyond inquiry without the aid of a model. The fact that neither original is in existence makes it essential that a model should somehow make allowance for, and deal with, this fact as part of the problem to be solved – a problem of the problem, so to speak – and as a feature that must itself be mirrored in the model.

Before leaving the discussion of 'sense' or 'direction', I must mention a mathematical feature of early stages in problem solving. The individual feels the problem is vast, or complicated, or otherwise out of reach. The model is an attempt to bring it into reach. When the individual is confronted with what, in comparison with himself, is an infinite number or quantity, he binds the 'innumerable' host by the name 'three' as soon as he has a feeling of 'threeness'. The 'infinite number' has now been made finite. A feeling of 'threeness' in himself has been 'bound' and what was infinity is now three. Infinity (or 'three') is the name for a psychological state and is extended to that which stimulates the psychological state. The same is true of 'three': it becomes the name for that which stimulates a sense of 'threeness'. 'Three' and 'infinity' are then instances of a peculiar form of model. They can be regarded as embodiments of a psychological state-like 'father'; or, like 'father', they can be regarded as relating to or disclosing an inescapable state of mind peculiar to the human being. From one vertex, 'three' binds a constant conjunction "won from the dark and formless infinite". It is a sign that precision has replaced imprecision. In what sense is 'three' precise and 'infinity' imprecise? Certainly not mathematically, because the mathematician strives to achieve a notation which, however inexact its genetic background, its role transplanted to a new domain is to convey the same meaning universally. In psychoanalysis precision is limited by the fact that communication is of that primitive kind which demands the presence of the object. Terms like 'excessive', 'hundreds of times', 'guilt', 'always', have a meaning provided that the object discussed is present. In a discussion between analysts it is *not* present; intercourse between them will tend to jargon – that is, to an arbitrary manipulation of psychoanalytic terms. Even when that does not happen, it presents an appearance of happening. The criticism of psychoanalysis that it is not mathematical and cannot therefore be scientific is based on a misapprehension of the nature of the problem and the nature of the kind of mathematics employed. The subject matter with which psychoanalysis deals cannot employ any form of communication which can cater for the requirements of a problem in the absence of the problem. It cannot even employ models which would provide an adequate substitute for the original of the problem. This has misled even friendly critics, because the language used by analysts often bears a close resemblance to ordinary conversation. Similarly, statements made in ordinary conversation appear to say exactly the same thing as psychoanalysts do – often better. I have heard a lay participant in a discussion on psychoanalysis in a BBC programme suggest that Freud said nothing we did not know already. When one considers that Freud merely drew attention to the existence of sex, such a criticism seems to have a kind of lunatic truth. The reality of the psychoanalytic experience soon demonstrates the falsity of such a supposition. A statement made about a sexual experience, in the presence of the sexual experience as it shows itself in the transference, has a meaning which the same words in another and different context cannot have.

Before passing on to consider the differences between the psychotic and the non-psychotic personalities, I must make a brief reference to **41** in which results are discussed. I shall often refer to the topic because the progress of psychoanalysis has led to a departure from the state of affairs in which ideas of 'treatment', 'cure' and 'results' had any meaning.

Analysis of the psychotic affords an opportunity for seeing what it means to work when insane. A distinction should be made in the use of the terms 'psychotic' and 'insane'; an analysand can be psychotic and insane, and psychotic and sane. It is useful to consider one kind of psychoanalytic progress as being from insane psychosis to psychotic sanity. When I wrote this section I had not appreciated the extent to which ideas of cure, based on a background of sensuous experience and the pleasure principle, pervaded not only psychoanalysis but the whole domain of mental or spiritual life. Scrutiny of the synoptic gospels will demonstrate the extent to which the religious approach to the domains of mental life activates the apparatus of expectation of 'cure' of 'painful' emotions and experiences in a way which would be appropriate to physical pain associated with physical relief and physical therapeutic measures. It did not require that St. Luke should be a doctor – this is plain from St. Mark's gospel – or that Freud's background was a training in physical medicine, to trigger off expectations of cure which are allied to a background of physical pain. It could be summed up: "There is a pain. It should be removed. Someone must remove it forthwith, preferably by magic or omnipotence or omniscience, and at once; failing that, by science". The conflict between the psychotic and non-psychotic personalities could be described as between a part of the personality which is religious and a part which is scientific. The contending views are alike in their bigotry. They are alike too in resembling contending personalities, success being marked by annihilation of the painful experience or awareness of it. Conversely, a sharpened awareness of painful emotional experiences would be a mark against the approach, scientific or religious, which was responsible. The analyst himself can act as if he embraced this view. It offers a simpler explanation and justification for the expense in time and money of psychoanalysis. Without it psychoanalysis becomes an activity which is hard to justify. Furthermore, it provides analyst and analysand with a 'memory' which gives both the sense of security that comes from a feeling that they are not engaged on any activity new to the human group.

In a paper to the British Psychoanalytical Society,[1] of which an abridged version has been published in the *Bulletin* of that Society, I drew attention to the recurrence of a certain configuration which I described as a relationship between container and contained (♀ ♂).

One manifestation of this relationship is in the stress between the 'establishment' of a group, and the 'mystic' who is a member of the group. The stress is found also in the relationship between an idea and the statement (verbal, pictorial, or artistic) that is intended to contain it. Psychoanalysis is itself such an idea: any formulation of it, or person entertaining it, or group (such as a psychoanalytic society) harbouring it, will show evidence of that stress. The abandonment of a protective shell of familiar ideas will expose the person or group

[1]['Catastrophic Change', see earlier, this volume. *Ed.*]

who abandons it to the disruptive (even if creative) force of the 'contained' idea. Therefore 'memory' is kept in constant repair as a defensive barrier. Prominent amongst these 'memories' in a psychoanalytic Society is the idea of cure. It is a preconception in K; that is a preconception (Category D) which is not to mate with a conception as part of K activity, but is to mate with a 'memory' to become a saturated element (similar to a beta-element) to prevent growth or catastrophic change. The analyst must not be surprised to find he is himself as unwilling as his analysand or his group, to abandon the desire for cure or its idea. Nor can abandonment be achieved by an act of will. It is a short step from abandonment of 'cure' to the discovery of the reality of psychoanalysis and the unfamiliarity of the world of psychoanalytic experience. The 'desire' for cure is one example of precisely the desire that must, in common with all desires, not be entertained by a psychoanalyst. The reader will find evidence in these papers that though I had suspected, I had not grasped the importance of this point.

The temptation to desire cure is intensified because anyone successfully undergoing psychoanalysis has an experience which resembles the popular idea of 'cure'; it is supposed he is 'cured' as a result of psychoanalytic 'treatment'. The idea of 'results' should be similarly suspect because it derives from an attitude, common to physical scientists whose experience is related to sensuous impressions – though the intervention of apparatus sometimes conceals this fact. It would be ironical if an idea which the physicist is tending to discard should be taken up by psychoanalysts; we should be amongst the first to have realized the inadequacy of models in which results occupy a prominent place. In **11,** I say that good work will be undone if the analyst reassures the patient: today I do not think it requires a psychoanalyst to reassure the analysand because the analysand can obtain reassurance through the apparent resemblance of psychoanalysis to the model of physical treatment and cure. Generations of experience of physical illness and treatment have established a model, a 'memory', which acts automatically as a barrier against the intrusion of disturbing facts. Complaints against ineffectual psychoanalysis can be seen as the obverse of the comforting beliefs associated with models of treatment and cure.

Abandonment of memories and models derived from physical medicine involves experience of problems which the psychoanalyst may regard as outside his province or capacity; often they appear to belong to disciplines to which his training has not extended. The psychoanalyst's experience of philosophical issues is so real that he often has a clearer grasp of the necessity for a philosophical background than the professional philosopher. The academic philosophic background and the realistic foreground of psychoanalytic experience approach each other; but recognition of the one by the other does not occur as often or as fruitfully as one might expect.

At the beginning of the paper on the 'Development of Schizophrenic Thought' (July 1955) [chapter 4], I report that the attempt to give clinical illustration was unsuccessful and that I restrict myself to theoretical description. The idea that the problem of communication would thereby be simplified I regard as optimistic. The clinical illustrations I regard as C category elements; they resemble reports of past events, transformations of visual images, models, but they cannot be described as any of these things because they do not satisfy psychoanalytic requirements. No solution lies in applying 'scientific' criteria as those are understood, but I cannot propose a better solution. Psychoanalysts who are not satisfied with the scientific quality of their work must look to themselves to produce better standards. The 'theoretical description' to which I thought to restrict myself is only the substitution of a sophisticated formulation for a formulation employing terms with a sensuous background. An experience about which I had no doubts sounds unconvincing to anyone without practical experience of psychoanalysis. Conviction cannot be carried even from one psychoanalyst to another unless their methods of working are extremely close. So far this has meant that two psychoanalysts share the same theoretical armoury and this involves the danger that the analyst sees what he wants to see. If two analysts are successful in minimizing the operation of memory and desire, they minimize the danger of collusion and increase the chance of sharing the same experience – 'seeing' the same mechanisms at work. The formulations used in this paper are verbal transformations of psychoanalytic intuitions.

Formulations of transference phenomena are unsatisfactory though correct as far as they go. In **41** I would now employ a geometrical formulation (H category) as a means of transforming the psychoanalytic experience into C category terms, that is into a visual image. To communicate the experience in psychoanalysis, I use a sophisticated category (H) in a primitive way (C). In the paper I speak of the transference as if it were a linear link – a line without breadth, joining analyst and patient. But I see this now as changing constantly in the stress of the psychoanalysis so that the transference link, which at one moment is a line, at the next transforms itself into a plane. The psychoanalyst who is bound by the tenuous and tenacious line suddenly finds himself in contact with a 'monomolecular' surface or plane. The patient has a precise contact with the analyst, who finds his every fleeting mood reflected in the transference. Should he be irritated by the buzzing of a fly, or a noise in the street, or the impact of some grievous or dangerous communication about a patient or relative, the mood will be reflected. But so slight is the depth (or thickness of the planar transference) that there is no discrimination of quality of these moods. They have the same value; the buzzing fly or a serious and distracting piece of news, cast an equal reflection; both are observed by the patient, the one is of no greater and no less significance than the other. The transference change can be represented pictorially from 'the line without breadth' to 'the plane without depth'.

Some of the difficulty experienced by analysts arises when they allow the intuition achieved to languish and to be replaced by what they have learned from their analyst's theories and experience. This impulse is easily stimulated, and the habit once contracted is difficult to check; the effect on the analyst's intuition is first bad and then disastrous; if analysts permitted themselves the conditions necessary in order to 'see' what is happening the realizations of psychoanalysis would assert themselves and the differences between analysts touching what they observe would assume more modest proportions. The problem of acknowledging indebtedness to earlier work is not difficult if it is excluded from the mind of the analyst when at work with an analysand.

The psychotic patient's hostility to mental apparatus, his own or another's, that puts him in touch with reality should be matched with his attitude to psychic reality. He appears to be peculiarly aware of, and persecuted by, psychic reality. I would not stress any particular aspect of it, such as the confusional states, painful though they certainly are, but to the whole of psychic pleasure or pain. The problem is associated with the dominance of the pleasure–pain principle, as would be expected, but it achieves its peculiar quality because the dominant pleasure–pain principle has to operate in the domain of endopsychic pleasure and pain. There is not therefore available the solution which is proper to problems of pleasure and pain which have their genesis in the world of external reality. It is as if the analysand felt he was required to deal with the kind of problem for which we now know psychoanalysis to be necessary at a time when at best he could only be expected to deal, in collaboration with a mother, with physical hunger. In other words, from the outset of life the patient feels his mental world requires special attention. This differs from having a *physical* endowment, say *physical* ill-health, which requires special attention.

With regard to the remaining sections of the paper, 44–50, descriptions are unlikely to lead to error if they are regarded as C category formulations and used by the reader as "disclosure models".[1] They are to be read, forgotten, but permitted to reappear, as part of the evolution peculiar to a particular psychoanalytic emotional situation. The comments in the conclusion (**50**) are related to a vertex in which 'cure' or 'improvement' appears as significant; at the time I did not recognize vertices, and had no reason for appreciating the inadequacy of the idea of 'cure'. My next paper shows clearly the extent to which I regarded this vertex as the only one. As it excludes many possibilities of which a psychoanalyst should be aware, I shall emphasize, by references to this paper, some of the disadvantages. In **51**, though I speak of developments 'which are analytically significant', I really meant that they were therapeutically significant.

I consider any idea that development is therapeutically significant as being of less importance than an idea that it is psychoanalytically significant. The development might be considered both therapeutically *and* psychoanalytically significant, but the latter idea I regard as of a different and more important category than the former. In the same paragraph I refer to improvements, but the 'improvement' must be in someone's opinion and according to some established (but unmentioned) standard. That assessment is useful in so far as it purports to measure change, however vaguely; but the assessment itself does not have the significance (still less the *only* significance) for psychoanalysis, in the sense that 'cure' and 'improvement' have a significance in the domain of physical medicine. Assessments of

[1]Ian T. Ramsey, *Models and Mystery* (Oxford University Press, 1964).

moral or social worth are borrowed from religion or morals or politics without consideration of their applicability to psychoanalysis. This is the more surprising in that the analysand's criteria are proper matters for investigation. I do not question the 'improvements'; I question the unquestioning acceptance of improvement as an aim or desire proper to a psychoanalyst. As I have said, there is no place for desire in psychoanalysis; there is no place for memory, as it is based on and inseparable from desires related to past activities different from psychoanalysis. A desire to be a good analyst obstructs *being* an analyst.

I would today not go further than my last sentence in **51**: "the improvements I have seen deserve psychoanalytic investigation". More than that imposes a standard of progress which precludes observation of the different standards of progress, their provenance and part in psychoanalysis.

The limited acknowledgements to previous work may seem surprising. It is an aspect of psychoanalytic work of which I have become more, not less, persuaded. A psychoanalyst needs a capacity to see the implications of both what his patients and his analytic predecessors say and not the quantity of ways in which they say it. The implications of Freud's paper 'Formulations on the Two Principles of Mental Functioning' (1911b) have been widely recognized by psychoanalysts, but this does not mean that they have been recognized by any particular psychoanalyst. Memory as usual offers a quick substitute, in appearance at least, for permitting an evolution to commence in the reader's mind. What I have said about the psychoanalytic sessions I consider applies to the *experience* of reading psychoanalytic work. Freud's paper should be read – and 'forgotten': only in this way is it possible to produce the conditions in which, when it is next read, it can stimulate the evolution of further development. There is time to do this only with the best papers; but only the best papers have the power to stimulate a *defensive* reading (of what the paper is about) as a substitute for experiencing the paper itself – what I have elsewhere[1] called Transformation under K, as contrasted with Transformation under O. The same comments hold for the papers of Melanie Klein that I have mentioned.

This view that psychoanalytic papers are to be treated as experiences which affect the development of the reader will not be subscribed

[1][*Transformations* – see Volume V. *Ed.*]

to by all psychoanalysts. I do not contend that it is a matter of conscious choice determined by the reader's wishes, but that certain books, like certain works of art, rouse powerful feelings and stimulate growth willy-nilly. As everyone knows, this was so with Freud.

As I have expanded this theme in my communication on 'Catastrophic Change',[1] I shall not pursue the matter further here. The works to which I have drawn attention here represent many hours of hard reading – which may not at first be apparent. I found them illuminating, but they have not been adequate; though my paper is inadequate I am still at a loss to suggest improvements beyond what I have said above about the psychotic transference; I therefore leave it as I wrote it. The views put forward in **58** are more fully dealt with in my paper 'Attacks on Linking' [chapter 8].

In **63–68**, I have given a description intended to represent the actual experience of a session. I think that the experience was exceptional; the patient was co-operative within the limits set by his mental state and he regarded himself in some sort as 'ill' and requiring 'treatment'. He also seemed to regard psychoanalysis as if it were treatment. I took this for granted as a reasonable view, but I think now that any view entertained by an analysand should be questioned. The psychoanalyst's tool is an attitude of philosophic doubt; it is of first importance to preserve such 'doubt', on which the analysis can be built. A patient making attacks on linking will show his dislike of the analyst's ability to preserve an attitude of doubt, and will make constant efforts to stimulate the analyst's desires and memory. The evidence of 'improvement' which impressed and pleased me was no part of psychoanalytic work.

This theme is embarked on at the end of **68** and discussed in **69**. When a patient is so disturbed that he earns a psychiatric diagnosis, it is not surprising that relatives, friends, the patient himself and the analyst tend to agree about 'treatment' and 'cure'. But the most disturbed patient can show flashes of intuition which are reminders of his mental life often lost to sight. Conversely, persons showing powerful insights are often attacked as mad. In the paper 'Catastrophic Change', I have drawn attention to one instance, well known in a Christian culture, and I pointed out a configuration in which this element is constantly repeated. It is necessary to be aware

[1][See earlier, this volume. *Ed.*]

of 'improvement' which may be denial of mystical qualities in the individual. The opposite error sees deep mental disturbance as evidence of genius. I leave that paper for further discussion, but repeat reasons for mistrusting 'cure' or 'improvement' – not because I doubt the existence of a realization which approximates to these terms, but because the tendency to equate psychoanalysis with 'treatment', and 'cure' with improvement, is a warning that the analysis is becoming restricted; limitation is being placed on the analysand's growth in the interest of keeping the group undisturbed. With the conclusion **70**, I have no quarrel in so far as it can be regarded as a plea for more psychoanalysis. Even so, I regard it as redundant, as psychoanalysis does not need anything that advertisement and political procedures can do for it. Conversely, those requiring the arts of the politician will not desire psychoanalysis.

When I wrote on hallucination, I thought 'independent' support for the diagnosis of schizophrenia important. Now it is more significant that these patients are able to inspire similar reactions in members of groups to which they belong. The more intimate associates (relatives chiefly and the patients themselves) wanted to claim that there was something wrong, but that the patients could not really be 'like that'; naturally what 'that' was, differed in the opinion of the doctors from what the relatives thought it was. I did not appreciate it at the time, but by making a psychoanalytic approach I was presupposing yet another 'that' that the patient was. I wanted support for the idea that I knew what the patient was; that the patient was what the medical profession said he was; that I agreed with the medical profession. I wanted to avoid the position in which it could be said that everyone knew what the patient was except myself and possibly, though not certainly, the patient. However that was soon the position in which *I did* find myself. As psychoanalyst I was committed to keeping an open mind, while feeling constant pressure, not least from myself, to take refuge in certainty. The patients showed themselves anxious to agree with an interpretation so as to build up a sense of security. Since I deprecate allowing rein to memory and desire, it is right to point out that exclusion of both exposes the analyst to the anxiety of being in a minority of one (possibly two when the patient throws in his lot with the analyst) by engaging on the analysis of such a patient.

Until co-operation evolves there is no question of 'observing hallucinations'. I do not believe this is possible if the analyst seeks the comfort of co-operation from anyone other than the patient himself. The analyst's position is not improved *vis-à-vis* relatives, friends the medical profession and others able and willing to co-operate, by what seems to be an uncooperative and possibly arrogant attitude. Nevertheless, the analysis of a schizophrenic is done with the patient alone, or not at all.

The 'clinical' description, **72**, is open to the objections already raised against this class of report. The description is in terms appropriate to a sensuous experience. The experience had psychic reality which no one would dispute, but it was not represented by its sensuous reality. I cannot improve on the description I gave in that paper though it could not carry conviction to anyone who did not want to be convinced, and might well put a strain on the credulity of someone who did. What then is to be done? I conclude that in addition to agreed procedures, analysis of the analyst and so on, there must be a conduct of the analyst's mental life which precludes his slipping into bad mental habits. It would help to avoid errors if, as a first step, psychoanalysts treated what are considered usually to be reports of analytic experiences as 'models' similar to those used by physical scientists. Scientific method must be followed with caution to profit by Freud's demonstration of unconscious motives. Psychoanalytic observation of our own faults is liable to mask the weaknesses of existing scientific method, even when recognized by scientists. The scientific method of psychoanalysis should be turned on its defects of communication. This is either meaningful, but inappropriate to a non-sensuous experience, or so 'abstract' that it simulates but does not represent a non-sensuous experience. The choice appears as picturesque inaccuracy or jargon. It may appear pedantry to scrutinize the descriptions which we give of psychoanalytic experiences, but not when the discussion centres on hallucinations which are, as far as the patient is concerned, sensuous experiences. To the analyst they are not, for he does not hear or see what the hallucinated patient hears or sees, but he must interpret the events which he witnesses.

In **76** I mention my inability to report the 'events' that led me to think the patient was hallucinated. I still find it hard to offer suggestions for determining the point at which awareness occurs. A patient may, for example, be making a series of hostile allegations. This can be a simple expression of hostility, but it may be part of a splitting attack on the analyst. On one occasion, the patient had no fear of hallucinations with which, he said later, he was quite familiar, but was using them as a weapon in his war with me. I do not consider here the *varieties of* experience with which the hallucinated patient confronts the analyst, but the analyst's experience of the patient's hallucination is usually a good example of what I mean by evolution. At one moment the facts appear to be a simple outpouring of hostility; suddenly they are transformed; the patient is experiencing hallucination. It is as if the analyst, whom the patient was attacking, had a 'skin' which floated off him and now occupied some position between the analyst and the patient. (It is characteristic that in this description I have to resort to spatial descriptions which have more 'body' than I like to give them, and are known by me to be inaccurate formulations.) The more experience an analyst has of psychotic phenomena, the less room he has for doubt of their reality. They 'evolve'; they are there and are replaced by a further 'evolution'. Fortunately for psychoanalysis, these events can be demonstrated between analyst and analysand, but unfortunately for the science they cannot be demonstrated *in the absence of the phenomena.* There is a curious parallel in the plight of the individual who cannot solve a problem of enumeration mathematically, but has to resort to manipulation of the objects to be numbered.

In this paper I have described the evacuatory function of hallucination as if it were the only one. I would now expect hallucinations and the 'use' to which they are being put to be constantly changing. The analyst needs to be in a position to 'intuit' hallucinations and ultimately the laws governing them and their changes. A rigid system cannot represent a changing realization. Ability to banish memory and desire is one of the conditions necessary for observation of hallucination. The moment an evolution takes place and reproaches directed at the analyst have been 'floated off' to an intermediate 'skin', the analyst must be able to 'intuit' and interpret it.

At **71**, I explain that existing descriptions of hallucinations are not good enough for practising analysts. The description I have just attempted may explain why I think analysts need to formulate their own descriptions. The transformation can be traced from hostile abuse of the analyst through its stages from fear of penetrating into him through violence of linear attack (and therefore confusion with him), to planar attack (the widespread, diffuse, unpenetrating associations) and thence to the 'floating-off' of the 'skin'. I am not optimistic about making my meaning clear to the reader by such a description, but once he is in a position to experience the realization he will not have any doubts of its reality.

The analyst must not allow himself to be deflected from the vertex from which the emotional events, when they have evolved, become 'intuitable'. The study of hallucination is at its beginning, not its end. Time has confirmed the conjecture made at the end of **82**.

In **83** of the paper 'On Arrogance' [chapter 7], I rehearse the Oedipus myth by way of making clear a connection between curiosity, arrogance and stupidity; the connection cannot so easily be established in psychoanalytic practice. I found more difficulty when I was relying on memory to provide the links than I do today when I allow the analytic situation to evolve, and then interpret the 'evolution'. It is essential for the analyst and his analysand that the operation of curiosity itself should be demonstrated – not its name. It has been objected, for example, that 'acting out' is an English translation of a phrase used by Freud to mean something different from the meaning attributed to it in English. The confusion arises because the discussion is thought to centre on the representation of a realization and not on the realization: Or vice-versa, not about the term 'acting out', but about the phenomena represented by that term. In the same way, I am not talking of occasions when patients use the word "curiosity", but of curiosity itself. The distinction must be, but is not always, borne in mind. If it were, the reproach of jargon would not so often be levelled at, or incurred by, psychoanalysts.

I state in **88** that the person on whose analysis this study is based did not at any time behave as a psychotic; this comment is valid if ordinary psychiatric usage is accepted.

Melanie Klein believed that psychotic mechanisms could be found in all analysands, and should be uncovered if the analysis was to be satisfactory. With this I agree: there is no applicant for psychoanalysis who is without fear of the psychotic elements in himself and who does not believe he can achieve a satisfactory adjustment without having those elements analysed. One solution of this problem is particularly dangerous for those concerned with training. The individual seeks to deal with his fear by becoming a trainee, so that his acceptance can be taken as an authoritative declaration of immunity by those best qualified to know. He can proceed with the aid of his analyst to evade coming to grips with his fear, and terminate by becoming a qualified analyst. His qualification is an ability, thanks to projective identification (in which he does not believe), to preen himself on freedom from the psychosis for which he looks down upon his patients and colleagues. The more psychosis, or even hallucinations, are psychoanalytically studied the more inadequate established ideas appear; as I have dealt with this development in greater detail in 'Catastrophic Change', I shall not discuss it here.

In **91**, the reference to the destruction of an important link is based on a number of observations, the cumulative effect of which led to the formulations in the paper, 'Attacks on Linking'. The ideas set out in it illuminate a number of situations which I did not have in mind when I wrote the paper. As I became able to observe the evolution of the psychoanalytic situation I was led to the frustrating aspects of memory and desire. Analysands stimulate both elements in the analyst as a method of destroying his link with the analysand. It is as if the patient were himself a psychoanalyst who discovered these elements and set about deliberately to stimulate them to destroy the link between the analyst and himself. Experience of attempting to exclude the operation of memory and desire has persuaded me of the value of doing so. The difficulty of successful exclusion makes it hard to define memory and desire with rigour, or to assess the nature of the sharpening of intuition associated with it. I regard the idea of causation, implicit throughout the paper, as erroneous; it will limit the perspicacity of the analyst if he allows this element in 'Attacks on Linking' to obtrude. The 'causal link' has apparent validity only with events associated closely in space and time. The fallacious nature of reasoning based on the idea of 'causes' is clearly argued by Heisenberg,[1] in terms which should evoke an understanding response in any psychoanalyst. Provided the analyst does not allow himself to be beguiled into searching for and proposing 'causes', except in conversational terms, the paper may stimulate enquiries of his own. The discovery of a 'cause' relates more to the peace of mind of the discoverer than to the object of his research.

This brings me to the problem of how the gap is to be bridged between reading the papers in this book and the psychoanalytic experience. My suggestion is that the papers should be read in the same conditions as those in which a psychoanalysis should be

---

[1] *Physics and Philosophy* (Allen & Unwin, 1958), p. 81.

conducted – without memory or desire. And then forgotten. They can be re-read; but not remembered. Such advice could be given with greater assurance if the nature of the communications, their status as formulations, were more certain. I have attempted to make that so by proposing that so-called clinical reports (supposedly F3) were regarded as C3-verbal transformations of sensory impressions. At this early stage, there is no adequate categorization which is likely to be more useful than popular repute.

The proper state for intuiting psychoanalytic realizations, which I have suggested in this review, can be compared with the states supposed to provide conditions for hallucinations. The hallucinated individual is apparently having sensuous experiences without any background of sensuous reality. The analyst must be able to intuit psychic reality which has no known sensuous realization. The hallucinated individual transforms and interprets the background of reality, of which he is aware, in different terms from those employed by the psychoanalyst. I do not consider that the hallucinated patient is reporting a realization with a sensuous background; equally I do not consider an interpretation in psychoanalysis derives from facts accessible to sensuous apparatus. How then is one to explain the difference between an hallucination and an interpretation of an intuited psychoanalytic experience? The charge is sometimes loosely and lightly made that psychoanalysts analysing patients who are psychotic are themselves psychotic. I would seek a formulation to represent the difference between the intuition (in my sense of the term) of a realization, which has no sensible component, and a hallucination of a realization which is similarly devoid of a sensible realization. The psychoanalyst has at least the opportunity which would allow him to contribute an answer; many supposedly sane and responsible people transform thoughts into actions which it would be charitable to call insane and are often, charitably, so called.

As a stimulus to further thought, I would draw attention to a peculiarity, known to all but not sufficiently regarded. Ordinarily the sense organs have their own objects of sense. It is true that the eye, subjected to pressure, will apparently 'see' light ('stars', according to pugilists). In the mental realm, the "sense organ of psychic reality" (to borrow a phrase from Freud) has no such limitation. It can indifferently appreciate all the counterparts of *all* the senses. The mental counterparts of smell, sight, etc., can *all* apparently be intuited by the same apparatus. The issue is of practical importance to the analyst whose analysand says, "I see what you mean" when he has an hallucination, say, of being sexually assaulted; what *he* means is that the *meaning* of what the analyst said appeared to him in a visual form and *not* that he understood an interpretation. This is the kind of problem to which the last paper, 'A Theory of Thinking' [chapter 9], is an introduction.

The fact that thinking and talking play such an important part in psychoanalysis is so obvious that it is liable to escape attention. It does not, however, escape the attention of the patient who is concentrating his attacks on linking, and in particular the link between himself and the analyst; such a patient makes destructive attacks on the capacity of both analyst and himself to talk or think. If these attacks are to be properly understood, the analyst needs to be aware of the nature of the targets being attacked. The paper is an attempt to elucidate this. With my present experience I would lay more stress, in **98**, on the importance of doubting that a thinker is necessary because thoughts exist. For a proper understanding of the situation when attacks on linking are being delivered, it is useful to postulate thoughts that have no thinker. I cannot here discuss the problems, but need to formulate them for further investigation, thus: – Thoughts exist without a thinker. The idea of infinitude is prior to any idea of the finite. The finite is "won from the dark and formless infinite". Restating this more concretely, the human personality is aware of infinity, the 'oceanic feeling'. It becomes aware of limitation, presumably through physical and mental experience of itself and the sense of frustration. A number that is infinite, a sense of infinity, is replaced, say, by a sense of threeness. The sense that an infinite number of objects exists is replaced by a sense that only three objects exist; infinite space becomes finite space. The thoughts which have no thinker acquire, or are acquired by, a thinker.

In practice I have found this formulation, or something like it, a helpful approximation to psychoanalytic realizations. The patient who suffers from what used to be known as 'disturbances of thought' will provide instances showing that every interpretation the analyst gives is really a thought of his. He will betray his belief that papers or books written by others, including of course his analyst, were really filched from him. This belief extends to what in more usual patients appears as the Oedipal situation. In so far as he or she admits the facts of parental intercourse, or verbal intercourse between the analyst and himself, he is simply a lump of faeces, the product of a couple. In so far as he regards himself as his creator, he has evolved out of the infinite. His human qualities (limitations) are due to the parents, by their intercourse, stealing him from himself (equated with God). The ramifications of this attitude, more clearly discerned if the analyst postulates "thoughts without a thinker", are so considerable that I require another book to attempt elucidation. Inadequate though this formulation is, I hope it will help the reader to find the continuation of the developments which I have tried to sketch out in these papers.

I would warn against the phrase, "empirically verifiable data", which I employ in **100**. I do not mean that experience 'verifies' or 'validates' anything. This belief as I have come across it in the literature of the philosophy of science relates to an experience which enables the scientist to achieve a feeling of security to offset and neutralize the sense of insecurity following on the discovery that discovery has exposed further vistas of unsolved problems – 'thoughts' in search of a thinker.

NOTES ON MEMORY AND DESIRE

1967

'Notes on Memory and Desire' was first published in 1967 in *Psychoanalytic Forum, 2* (No. 3). Reprinted, by kind permission of John A. Lindon, MD, Editor, in *Cogitations* [New Extended Edition], edited by F. Bion (London: Karnac Books, 1994). It was also reprinted in E. Bott Spillius (Ed.), *Melanie Klein Today Vol. 2: Mainly Practice* (London: Routledge, 1988), pp. 17–21.

Notes on Memory and Desire

Memory is always misleading as a record of fact since it is distorted by the influence of unconscious forces. Desires interfere, by absence of mind when observation is essential, with the operation of judgement. Desires distort judgement by selection and suppression of material to be judged.

Memory and Desire exercise and intensify those aspects of the mind that derive from sensuous experience. They thus promote capacity derived from sense impressions and designed to serve impressions of sense. They deal, respectively, with sense impressions of what is supposed to have happened and sense impressions of what has not yet happened.

Psychoanalytic 'observation' is concerned neither with what has happened nor with what is going to happen, but with what is happening. Furthermore, it is not concerned with sense impressions or objects of sense. Any psychoanalyst knows depression, anxiety, fear, and other aspects of psychic reality, whether those aspects have been or can be successfully named or not. These are the psychoanalyst's real world. Of its reality he has no doubt. Yet anxiety, to take one example, has no shape, no smell, no taste; awareness of the sensuous accompaniments of emotional experience are a hindrance to the psychoanalyst's intuition of the reality with which he must be at one.

Every session attended by the psychoanalyst must have no history and no future.

What is 'known' about the patient is of no further consequence: it is either false or irrelevant. If it is 'known' by patient and analyst, it is obsolete. If it is 'known' by the one but not the other, a defence or grid category 2 element (1,2) (see Grid, [p. vii, this volume]) is operating. The only point of importance in any session is the unknown. Nothing must be allowed to distract from intuiting that.

In any session, evolution takes place. Out of the darkness and formlessness something evolves. That evolution can bear a superficial resemblance to memory, but once it has been experienced, it can never be confounded with memory. It shares with dreams the quality of being wholly present or unaccountably and suddenly absent. This evolution is what the psychoanalyst must be ready to interpret.

To do this, he needs to discipline his thoughts. First and foremost, as every psychoanalyst knows, he must have had as thorough an analysis as possible; nothing said here must be taken as casting doubt on that. Second, he must cultivate a watchful avoidance of memory. Notes should be confined to matters that *can* be recorded – the programme of appointments is an obvious example.

Obey the following rules:

1. *Memory:* Do not remember past sessions. The greater the impulse to remember what has been said or done, the more the need to resist it. This impulse can present itself as a wish to remember something that has happened because it appears to have precipitated an emotional crisis: *no* crisis should be allowed to breach this rule. The supposed events must not be allowed to occupy the mind. Otherwise the evolution of the session will not be observed at the only time when it can be observed – while it is taking place.
2. *Desires:* The psychoanalyst can start by avoiding any desires for the approaching end of the session (or week, or term). Desires for results, 'cure' or even understanding must not be allowed to proliferate.

These rules must be obeyed *all* the time and not simply during the sessions. In time the psychoanalyst will become more aware of the pressure of memories and desires and more skilled at eschewing them.

If this discipline is followed, there will be an increase of anxiety in the psychoanalyst at first, but it must not interfere with preservation of the rules. The procedure should be started at once and not abandoned on any pretext whatever.

The pattern of analysis will change. Roughly speaking, the patient will not appear to develop over a period of time, but each session will be complete in itself. 'Progress' will be measured by the increased number and variety of moods, ideas, and attitudes seen in any given session. There will be less clogging of the sessions by the repetition of material that should have disappeared and, consequently, a quickened tempo within each session every session.

The psychoanalyst should aim at achieving a state of mind so that at every session he feels he has not seen the patient before. If he feels he has, he is treating the wrong patient.

This procedure is extremely penetrating. Therefore the psychoanalyst must aim at a steady exclusion of memory and desire and not be too disturbed if the results appear alarming at first. He will become used to it and he will have the consolation of building his psychoanalytic technique on a firm basis of intuiting evolution and NOT on the shifting sand of slight experience imperfectly remembered, which rapidly gives way not to experience, but to neurologically certain decay of mental faculty. The evolving session is unmistakable, and the intuiting of it does not deteriorate. If given a chance, it starts early and decays late.

The foregoing is a brief account distilled from putting the precepts advocated into practice. The theoretical implications can be worked out by each psychoanalyst for himself. His interpretations should gain in force and conviction – both for himself and his patient – because they derive from the emotional experience with a unique individual and not from generalized theories imperfectly 'remembered'.

DISCUSSANTS

The discussants commenting on this paper were: Thomas French, MD (Chicago, Illinois, USA); John A. Lindon, MD (Los Angeles, California, U.S.A.); Avelino González, MD (Mexico DF, Mexico); Marjorie Brierley, MBBS (Keswick, Cumberland, England); Herbert H. Herskovitz, MD (Bala-Cynwyd, Pennsylvania, USA).

AUTHOR'S RESPONSE

The discussants of my 'Notes on Memory and Desire' help to make it clear that some of the confusion arises through the ambiguity of the terms 'memory' and 'desire'. I realize that it would be helpful if I could distinguish between two different phenomena that are both usually and indifferently called 'memory'. This I have tried to do by speaking of one as 'evolution', by which I mean the experience where some idea or pictorial impression floats into the mind unbidden and as a whole. From this I wish to distinguish ideas that present themselves in response to a deliberate and conscious attempt at recall; for this last I reserve the term 'memory'. 'Memory' I keep for experience related predominantly to sensuous impressions: 'evolution' I regard as based on experience that has no sensuous background but is expressed in terms that are derived from the language of sensuous experience. For example, I 'see' meaning I intuit through the medium of a visual impression.

'Desire' should not be distinguished from 'memory', as I prefer that the terms should represent one phenomenon that is a suffusion of both. I have tried to express this by saying 'memory' is the past tense of 'desire', 'anticipation' being its future tense.

These definitory hypotheses have a limited value, and I suggest that every psychoanalyst should make up his mind for himself by simple experimentation as to what these terms represent. For example, he should school himself to avoid thinking of the end of the session, week, or term (having made previous provision for terminating the session at the correct time as a matter of administration), and when he has done this for a sufficient period without trying to hurry himself, make up his mind about what *he* would call 'Memory' and 'Desire'. When he has done this, he can proceed to the next stage of extending his suppressions of the experience he has discovered in this way. I must warn psychoanalysts that I do not think they should extend this procedure hurriedly or without discussion with other psychoanalysts with a view to consolidating each step before taking another.

This procedure seems to me to approximate a state which Freud described in a letter to Lou Andreas-Salomé, 25 May 1916: "I know that I have artificially blinded myself at my work in order to concentrate all the light on the one dark passage." In my experience this procedure makes it possible to intuit a present 'evolution' and lay the foundations for future 'evolutions'. The more firmly this is done, the less the psychoanalyst has to bother about remembering.

I hope this makes clear some of the points to which Dr French objects, though I am doubtful whether this method should be used if he really feels that he is 'completely unable' to understand. Indeed, I would not 'desire' anyone to employ this approach unless, like Dr Lindon, he feels it has some meaning for him.

The experience that Dr Lindon describes appears to me to afford the foundation for exploring the whole question of psychoanalytic observation. I agree with his feeling that 'memory' and 'desire' are obstacles intervening between the psychoanalysts and the emotional experience of the session. When it is considered how little opportunity even five sessions a week affords the psychoanalyst, any obstacle to appreciation becomes serious.

Dr González draws attention to a defect of which I am very conscious. My own feeling is that my views have 'evolved', and although this must mean they have changed, I think the 'change' less significant than the 'evolution'.

I think the expressions he rightly quotes from *Elements of Psycho-Analysis* are wrongly framed, but wrong though the formulations now seem to me to be, they were good enough to lead me to my present formulations, which I think are better. In particular, I think the use of language based on the experience of the senses led me to fail to recognize that one does not in fact 'see' (feel, touch, smell, etc.) anxiety. I hope that my experience will be repeated by others who have tried to read these earlier formulations. If it is, I shall feel less remorseful.

I hope that my quotation from Freud will convince Dr Brierley that I am attempting to elaborate on the importance of rapport. I feel some unease if it is suggested that I am departing from psychoanalytic technique, not because I have any objection to innovation if it seems to be necessary, but because it is unlikely that the intuitions of experienced psychoanalysts can be lightly laid aside. I do hope, however, that the points I make may help psychoanalysts to think themselves into closer contact with the psychoanalytic experience.

Darwin expressed the view that judgement was inimical to observation, but, as Dr Brierley points out, the psychoanalyst has to formulate judgements while observations are being made. I hope the distinction I have tried to draw between 'evolution' and 'memory' may help to meet her objections. I believe it would go some way towards meeting Dr Herskovitz's objection to 'illogicalities'. I do in any case feel doubts about the value of a logical theory to represent the realizations of psychoanalysis. I think the 'logical' theory and the 'illogicalities' of the psychoanalytic experience should be permitted to coexist until the observed disharmony is resolved by 'evolution'.

ATTENTION AND INTERPRETATION: A SCIENTIFIC APPROACH TO INSIGHT IN PSYCHO-ANALYSIS AND GROUPS

1970

Attention and Interpretation: A Scientific Approach to Insight in Psycho-Analysis and Groups was published by Tavistock Publications, London, in 1970 and reprinted by Karnac Books, London, in 1984. It was included in *Seven Servants*, published by Jason Aronson, New York, in 1977

Chapter 12, 'Container and Contained Transformed', is an amended version of 'Catastrophic Change', published in the *Bulletin of the British Psychoanalytical Society, 5* (1966).

EDITOR'S INTRODUCTION

This work was published in 1970, when Bion had been living and working for two years in Los Angeles. As André Green (1973) suggested in his review of the book, readers who turn to this work hoping to find a definitive theory either of attention or of interpretation will be disappointed, the former term not even making an appearance in the book's index. Reflecting, however, on the definition of attention used by Bion and Freud, Green had a flash of realization: if the function of attention is, "periodically to search the outer world in order that its data might be already familiar if an urgent need should arise" (Freud, 1911b, p. 220), and "Its activity meets the sense impressions half way, instead of awaiting their appearance", then Bion's book could be understood as fulfilling just such a function – that of meeting the reader half-way. So, wrote Green, "Attention was not what was *in* the book, it was the book itself."

This is an interesting and accurate statement, and one that holds true specifically for *Attention and Interpretation* and generally in terms of Bion's overall project, which was to address the problem of "how to make the emotions which permeate the abstract formulations of psychoanalytical theories come alive for the reader or the listener" (Bion Talamo, 1981):

> This sort of problem has been present in Bion's work from *Second Thoughts* onwards, when he states that: "The subject matter with which psychoanalysis deals cannot employ any form of communication which can cater for the requirements of a problem in the absence of the problem." It seems to me that this statement implies Bion's desire to make the subject of the discussion emotionally present for the reader so that it is then possible to discuss it at once with an immediate awareness of the emotional aspects. [Bion Talamo, 1981, p. 626]

In *Attention and Interpretation* Bion encourages the capacities of patience and faith in the reader, as he did in *Learning from Experience*, and he produces a series of experiences that in their basic underlying structure resemble the operation of the concepts under discussion – something that has been remarked on by David Bell (2010), who likens the effect of Bion's writing to that of Wittgenstein:

> Bion is a writer who has an effect on his reader, and one that is most peculiar. It is as if the very thing that he discusses takes place in the act of reading him; there is a reflexivity in his writing. This seems also to be true of Wittgenstein, referred to by Stanley Cavell (1969), when he stated that in reading Wittgenstein one feels exposed to the peculiar experiences he describes. [Bell, 2010, p. 81]

André Green (1992), in his review of *Cogitations*, stated that Bion, "makes us witnesses to the process of the unfolding of his thought. We literally follow him." In this process Bion's formulations promote experiential realizations, particularly in those readers who have an opportunity to meet the phenomena in the analytic encounter – by being exposed to transference and countertransference phenomena – and in a concentrated form in work with patients whose thought and learning processes are disturbed. This is what Bion meant in his many references to aspects of the writing being particularly aimed at practising analysts.

Readers can find themselves experiencing – often some time afterwards – a coming-together of preconceptions (states of half-expectation) and impressions appropriate to them to form conceptions. This process Bion calls 'realization', and in Chapter 3, 'Reality sensuous and psychic', he warns the reader against "too great a regard" for what he has written, because to do so risks obstructing that experience of personal realization, in the analytic situation, of what Bion has been sketching out.

Bion's recommendations concerning memory and desire are elaborated in this book. His 1966 paper 'Catastrophic Change', which further describes his container–contained (♀♂) model, is repeated with only small amendments as Chapter 12.[1] These recommendations can be read in conjunction with his original exposition of the ideas in the 1965 presentation of his paper 'Memory and Desire' (this volume).

---

[1] A line-by-line comparison of the two texts is provided in Appendix C of Volume XV.

Chapter 4 is headed, 'Opacity of memory and desire'. If we are to be strictly logical about the terms Bion is using here, there is a case for considering that the opacity is a characteristic not of memory and desire, but of *F* (Faith), with the interfering effects of memory and desire operating as 'effacing light' to the analyst's receptivity towards *F* as an aspect of what Bion indicates as 'O' (see below).

Two final points: First, a word about the complete title of the book – *Attention and Interpretation: A Scientific Approach to Insight in Psycho-Analysis and Groups*. The second part of the title tends, for brevity, to be left out when the book is quoted, but it does contain an important reference to Bion's correlation of group mentality and the inner world of the individual in analysis, to provide something that functions in an analogous manner to 'binocular vision'. In this correlation Bion felt that there existed the germ of a scientific function, as he stated in his introduction to *Experiences in Groups and Other Papers* (1961):

> I am impressed, as a practising psycho-analyst, by the fact that the psychoanalytic approach, through the individual, and the approach these papers describe, through the group, are dealing with different facets of the same phenomena. The two methods provide the practitioner with a rudimentary binocular vision. The observations tend to fall into two categories, whose affinity is shown by phenomena which, when examined by one method, centre on the Oedipal situation, related to the pairing group, and, when examined by the other, centre on the sphinx, related to problems of knowledge and scientific method. [p. 101]

Finally, an important aspect of *Attention and Interpretation: A Scientific Approach to Insight in Psycho-Analysis and Groups* is Bion's discussion of what he indicates as O.

Bion's O is one of the later ideas which undoubtedly has proved most off-putting to many British psychoanalysts. As Caper (1998) has pointed out, the notion, and Bion's exposition of it, lends itself to being understood as belonging to mysticism. A careful reading of Bion, however, allows us to see that it is an epistemological idea relating to *the limits of representation*.

One can see this notion, 'O', as representing the unknowable dimension of real life that lies behind what we can apprehend through the senses or articulate in language, and to which Wittgenstein was referring in his *Tractatus Logico Philosophicus* (1922/1974, p. 7) when he wrote, "Whereof one cannot speak, thereof one must be silent", and which Bertrand Russell (1922) clarified in the following sentences from his introduction to that work:

> In order that a certain sentence should assert a certain fact there must, however the language may be constructed, be something in common between the structure of the sentence and the structure of the fact. This is perhaps the most fundamental thesis of Mr Wittgenstein's theory. That which has to be in common between the sentence and the fact cannot, he contends, be itself in turn *said* in language. It can, in his phraseology, only be *shown*, not said, for whatever we may say will still need to have the same structure. [p. x]

When Russell goes on to state the following, about Wittgenstein, we can see some links to Bion's use of Hume's (1896) term 'constant conjunction' and that of 'invariant'. Russell writes:

> He compares linguistic expression to projection in geometry. A geometrical figure may be projected in many ways: each of these ways corresponds to a different language, but the projective properties of the original figure remain unchanged whichever of these ways may be adopted. These projective properties correspond to that which in his theory the proposition and the fact must have in common, if the proposition is to assert the fact. [p. xi]

Bion uses the deliberately empty sign 'O' to point towards this unspeakable and unknowable reality, which, he says, can be 'intersected with' but not grasped. Tempting though it is to attach words to it, such as 'Origin', or 'totality', as many have done, forming their own associations to the letter used by Bion, I recommend for the time being that it rests undeciphered or (as Bion would say) unsaturated in the reader's mind, in order to be open to Bion's signification. In the opening passages of Transformations (1965) Bion's comments about a painting of a field of poppies hold a remarkable resemblance to parts of Wittgenstein's picture theory of meaning, as set out in his *Tractatus*. As Bertrand Russell (1922) pointed out in his introduction to that work, the picture and the objects pictured must exhibit the same 'logical manifold', which 'cannot be itself represented since it has to be in common between the fact and the picture' (p. xii). In other words, there are elements responsible for and essential to meaning which are ineffable. It was on this point that Wittgenstein had ended the work containing his first theory of language with the telling proposition, "Whereof one cannot speak, thereof one must be silent".

A personal communication from the analyst Neville Symington (2011) is of relevance here. By way of his combined theological and psychoanalytic experience he considered Bion's obscure concept as pointing to the Ontological, which I believe to be right. I now view Bion's 'O' as the beginning of an unfinished work, begun in 1965, on the psychoanalytic implications of the distinction between knowing and being. In other words, although Bion begins by writing as though 'O' indicates the unknowable reality of the 'objective presence' of things, his later clinical use of the idea moves towards helping the patient in analysis to navigate transitions between 'knowing about' objects and the self to being and becoming real.

In *Attention and Interpretation* Bion argues for its relevance to the analytic situation, and I end this introduction with Green's (1973) view of the relevance of Bion's O to clinical thinking:

> This 'beyond the scope of knowledge' idea is essential not because it represents a limit to knowledge or because it leads us to take refuge in fundamental obscurity, but because it is the starting point of what there will be to know. If, from the beginning, we assign a place to an object we are in contact with through immediate knowledge – whatever reservations we might establish as to the mode of knowledge, saying, for instance, that it is cathected before it is perceived – we prematurely fill this object with some content which perhaps prevents us from following the sequence of states that will take place in our contact with the object. It is as essential for the assumptions of preconception as for that of the thing in itself that we keep an open mind as to the perspectives of transformation. In other words, it is important for the constant psychic component to appear as non-saturated so that we can follow the sequence of events that will lead us to the knowledge of the particular modes of saturation of the general form.
>
> From what we are able to know through the realizations which accomplish themselves by saturation, we will be able to evaluate how we came to accept the experience of going from the infinite to the finite, the non-formal to the formal, the unlimited to the limited. At one point or another, any preconception can be subjected to the impossibility of finding its realization. The development of thought depends on this non-realization, which engenders a form of limitation similar to that due to realization through the senses, but which in this case creates a counterpart of sensual experience in as much as it is associated with language. [Green, 1973, p. 117]

Attention and Interpretation

A Scientific Approach to Insight in Psycho-Analysis and Groups

1

Introduction

I doubt if anyone but a practising psychoanalyst can understand this book although I have done my best to make it simple. Any psychoanalyst who is *practising* can grasp my meaning because he, unlike those who only read or hear *about* psychoanalysis, has the opportunity to experience for himself what I in this book can only represent by words and verbal formulations designed for a different task. They were developed from a background of sensuous experience. Reason is emotion's slave and exists to rationalize emotional experience. Sometimes the function of speech is to communicate experience to another; sometimes it is to miscommunicate experience to another. Sometimes the object is to achieve access to, and permit access from, a good spirit; conversely, to deny access to a bad spirit. The vocabulary forged from such material serves, though inadequately, when, as in psychoanalytic practice, the object being studied is present. In mathematics, calculations can be made without the presence of the objects about which calculation is necessary, but in psychoanalytic practice it is essential for the psychoanalyst to be able to demonstrate as he formulates. This is not possible the moment the conditions for psychoanalysis, in the narrow technical sense, do not exist. Some of us have sought to extend psychoanalytic method so that it can be employed in a group setting. Such a development, if it can be done without mutilation of the fundamental character of psychoanalytic method, would initiate the change from private to public communication. Language does just that in the domain of sensible experience. Poetic and religious expressions have made possible a degree of 'public-ation' in that formulations exist which have achieved durability and extensibility. To say the same thing differently, the carrying power of the statement has been extended in time and in space. *Vixere fortes ante Agamemnona multi,*[1] and *Not marble, nor the guilded monuments / Of princes, shall outlive this powerful rhyme*[2] are expressions of that belief; they are interpretations of human experience. In his sphere the psychoanalyst's attention is arrested by a particular experience to which he would draw the attention of the analysand. To do this he must employ the Language of Achievement. That is to say, he must employ methods which have the counterpart of durability or extension in a domain where there is no time or space as those terms are used in the world of sense.

What I have said with regard to this book also applies to the psychoanalytic session; it is certainly my impression that the experience of psychoanalysis is supposed or intended to have an enduring effect. Unlike this book the session affords me and others an opportunity for drawing attention to the actual phenomena to which I think the analysand should attend, and this might reinforce the effect of my communication. A similar advantage seems to me to be available in a psychoanalytic approach to groups; it is possible to hope that the capacity of the artist, though useful, may not be essential to the psychoanalyst. Indeed, it may be a disadvantage in so far as the artist's capacity may enable him to provide, as Plato feared, a *substitute* for the truth.

In this book I have made a few tentative approaches to a matter which I think has not received proper attention in psychoanalysis, namely, lying. The disposition to lie may be regarded as a symptom of a severely disordered personality. It certainly contributes many difficulties to any attempt at a psychoanalytic approach, but on the other hand my experience of psychoanalysis makes me feel that the aptitude for lying, so universal that only a liar could disregard its all-pervading nature, has its own place as an object for study and is ignored at a dangerous cost to analyst and analysand. In short, I agree that it is often a symptom of a disordered personality but submit that it is not necessarily a contraindication for analysis. Here I can only indicate one or two aspects.

It is too often forgotten that the gift of speech, so centrally employed, has been elaborated as much for the purpose of concealing thought by dissimulation and lying as for the purpose of elucidating

[1] [Horace, Ode ix.25. *Ed.*]
[2] Shakespeare, Sonnet 55.

or communicating thought. Therefore, the Language of Achievement, if it is to be employed for elucidating the truth, must be recognized as deriving not only from sensuous experience but also from impulses and dispositions far from those ordinarily associated with scientific discussion. Freud, like others before him, felt the need to isolate himself – insulate himself? – from the group in order to work. This would mean insulating ourselves against the very material we should study. We should, therefore, re-orientate our views on such matters as rationalization and the employment of reason generally. The patient says, "Suddenly, just as I finished lunch he threw a mug of beer in my face without any warning. I kept my head and showed no resentment at all remembering what you had said about psychoanalysis. So it passed off without anyone noticing." Is he lying? Is he verbalizing a present hallucination? Matters of this kind are occurring throughout a psychoanalysis and demand correct assessment by the psychoanalyst. Yet we have not elaborated instruments – I have tried to do so with the Grid[1] – for making the assessment. I am not speaking of making the *interpretation* or of the many theories that facilitate the making of an interpretation; the Grid is of a different category altogether, analogous to a ruler in physical science, formed from a matrix of theories to aid observation and not as a substitute for observation. I commend to others a proper study of the lie and its differential diagnosis from phenomena which appear similar. The psychoanalyst must employ the Language of Achievement, but he must remember that the language was elaborated as much for the achievement of deception and evasion as for truth. This aspect is particularly clear when the prevalent emotional field is one of rivalry and hostility such as I have described, in group situations, as peculiar to the fight–flight basic assumption (*Experiences in Groups and Other Papers* [Volume IV, p. 148]). The individual is similarly affected by the *group* emotional situation. It is, therefore, impossible to give correct interpretations, save by accident, unless that *situation* is assessed. For example, drug addiction is exploited as a cover for psychosis, lying is often excused as an aspect of drug addiction, and vice versa.

Psychoanalysts should determine whether they are talking of means of communication, including verbal communications, as

---

[1]See *Elements of Psycho-Analysis* [Volume V], where the Grid system is more fully discussed.

things-in-themselves or whether they are talking of other things-in-themselves which these communication elements, gestures, actions, silences, and verbal formulations, are being used to represent. The Grid is intended to remind the psychoanalyst that it is necessary to discriminate one element in his psychoanalytic experience from another and, in particular, to recognize that what matters is both the communication and the use to which it is being put. He must observe whether the presenting feature (or the feature to the obtrusion of which he wants to draw attention) is intended to further illumination or deception, and where in the genetic spectrum it belongs (primitive communication or sophisticated).

Although the Grid is unsatisfactory in its present form, it will not, I hope, mislead but lead to an improved version. I have used the following signs[1]:

T–transformation

Tα – the point from which the transformation starts

Tβ – the point at which the transformation is presumed to be complete

Ta – the psychoanalyst's transformation

Tp – the analysand's transformation

O – the experience (thing-in-itself)

Analogies are frequently used. The things used and what those things represent are dissimilar. It is supposed that a rifle and a penis are similar. But what should be exact is the *relationship* between the particular objects in the particular analogy and not the objects themselves. Thus: as the breast is to the baby's mouth so the surgeon's knife is to the X. In any particular instance the inexactitude of the *relationship* merits criticism and appraisal. The objects are faulty and to be condemned if they *are* similar. For example, 'The knife is to the fork as the knife is to the fork' is a 'non-analogy'. 'The eyes are to the mind as the mouth is to the food' is a correct analogy and draws attention to the matter that is to be observed, namely, the relationship between the two.

[1]Originally in *Transformations* [Volume V].

2

Medicine as a model

Most people think of psychoanalysis, as Freud did, as a method of treatment for a complaint. The complaint was regarded as similar to a physical ailment which, when you know what it is, has to be treated in accordance with the rules of medicine. The parallel with medicine was, and still is, useful. But as psychoanalysis has grown, so it has been seen to differ from physical medicine until the gap between them has passed from the obvious to the unbridgeable. For most purposes the similarity yields illuminating comparisons and models that facilitate discussion. But the more we see of psychoanalysis the more the models become inadequate to define, report, or apply psychoanalysis. Differentiation has meant that models which were illuminating have become opaque and often misleading even to psychoanalysts. Let us see why. We may start by discussing the obvious and simple reasons, though they will not remain either for long.

In physical medicine the patient may have a pain in his chest for which he can go to his doctor. To him he can explain its nature and its history and from him he can receive instructions to undergo further examination, say, by X-rays or microscopy, or certain forms of treatment. Or so it appears; later we may have reason to question this account. For the present it will serve to point the divergence of physical medicine and psychoanalysis.

Suppose the patient complained not of physical but of mental pain; no one doubts the existence of anxiety or sees any incongruity in seeking help to cure it. We find it necessary to differentiate between the pain of a broken leg and the pain, say, of bereavement; sometimes we prefer not to, but exchange mental for physical pain and vice versa. Physician and psychoanalyst are alike in considering that the disease should be recognized by the physician; in psychoanalysis recognition must be by the sufferer too. The physician considers recognition of the pain subordinate to its cure; the psychoanalyst's view is expressed by Doctor Johnson's letter to Bennet Langton[1]: "Whether to see life as it is, will give us much consolation, I know not; but the consolation which is drawn from truth, if any there be, is solid and durable; that which may be derived from error must be, like its original, fallacious and fugitive."

The point that demonstrates the divergence most clearly is that the physician is dependent on realization of sensuous experience in contrast with the psychoanalyst whose dependence is on experience that is not sensuous. The physician can see and touch and smell. The realizations with which a psychoanalyst deals cannot be seen or touched; anxiety has no shape or colour, smell or sound. For convenience, I propose to use the term 'intuit' as a parallel in the psychoanalyst's domain to the physician's use of 'see', 'touch', 'smell', and 'hear'.

I shall now give three different formulations of the same episode occurring in the psychoanalysis of a woman. More could easily be given to demonstrate the problem of communication and publication that faces the psychoanalyst.

The patient produced an association to express, though in a disguised manner, her hostility to parents whose relationship to each other she represented as that between pander and whore. She intended also to evoke a response from the analyst such that he would be wrong whatever facet of a multi-dimensional association he selected for interpretation. Choice of dimension and interpretation could be 'proved' to reflect the analyst, not the analysand; he could hesitate impotently before the wealth of alternatives presented to him.

A version employing more analytically recondite Kleinian intuitional formulations: the patient was directing an attack on the analyst's psychoanalytic potency; the 'missile' was the association – which therefore is to be regarded as an object of Grid category A6. The characteristics of the association are either that it subjects the analyst's intuition to splitting because of his inability to formulate simultaneous expressions of diverse and possibly incompatible interpretations, or that it has the ability to compel the analyst, through the need to act, to adopt a moral standpoint for interpretation because the scientific

[1][A quotation often drawn upon by Bion, and a favourite of Melanie Klein's. *Ed.*]

standpoint involves being 'split' between alternative interpretations. The close relationship between moral attitudes and action, as contrasted with thought or meditation, will be investigated later. The first problem is to choose what interpretation to give. Any one of many facets of the patient's statement may be noticed rather than any other. It can be considered as a statement or as a transformation; as multidimensional or multi-faceted; it could be represented by a visual image of a figure in which many planes meet or lines pass through a common point. I can represent it to myself by a visual image of a geometric solid with an infinite number of surfaces. It depends on a realization, derived from space, of sensuous experience. The attempt to externalize the visual image is restricted as if the representation by points and lines was itself a 'space' too restricted to 'contain' the visual image; thus, – has breadth whereas the *mental* visual image of a line or a point has not.

Projective identification has hitherto been formulated in terms derived from a realization of the ordinary man's, or woman's, idea of three-dimensional space. The usual Kleinian formulations depend on a visual image of a space containing all kinds of objects. Into these objects in this space it is supposed that the patients project parts of their personality that they have split off. Melanie Klein, who discovered this mechanism, considered it to be observable in psychotic and borderline psychotic patients. Later, she and her co-workers considered that the theory had a more extended application and that realizations approximating to it could be detected in neurotic and normal personalities. She stressed the degree of fragmentation and the distance to which the fragments were projected as a determining factor in the degree of mental disturbance the patient displayed in his contact with reality. With this view I agree; as my practice with disturbed patients increased, it became evident that more rigorous formulation of the theory was needed if the gap between representation and realization was to be bridged by the analyst's interpretation. This was brought home to me in circumstances adumbrated in *Learning from Experience* and *Elements of Psycho-Analysis*. I shall recapitulate briefly some of what I wrote then, and later in *Transformations*.

There are patients whose contact with reality presents most difficulty when that reality is their own mental state. For example, a baby discovers its hand; it might as well have discovered its stomach-ache, or its feeling of dread or anxiety, or mental pain. In most ordinary personalities this is true, but people exist who are so intolerant of pain or frustration (or in whom pain or frustration is so intolerable) that they feel the pain but will not suffer it, and so cannot be said to discover it. *What* it is that they will not suffer or discover we have to conjecture from what we learn from patients who *do* allow themselves to suffer. The patient who will not suffer pain fails to 'suffer' pleasure and this denies him the encouragement he might otherwise receive from accidental or intrinsic relief. Where one patient would understand a word to mark a constant conjunction, this patient experiences it as a thing that is not there, and the thing that is not there, like the thing that *is* there, is indistinguishable from an hallucination. Since the term 'hallucination' has a penumbra of associations which would be inappropriate I have named these objects beta-elements.

These descriptions of how these objects appear to the patient and how they appear to me are intended to aid the reader's understanding, but are not sufficiently rigorous for use in practice. The formulations have the status of elements in Grid category C.

Suppose the patient is capable of tolerating frustration and pain: his story will differ in important respects from the above. To him the name represents a 'no-thing', but his capacity for toleration enables him to observe a constant conjunction, to bind it with a name or to use it when it has already been named. Patient A, for I shall now call the intolerant patient so, has then at his disposal beta-elements or bizarre objects and his case differs in this respect from patient B, as I now designate the second patient, who can tolerate and therefore name (even if the name is no more than a grunt or a yell) a constant conjunction and so investigate its meaning. Whether the beta-element or the bizarre object is to be classified as thought or not is a matter of scientific convenience which may be determined later. I suggest provisionally that all beta-elements are distinguished from elements that pervade the mental processes of patient B, by considering the latter to be thoughts and the former not. The most genetically primitive elements of thought I shall group together as alpha-elements, in distinction to beta-elements.

I shall now use the geometrical concepts of lines, points, and space (as derived originally not from a realization of three-dimensional space but from the realizations of the emotional mental life) as returnable to the realm from which they appear to me to spring. That is, if the geometer's concept of space derives from an experience of 'the place where something was' it is to be returned to illuminate the domain where it is in my experience meaningful to say that 'a feeling of depression' is 'the place where a breast or other lost object was', and that 'space' is 'where depression or some other emotion used to be'.

I have pointed out that this space, these points, and these lines differ in one important respect, namely, that in the domain of mental visual images an infinite number of lines may pass through one point but, were I to attempt to represent such a visual image by point and lines on a piece of paper, there would be a finite number of lines. This limiting quality inheres in all realizations of three-dimensional space that approximate to the points, lines, and space of the geometer. It does not inhere in mental space until an attempt is made to represent mental space by verbal thought. I am thus postulating mental space as a thing-in-itself that is unknowable, but that can be represented by thoughts. In thought I include all that is primitive, including alpha- elements as I have so far described them. I exclude, arbitrarily by definition, beta-elements. Thoughts may be classed with the realizations of all objects approximating to the representations of three-dimensional space in this particular: they are intolerable to patient A because they share the frustrating quality of all realizations. Yet to the 'ordinary man' thoughts do not have this restrictive character until it is necessary to apply them to pre-verbal material. Material may be pre-verbal because the individual who seeks to verbalize it has not had sufficient experience of the material to observe a constant conjunction. He is in a state analogous to that seen in a number of similar configurations such as: having pain without suffering it; not understanding planetary movement because the differential calculus has not been invented; not being conscious of a mental phenomenon because it has been repressed; not knowing an event because the event has not occurred.

In all these situations the associated problems require thought for their solution. In all of them thought is restrictive and can be directly experienced as such as soon as an intuition demands representation for private communication. Since thought liberates the intuition there is conflict between the impulse to leave the intuition unexpressed and the impulse to express it. The restrictive element of representation therefore obtrudes in transformation $T\alpha \rightarrow T\beta$ of preverbal material. One man achieves the transformation; the other, who cannot tolerate restriction, does not. He therefore forfeits the relief from frustration that thought, were he able to tolerate it, would give. The onset of the reality principle is thus imperilled. In my definition of thought, he will not generate alpha-elements and will not be capable of thought. Whatever substitute he finds for thought is not to be classified as thought. When I discuss psychotic verbalization this point will be considered again.

The failure of alpha-function, which should produce alpha-elements, involves the absence of mental visual images of points, lines, and space. Patient A therefore lacks equipment that would help him to map the realization of mental space. His position is analogous to that of the geometer who had to await the invention of Cartesian co-ordinates before he could elaborate algebraic geometry.

Now consider patient A confronted with an experience in which B would resort to projective identification as adumbrated by Melanie Klein. The restrictive character of reality and the dependence of projective identification on recognition of objects preclude projection of parts of the personality because there is no conception of containers into which the projection could take place. The explosive projection is therefore felt to take place in what is, to the analyst, the *realization* of mental space: a mental space that has no visual images to fulfil the functions of a co-ordinate system, either the 'faceted solid' or the multi-dimensional, multi-linear figure of lines intersecting at a point. The mental realization of space is therefore felt as an immensity so great that it cannot be represented even by astronomical space because it cannot be represented at all.

Paradoxically this explosion is so violent and is accompanied by such immense fear – hereafter referred to as psychotic fear or psychotic panic – that the patient may express it by sudden and complete silence (as if to go to an extreme as far as possible from a devastating explosion).

The ensuing state can be most easily expressed by using surgical shock as a model: in this the dilatation of the capillaries throughout the body so increases the space in which blood can circulate that the patient may bleed to death in his own tissues. Mental space is so vast compared with any realization of three-dimensional space that the patient's capacity for emotion is felt to be lost because emotion itself is felt to drain away and to be lost in the immensity. What may then appear to the observer as thoughts, visual images, and verbalizations must be regarded by him as debris, remnants or scraps of imitated speech and histrionic synthetic emotion, floating in a space so vast that its confines, temporal as well as spatial, are without definition. The events of an analysis, spread out over what to the analyst are many years, are to A but the fragments of a moment dispersed in space. The distance in time separating one statement from another can be taken as a measure of the distance in space of one element from another in which all are contemporary. Thus A says he could buy no ice-cream. Six months later he says he cannot even buy ice-cream. Three days later he mentions his being too late to buy ice-cream: there was no ice-cream left. Two years later he says he supposes there was no ice-cream. Had I known, when the topic was mentioned first, what I know now I might have noted the time and place of the reference, but I did not know and therefore could not attend to this statement or note it. When I did, it was because of the obtrusive 'I scream' theme. It was later still that I grasped the significance of 'no – I scream'. By this time, I could make only the vaguest reference to previous appearances of the material. As it turned out this difficulty did not appear to matter and my interpretation was taken. Yet I would feel happier if I thought that my gain in experience could lead to earlier observation and use of the material. I now know that a violent attack had been delivered on a relationship in which the link between the two personalities had been 'I scream'. This had been destroyed and the place of the link 'I scream' had been taken by a 'no – I scream'. The 'I scream' link had itself previously been food, 'ice-cream', a 'breast', until envy and destructiveness had turned the good breast into an 'I scream'. In narrative form: he had been linked to his object by a good breast (he liked ice-cream). This he had attacked, possibly bitten it in actuality. The place of the breast as link was then taken by an 'I scream'. Further attacks made it a 'no – I scream'. The destruction of the link by explosion now took place in the domain of mental realization. Mental space being infinite, the fragments of the link are dispersed instantaneously over infinite space. The 'distance' between one piece and another is measured in time.[1]

---

[1]The account I have just given is an example of taking Tpβ as my TaO, and by Taα proceeding to Taβ. Taβ is my attempt at a reconstruction of TpO, Tpα, Tpβ. When this degree of private communication has been attained, the problem becomes one of publishing it – formulating it in conversational English that the patient can understand (see *Transformations* [Volume V], p. 153).

The patient should be shown the evidence on which the interpretation is based; if the evidence is scattered sparsely over a period of years of acting-out, the problem of interpretation assumes serious proportions, because the medium in which the patient is effecting his transformation is not predominantly conversational English, but acting-out. The analysis may be regarded as one moment in time stretched out so that it becomes a line or surface spread out over a period of years – an extremely thin membrane of a moment. Regarded thus, the total analysis can be seen as a transformation in which an intense catastrophic emotional explosion O has occurred (elements of personality, link, and second personality having been instantaneously expelled to vast distances from their point of origin and from each other). This explosive event O is then transformed, in the medium of acting-out and by virtue of beta-elements, to $Tp\beta$, in which space, being restrictive and not amenable to adequate formulation of distance between beta-elements, is replaced by the realization corresponding to time. Though there is no representation of mental space available to the patient and though the realization of three-dimensional space is too restrictive for a temperament intolerant of frustration, the realization of mental space, being unbounded, permits of a continuous and continuing expansion and separation of beta- elements. For the investigation of this mental state the patient cannot, but the analyst can, employ points, lines, and space. The geometer has used them for the investigation of three-dimensional space and, by the substitution of algebraic geometry for the figurative geometry of Euclid, has been able to extend his investigation to multi-dimensional space and leave Euclidean space to be used for psychological preparation for the non-Euclidean geometries now available. Can we similarly use the concepts of Euclidean geometry to get back to the emotional realizations from which I believe it originally sprang? The need is for a formulation so general that a multiplication of theories to meet a diversity of realizations bearing the same configuration is obviated, yet so precise that it will not cover configurations whose similarity is only apparent, or whose appearance of similarity is due to irrelevant C category visual imagery.

The impossibility of communication without frustration is so familiar that the nature of the frustration is forgotten. Most people are aware of it as a transient phenomenon experienced on relatively few occasions. In psychoanalytic work the problems are more obtrusive than usual because the subject is novel and its difficulties are uncharted; difficulties become still more marked when the material to be communicated is pre- or non-verbal. The psychoanalyst can employ silences; he, like the painter or musician, can communicate non-verbal material. Similarly, the painter can communicate material that is non-visual and the musician material that is inaudible. The pre-verbal matter the psychoanalyst must discuss is certain to be an illustration of the difficulty in communication that he himself is experiencing. Ability to use points, lines, and space becomes important for understanding 'emotional space', for the continuance of the work and avoidance of a situation in which two inarticulate personalities are unable to release themselves from the bondage of inarticulation. This mutually sterile relationship provides a model for some relationships of the self with itself. When the relationship of the self with itself is of this kind, either the container or the contained must be destroyed. Finally, the individual cannot contain the impulses proper to a pair and the pair cannot contain the impulses proper to a group. The psychoanalytic problem is the problem of growth and its harmonious resolution in the relationship between the container and the contained, repeated in individual, pair, and finally group (intra- and extra-psychically).

Any definitory hypothesis, be it exclamation, name, theoretical system, or extended statement such as a book, has, and has always been recognized to have, a negative function. It must always imply that something *is*; equally it implies that something is *not*. It is therefore open to the recipient to infer one or other according to his temper. If the personality is incapable of tolerating frustration there seems to be no reason why he should not develop on the assumption that the definitory hypothesis means that something is. The statement is then allowed to become a pre-conception and the way is open for the unsaturated element to become saturated. But suppose that the inability to tolerate frustration is 'excessive': the personality may react against the statement, seeing only its negative implications and, in the extreme case, refusing to allow the statement, to him a 'nothing', even to exist. The attempt then is to annihilate the statement in its function of definitory hypothesis. A model would be the infant who cannot tolerate weaning because it is dominated by the *loss* of the breast and who therefore cannot accept what it might have instead. The patient cannot tolerate the definitory hypothesis and therefore does not achieve the pre-conception (D4).

Knowledge of loss, of the negative aspect of the definition, of the 'thought' as a 'no-thing', is immediate; knowledge of gain, if any, has to wait upon the fruits of permitting the thought, or other statement, to be a pre-conception ($\Psi(\xi)$). Therefore 'excessive' inability to tolerate frustration is likely to obstruct development of pre-conception (D4 functions). 'Excessive' intolerance is likely to obstruct awareness of realizations. The 'no-thing' with its corresponding realization (of some object not present) will be liable to destruction, whereas 'hallucination' will be favoured for its immediacy. Another formulation of this is to say that the domain of realizations and all that might represent realizations is felt not to afford enough 'space' for freedom, whereas the domain of hallucination does. In passing, I must draw attention to the fact that the sense of loss in the definitory hypothesis and the sense of gratification in hallucination both depend on a restricted mental range. In both instances the reaction, of intolerance in one and gratification in the other, might be said to be associated with a short-sighted 'view'. Thought consequently is not seen as offering freedom for development, but is felt as a restriction; by contrast, 'acting-out' is felt to yield a sense of freedom. *A fortiori* an hallucination is designed through its quality as the-thing-itself (not the thought of a breast but the breast itself) to be indistinguishable from freedom. The patient then may be seen as facing a choice: either he may allow his intolerance of frustration to use what might otherwise be a 'no-thing' to become a thought and so achieve the freedom Freud (1911b) describes, or he may use what might be a 'no-thing' to be the foundation for a system of hallucinosis.

From this last will spring the set of transformations in hallucinosis which it will be necessary to differentiate from transformations in painting, music, mathematics, and the domain of verbal communication. The importance of making this last distinction is enhanced by the fact that words are used both in the expression of verbal communication and in transformations in hallucinosis. Yet consideration of the nature of the differing reaction to the 'no-thing' will show that the word representing a thought is not the same as the identical word when it is representing an hallucination. Since the similarity may be extremely close in the words employed in both systems and sometimes in the method by which they appear to be combined, it is important to discover in what the difference lies. The difference between philosophy (and even theoretical psychoanalysis) and the practice of psychoanalysis can be seen by considering what the detection of this difference means for the philosopher or theoretician and what it means for the practising psychoanalyst who has to decide in the emotional situation itself whether the patient's statements represent an hallucination or a fact of external reality. It is for this reason that the psychoanalyst must be experienced in non-sensuous realities and able to ignore sensuously derived experience as it appears formalized in memory. The word 'dog' represents different realizations in scientific inquiry and hallucinosis; but the word 'dog' is itself not the same when it is representing a realization in scientific inquiry and when it is an element belonging to the domain of hallucinatory transformations. It is sometimes useful to regard it as analogous to the visual image in a reversible perspective: in the visual image the marks of a drawing on paper remain unchanged but 'mean' two faces or a vase; similarly, 'dog' may mean dog or God (to take but one example). In non-psychotic transformations the invariant is insignificant: the resemblance to ordinary speech, the fact that the word is identical in psychotic and non-psychotic transformation, is accidental.

Verbal, musical, artistic modes of communication all meet with realizations that they appear to represent only very approximately. Hallucination may be regarded, wrongly, as a representation and therefore as unsuited to some activities. As verbal, musical, and artistic transformations have compensating values arising from their being *transformations* of O, it is natural to consider the like possibility with hallucinosis. But hallucinations are *not* representations: they are things-in-themselves born of intolerance of frustration and desire. Their defects are due not to their failure to represent but to their failure to *be*. Thus we need to consider the difference between psychic and external reality.

As I am primarily concerned with the formulation of theory, the illustrations I am about to give are by way of C formulations, not records of clinical experience. The intention is to approach to more rigorous theoretical presentation, that is, presentation less open to misunderstanding through logical defect, or over-flexibility in an attempt to represent different configurations of the same fundamental structures and functions, or failure to represent, through over-rigidity, realizations in which the fundamentals are invariant but the accidentals diverse. The illustrations are C category elements used as preparation for theoretical formulations that can stand by themselves: the reader should regard the 'illustrations' as psychological aids to understanding the theories proper. From this point to the end of the chapter emotional experiences will be represented by C formulations.

1. The patients, for the treatment of whom I wish to formulate theories, experience pain but not suffering. They may be suffering in the eyes of the analyst because the analyst can, and indeed must, suffer. The patient may say he suffers but this is only because he does not know what suffering is and mistakes feeling pain for suffering it. The theory will need to be such that it represents the realization in which this is possible and shows how it comes about. The *intensity* of the patient's pain contributes to his fear of suffering pain.
2. Suffering pain involves respect for the fact of pain, his own or another's. This respect he does not have and therefore he has no respect for any procedure, such as psychoanalysis, which is concerned with the existence of pain.
3. Frustration and intense pain are equated.
4. Pain is sexualized; it is therefore inflicted or accepted but is not suffered – except in the view of the analyst or other observer.
5. For purposes of this exposition the following conjunction is described in narrative form, the elements being sequential and bound in a chain of causation. The realization of the constant conjunction does not have any element that approximates to the sequential or causal elements of the narrative representing it. These features belong only to the C category representation, not to the realization they represent. The patient feels the pain of an absence of fulfilment of his desires. The absent fulfilment is experienced as a 'no-thing'. The emotion aroused by the 'no-thing' is felt as indistinguishable from the 'no-thing'. The emotion is replaced by a 'no-emotion'. In practice this can mean no feeling at all, or

an emotion, such as rage, which is a column 2 emotion, that is, an emotion of which the fundamental function is denial of another emotion.

6. As a column 2 element, all felt emotion is a 'no-emotion'. In this respect it is analogous to 'past' or 'future' as representing the 'place where the present used to be' before all time was annihilated.
7. The 'place' where time was (or a feeling was, or a 'no-thing' of any kind was) is then similarly annihilated. There is thus created a domain of the non-existent. I have not come across any realization that corresponds to such a state though I can imagine a stupor so intense that it might seem to do so. It is nevertheless useful to postulate it partly because there are occasions when it is convenient to suppose that the patient holds such a belief, and partly because it is convenient for the analyst. As will be seen, meanings other than sophisticated meanings creep back into the relatively meaningless state of the term 'non-existent' as E1 category. Some patients with whom I am familiar achieve a state to which I wish to apply the term 'non-existence' for a few moments at most; this is followed by an externalization or evacuation of 'non-existence'. 'Non-existence' immediately becomes an object that is immensely hostile and filled with murderous envy towards the quality or function of existence wherever it is to be found. 'Space', either as a representation or the realization the term derives from or represents, becomes terrifying or terror itself: "*Le silence de ces espaces infinies m'effraie.*" The space of the ordinary man, the astronomer, or the physicist, becomes confounded with 'mental space', and its objects with the objects of 'mental space'.
8. The scientific or sophisticated approach tends to become confounded with the realizations its formulations are intended to represent. The point (.) and the line (—) are regarded as if they were analogous to representations of reversible perspective. Their significance therefore varies according to the point of view (or vertex) with which they are associated. Vertices may have as their approximate realizations various recognized disciplines such as religion, mathematics, physics, music, painting, and other arts. The formulations associated with a particular vertex may be categorized in accordance with the Grid.

9. The following illustration is to facilitate an approach to a more rigorous representation of 'points of view' or vertices. The patient corresponds to the A personality, the analyst to B. The analytic exchange described is at an advanced stage in the analysis, in the sense that what was an extremely disturbed patient has become better adjusted to what the psychoanalyst regards as reality. The psychoanalyst similarly has become better adjusted to what the patient regards as reality. 'Somewhere' there is present a 'super-ego' that is cruel, denuded of all the characteristics usually associated with the super-ego, and, finally, of 'existence' itself. It therefore has the characteristics of 'non-existence' described in 7 above. I use the term 'super-ego' as a psychoanalytic intuitive theory, now with the status of a realization, which I want to reformulate in terms of another intuitive theory.

The patient talks freely, but his communications are disjointed sentences which would, anywhere but in analysis, be described as 'incoherent'. Such a term is insufficiently illuminating to lead to a psychoanalytic interpretation, but the 'vertex' (the 'point of view' provided by regarding an analysis as an ordinary conversation) gives me a descriptive term suitable for the immediate purpose. As it is not suitable for continuing the psychoanalytic discussion, the term 'incoherence' must be observed more critically.

As time passes, and it may require many months of observation, 'incoherence' displays many characteristics which are changing constantly. The patient may, in a fit of impatience, describe them as pointless; and so they may prove to be, for sentences can indeed communicate everything but the point. The sentences were mutilated. Personal pronouns were used without indication of the person to whom they might relate. Important parts of speech were missing; and so on. The mutilations varied in form and in effect; they did not always make sentences pointless, though sometimes 'pointlessness' was the 'point'. This type of peculiarity is but one manifestation of attacks on linking, the technique of psychoanalysis and indeed articulate speech itself being the link. My immediate concern is not with attacks on linking but with an aspect of transformation (*Transformations*, Chapter 2). The patient, having delivered himself of a series of statements, listens to the interpretation and then continues, to all outward appearance, in much the same way. Further observation reveals that there has in fact been a change. If my interpretation was intended to show him that he was speaking to conceal, rather than to reveal, something about his sexual life, he will identify himself with a 'point of view', a vertex, such that only certain elements in my interpretation are illumined. Thus he emulates the mathematician whose formula effects a transformation in vector space. What takes place I now represent by a slow-motion model:

The patient grasps the gist of what I say. The totality of the statement, including the implication that I am the analyst, is evacuated (the mechanism represented by the theory of projective identification). He identifies himself with the analyst, and by virtue of his intuition is able to 'see' the meaning of my interpretation. The meaning that he thus 'sees' is that I am annoyed, jealous, envious at my exclusion from participation in, or understanding of, his sexual life. He then exclaims, "Oh that frightful noise!"

His remark, without the interpolated story, appears to be a *non sequitur*; if the account given is assumed to represent the mental events, unexpressed in the interval between interpretation and rejoinder, incoherence disappears. Many assumptions can be made about the link between interpretation and response. One set assumes that it should be compatible with respect for the truth; another that it should conform to respect for omniscience; yet another that it should be compatible with both. The role of desire, in pre-conception, is determinant.

In this episode there are some of the unsatisfactory features to which I would draw attention. There is no evidence to support the particular assumption made. To produce it would involve the impossible task of explaining the history of my mental development, or even that limited part of it shared with the patient, that has led to accretions of 'desires' to original beliefs (Grid category C1) that my analysand was my patient.

Furthermore, I have used terms ('omniscient' is one of them) that represent similar developments of meaning in order that the term should become the premise of further developments. 'Omniscient' is therefore an element categorized as $\overleftarrow{C}3$ and $\overrightarrow{D4}$.

The patient may categorize the same statements in an entirely different way, as is apparent from the description I have given of his interpretation of my interpretation. To meet this difficulty I propose to construct a figure that will serve to represent the invariants of an ever-changing situation.

By way of psychological preparation for the reception of a system that is independent of the particular situations it is intended to serve, I shall use descriptions that lack rigour but have definition. This makes for a lack of flexibility in the final formulation which is intended to combine flexibility with rigour. The system may be regarded as being contained within an emotional space within itself – an 'exo-skeleton' or an 'endo-skeleton'.

To construct this I differentiate an awareness of reality from a denial (or ignoring, or ignorance) of reality. A will ignore reality; B will accept it. With vertex A, reality will be restrictive and frustrating; with vertex B, reality will be liberating and conducive to growth.

Further, I assume an axiomatic approach in all theoretical formulations; axiomatic statements are not differentiated from postulates and premises: they are treated as indistinguishable from each other and from definitory hypotheses. Definitory hypotheses are statements marking the binding of a constant conjunction whatever the content of the formulation may be. I regard any theorem as capable of one of the uses of the horizontal axis. But when a column 1 → columns 3 and 4, it means the category has changed to row D. Any theorem may illuminate facts it was not designed to display, but, conversely, any deductive system will be seen, as soon as it is used, to accumulate meaning in a manner analogous to that of the pre-conception and, in doing so, to require axioms that have not been necessary for the completion of the system.

Any deductive system may appear to be consistent within itself provided it remains definitory, that is to say, with characteristics that qualify it for column 1. The deductions may appear to be consistent and logically necessary so long as it is not asked 'necessary to what?' or 'to whom?' But if they are said to be logically necessary this is itself a statement about the system, and this statement cannot be refuted unless it is used. But if it *is* allowed to become saturated, that is to say *used* as a pre-conception, then the pre-conception mates with the realization to produce a conception (E) and again to produce a concept (F). The conception (E) has the characteristic not only that it records by implication (a realization exists which approximates to the pre-conception) but that a realization exists which approximates to the conception although its existence was not known when the pre-conception was formulated. As soon as the deductive system proves its value as an exploratory tool, the self-consistency, which appeared to exist when the domain in which the system applied was limited, is imperilled because readjustments become necessary to fit the theorem to its extended domain. As the system illuminates facts whose significance was unknown before (the elements of the paranoid-schizoid position) and thus imperils its self-consistency, it throws off the limitations of the domain in which it applies. It approximates to illimitability and universality. The dilemma can be stated thus: the system, if consistent within itself, is limited; if not limited, then it cannot be regarded as self-consistent because its self-consistency is contingent. Furthermore, its statements can be seen to depend on an axiomatic statement whose existence was not even suspected, let alone regarded as logically necessary, when the system was formulated and had the status common to column 1 categories.

3

Reality sensuous and psychic

The illustrations in the previous chapter are not satisfactory and I propose to consider some reasons for this.

Psychoanalytic events cannot be stated directly, indubitably, or incorrigibly any more than can those of other scientific research. I shall use the sign O to denote that which is the ultimate reality represented by terms such as ultimate reality, absolute truth, the godhead, the infinite, the thing-in-itself. O does not fall in the domain of knowledge or learning save incidentally; it can be 'become', but it cannot be 'known'. It is darkness and formlessness but it enters the domain K when it has evolved to a point where it can be known, through knowledge gained by experience, and formulated in terms derived from sensuous experience; its existence is conjectured phenomenologically.

The events of the psychoanalytic experience are transformed and formulated. The value of these formulations can be assessed according to the conditions under which the transformations are effected. Formulations of the events of analysis made in the course of analysis must possess value different from that of formulations made extra-sessionally. Their value therapeutically is greater if they are conducive to transformations in O; less if conducive to transformations in K.

The experience of psychoanalysis affords material impossible to equal from any other source. It follows that this material should be available in full to the psychoanalyst. The analysis that every psychoanalyst is obliged to undergo as part of his training is necessary because it removes obstacles to participation in the psychoanalytic experience; it has many facets, but for the psychoanalyst none can compare in importance with this; what I have to say is ancillary to this. It is impossible to undergo an analysis without learning about psychoanalysis as practised by one particular psychoanalyst; this is a misfortune rather than an advantage. Furthermore, established beliefs and conventions, hardened habits of thought, unless subjected to vigilance, re-establish themselves and encroach upon the freedom the psychoanalyst has won by being psychoanalysed and lead to deterioration of his efficiency.

In the course of analysis it is inevitable that the analysand imparts a great deal of information *about* himself just as the analyst imparts information *about* analysis. This information is worthless at best and, at worst, harmful because every analysis is unique; talk about analysis is not.

The analyst must focus his attention on O, the unknown and unknowable. The success of psychoanalysis depends on the maintenance of a psychoanalytic point of view; the point of view is the psychoanalytic vertex; the psychoanalytic vertex is O. With this the analyst cannot be identified: he must *be* it.

Every object known or knowable by man, including himself, must be an evolution of O. It is O when it has evolved sufficiently to be met by K capacities in the psychoanalyst. He does not know the 'ultimate reality' of a chair or anxiety or time or space, but he knows a chair, anxiety, time, and space. In so far as the analyst becomes O he is able to know the events that are *evolutions* of O.

Restating this in terms of psychoanalytic experience, the psychoanalyst can know what the patient says, does, and appears to be, but cannot know the O of which the patient is an evolution: he can only 'be' it. He knows phenomena by virtue of his senses but, since his concern is with O, events must be regarded as possessing either the defects of irrelevancies obstructing, or the merits of pointers initiating, the process of 'becoming' O. Yet interpretations depend on 'becoming' (since he cannot know O). The interpretation is an actual event in an evolution of O that is common to analyst and analysand.

A fallacious but helpful description is that the practising analyst must wait for the analytic session to 'evolve'. He must wait not for the analysand to talk or to be silent or to gesture, or for any other occurrence that is an actual event, but for an evolution to take place so that O becomes manifest in K through the emergence of actual events. Similarly, the reader must disregard what I say until the O of the experience of reading has evolved to a point where the actual events of reading issue in his interpretation of the experiences. Too great a regard for what I have written obstructs the process I represent by the terms, 'he becomes the O that is common to himself and myself'.

The reasons for this are as follows: there can be no genuine outcome that is based on falsity, therefore the outcome depends on the closeness with which the interpretative appraisal approximates to truth. The psychoanalyst and his analysand are alike dependent on the senses, but psychic qualities, with which psychoanalysis deals, are not perceived by the senses but, as Freud says, by some mental counterpart of the sense organs – a function that he attributed to consciousness. Without wishing to discard this possibility I prefer to consider it as an open question and substitute a more general postulate which I represent by O. To put it in more popular terms, the more 'real' the psychoanalyst is, the more he can be at one with the reality of the patient. Conversely, the more he depends on actual events, the more he relies on thinking that depends on a background of sense impression.

In the primitive phase, which Freud regards as dominated by the pleasure principle and from which he excludes the operation of memory, this last being dependent on the prior development of a capacity for thought, the prototype of memory appears to reside in one of the aspects of projective identification. This mechanism, employed to fulfil the duties of thought until thought takes over, appears as an interchange first between mouth and breast, and then between introjected mouth and introjected breast. This I regard as reaction between container ♀ and contained ♂. ♀ seems to be the element which is nearest in this phase to the memory. The terms I use must be regarded as verbal representations of visual images; the whole description will be in these C category terms because I find them easier to employ and more likely to be understood. Later, I may attempt more sophisticated formulations.

♂ evacuates unpleasure in order to get rid of it, to have it transformed into something that is, or feels, pleasurable, for the pleasure of evacuation, for the pleasure of being contained. ♀ takes in the evacuations for the same motives. The nature of the relationship needs investigation. ♀, which may evacuate or retain, is the prototype of a forgetful or retentive memory. Pleasure may be retained if possession is the dominant concern; grievance if a store of ammunition is the main concern. Evacuation may be forcible as if to convert the evacuated object into a missile; introjection likewise as fulfilment of greed. Developments of memory that are inevitable to the psychoanalyst are C category elements, the dominance of ♀♂, the primacy of pleasure-pain (in contrast with reality or truth), and 'possession' with its reciprocal, fear of loss; all have been acquired in close association with the senses.

The impulse to be rid of painful stimuli gives the 'content' of the memory (♀) an unsatisfactory quality when one is engaged in the pursuit of truth O. The more successful the memory is in its accumulations, the more nearly it approximates to resembling a saturated element saturated with saturated elements. An analyst with such a mind is one who is incapable of learning because he is satisfied. Furthermore, because of its primitive nature, his memory is believed to be filled only with objects giving rise to feelings of pleasure and to be empty of unpleasure components, or vice versa. The attitude towards the 'memory' or 'unconscious' depends on the idea that it is a container for the 'evacuations' of projective identification. Such a 'memory' is no equipment for an analyst whose aim is O, as may be seen by considering what is represented by this sign.

O stands for the absolute truth in and of any object; it is assumed that this cannot be known by any human being; it can be known about, its presence can be recognized and felt, but it cannot be known. It is possible to be at one with it. That it exists is an essential postulate of science but it cannot be scientifically discovered. No psychoanalytic discovery is possible without recognition of its existence, at-one-ment with it and evolution. The religious mystics have probably approximated most closely to expression of experience of it. Its existence is as essential to science as to religion. Conversely, the scientific approach is as essential to religion as it is to science and is as ineffectual until a transformation from K → O takes place.

In order to know about the analysand, the analyst has recourse to K. Memory is a part of K. Notation (Freud, 1911b), in the wide sense of the term, is its servant. But memory depends on the senses. It is limited by the limitations of the senses and their subordination to the pleasure-pain principle; memories are therefore fallacious and memory has the defects of its origin in functions of possessiveness and evacuation.

The psychoanalyst is concerned with O, which is incommunicable save through K activity. O may appear to be attainable by K through phenomena, but in fact that is not so; K depends on the evolution of

O → K. At-one-ment with O would seem to be possible through the transformation K → O, but it is not so. The transformation O → K depends on ridding K of memory and desire. I turn accordingly to consider 'desire'.

It may not seem necessary to postulate desire as well as memory; if memory could be dispensed with, desire would likewise disappear, and vice versa. But this would involve loss of meaning which I wish to retain. So, in addition to memories, I wish to consider thoughts which are formulations of desire, and probably, but not certainly, objects we represent by the term 'desire'. They are not verbal formulations merely, or even verbal formulations of elements of C category. The desires that can be represented verbally are relatively simple to deal with. For example, the thought occurs that one would like to go abroad for the annual holiday; this can be followed by further ideas, more or less detailed elaborations of the main theme. These thoughts are typical 'desires'; they are extremely common and can be harboured almost unaware; they may be reminiscences or anticipations.

The 'memories' and 'desires' to which I wish to draw attention have the following elements in common: they are ready formulated and therefore require no formulation; they derive from experience gained through the senses; they are evocations of feelings of pleasure or pain; they are formulations 'containing' pleasure or pain. In so far as they are column 2 statements, their function is to prevent transformation of the K → O order.

The above characteristics cannot be indulged by the psychoanalyst without impairment of analytic capacity. For any who have been used to remembering what patients say and to desiring their welfare, it will be hard to entertain the harm to analytic intuition that is inseparable from *any* memories and *any* desires.

The first point is for the analyst to impose on himself a positive discipline of eschewing memory and desire. I do not mean that 'forgetting' is enough: what is required is a positive act of refraining from memory and desire.

It may be wondered what state of mind is welcome if desires and memories are not. A term that would express approximately what I need is 'faith' – faith that there is an ultimate reality and truth – the unknown, unknowable, 'formless infinite'. This must be believed of every object of which the personality can be aware: the evolution of ultimate reality (signified by O) has issued in objects of which the individual can be aware. The objects of awareness are aspects of the 'evolved' O, and are such that the sensuously derived mental functions are adequate to apprehend them. For them faith is not required; for O it is. The analyst is not concerned with such sensuously apprehended objects or with knowledge of such objects. Memories and desires are worthless but inevitable features that he encounters in himself as he works. He *is* concerned with these objects in his analysand because he is concerned with the working of the analysand's mind. His analysand will express his awareness of O in people and things by formulations representing the intersection of evolutions of O with the evolution of his awareness.

It is not possible to say that such formulations by the analysand are not to be interpreted: no such rule can be laid down far from the situation in which it is to be applied because the criteria for it do not exist. Nor can the criteria be established in the situation of the analysis, for they are part of an ineffable experience. There can be no rules about the nature of the emotional experience that will show that the emotional experience is ripe for interpretation. Instead I can only suggest rules for the analyst that will help him to achieve the frame of mind in which he is receptive to O of the analytic experience. If he is able to be receptive to O, then he may feel impelled to deal with the intersection of the evolution of O with the domain of objects of sense, or of formulations based on the senses. Whether he does so or not cannot depend on *rules* for O, or O → K, but only on his ability to be at one with O.

My last sentence represents an 'act' of what I have called 'faith'. It is in my view a scientific statement, because for me 'faith' is a scientific state of mind and should be recognized as such. But it must be 'faith' unstained by any element of memory or desire. If it reveals an aspect of O which has to be formulated, then the *transformation* will require the operation of memory and desire; even so the formulation will require the negative characteristics of column 1 elements – that is to say that the statements must affirm implicitly that the object defined is *not* any of the elements whose names are used in the definitory hypothesis, but is a constant conjunction whose meaning will declare itself only when all traces of memory and desire have been removed from the elements invoked to produce the new formulation. Failure to observe the nature of transformation O → K (that is, the use of objects of memory and desire to mark a new constant conjunction, and the need to discard the evocative characteristics of memory and desire so that the formulation representing the new constant conjunction is unsaturated) has obscured the only sense in which the term 'abstraction' has any useful meaning. A formulation has the quality of an abstraction only in so far as it is divorced from the sensuous background inherent in and essential to memory and desire. The abstract statement must not stimulate memory and desire, though memory and desire have contributed elements to its formulation.

Memory and desire are essential elements in the composition of the new formulation, but a distinction must be made between two classes of mental event. One is an evocation of memory and desire with impulses of possessiveness and sensuous greed: the impulses generate memory and desire; memory and desire generate sensuous greed. The other is the evocation of memories and desires because the experience of at-one-ment *resembles* possession and sensuous fulfilment. The classes differ because the mode of selection differs, and since the classes differ the interpretation (the formulation by the analyst) will differ. The evocation of that which provided a container for possessions, and of the sensuous gratifications with which to fill it, will differ from an evocation stimulated by at-one-ment. The exercises in discarding memory and desire must be seen as preparatory to a state of mind in which O can evolve. The facilitation of 'constellation'[1] must in turn be seen as a step in the process of at-one-ment, the transformation $O \rightarrow K$. In practice this means not that the analyst recalls some relevant memory but that a relevant constellation will be evoked during the process of at-one-ment with O, the process denoted by transformation $O \rightarrow K$.

To what then *is* the analyst's memory relevant and why can there not be a constellation that has a relevance other than relevance to analysis?

It is difficult to conceive of an analysis having a satisfactory outcome without the analysand's becoming reconciled to, or at one with, himself. It is tempting to suppose that such an outcome, or the desire for such an outcome, might provide a criterion for relevance. Conversely, it would be convenient if the analyst's memories, as reminiscences of sensuous experience, could be disregarded as column 2

---

[1] I use the term 'constellation' to represent the process precipitating a constant conjunction.

phenomena mobilized to keep at bay the experience inseparable from the transformations in O. If the objection to memory can be sustained because all memory is a special case of keeping (possessing) a theory known to be (or suspected of being) false in order to prevent the psychological upheaval inseparable from mental growth, it will have the advantage of decreasing the number of theories required to extend, as I propose to do, the theories of resistance. It is sometimes said that a particular interpretation is inadvisable because it increases resistances, but any approach produces its proper resistances; it is as possible to identify an approach by its resistances as it is to judge a tree by its fruit. Resistance to growth is endo-psychic and endo-egregious; it is associated with turbulence in the individual and in the group to which the growing individual belongs.

All C category elements, developed from experience gained by the senses, have gratificatory quality associated with dominance of the pleasure – pain principle. Objections to 'memories' and 'desires' are therefore objections to C3 and C3(2) statements. Later it will be necessary, when we deal with hallucinations, to distinguish between C elements having a background of visual sensation and those with other sense backgrounds.

The discipline that I propose for the analyst, namely avoidance of memory and desire in the sense in which I have used those terms, increases his ability to exercise 'acts of faith'. An 'act of faith' is peculiar to scientific procedure and must be distinguished from the religious meaning with which it is invested in conversational usage; it becomes apprehensible when it can be represented in and by thought. It must 'evolve' before it can be apprehended and it is apprehended when it is a thought, just as the artist's O is apprehensible when it has been transformed into a work of art.

But the 'act of faith' is not a statement, not even a column 6 statement, though it has resemblances to column 6 elements. All Grid elements have a background of O from which they have evolved and it is only when O has evolved sufficiently to be apprehended that it can be represented by a Grid element. It is only when it has evolved to the point where it can be represented by a Grid element that it can be apprehended. When it is apprehended the element can be represented by a Grid category.

The 'act of faith' has no association with memory or desire or sensation. It has a relationship to thought analogous to the relationship of *a priori* knowledge to knowledge. It does not belong to the ±K system but to the O system. It does not by itself lead to knowledge 'about' something, but knowledge 'about' something may be the outcome of a defence against the consequences of an 'act of faith'. A thought has as its realization a no-thing. An 'act of faith' has as its background something that is unconscious and unknown because it has not happened. Thoughts have as their background realizations that are sensible: anxiety, fear, sex can be thought about only when O has evolved to a point where it is apprehensible in sense and has become amenable to transformations in K. Anxiety is 'known' by its secondary qualities. Yet no one has any doubt about anxiety or about 'feeling' the reality, though what is felt is sensations associated with anxiety and not anxiety itself. Similarly, no one who denudes himself of memory and desire, and of all those elements of sense impression ordinarily present, can have any doubt of the reality of the psychoanalytic experience which remains ineffable.

Receptiveness achieved by denudation of memory and desire (which is essential to the operation of 'acts of faith') is essential to the operation of psychoanalysis and other scientific proceedings. It is essential for experiencing hallucination or the state of hallucinosis.

This state I do not regard as an exaggeration of a pathological or even natural condition: I consider it rather to be a state always present, but overlaid by other phenomena which screen it. If these other elements can be moderated or suspended, hallucinosis becomes demonstrable; its full depth and richness are accessible only to 'acts of faith'. Elements of hallucinosis of which it is possible to be sensible are the grosser manifestations and are of secondary importance; to appreciate hallucination the analyst must participate in the state of hallucinosis. From what I have said it will be clear that this is so, for I have postulated that a K link can operate only on a background of the senses, is capable of yielding only knowledge 'about' something, and must be differentiated from the O link essential to transformations in O. Before interpretations of hallucination can be given, which are themselves transformations $O \rightarrow K$, it is necessary that the analyst undergoes in his own personality the transformation $O \rightarrow K$. By eschewing memories, desires, and the operations of memory he can approach the domain of hallucinosis and of the 'acts of faith' by which alone he can become at one with his patients' hallucinations and so effect transformations $O \rightarrow K$.

A type of hallucination worthy of study is that which one may describe provisionally as visual. I have described a patient who seemed to think that my words flew over his head and could be detected in what to me were the patterns on a cushion. I have since found that the pattern on the cushion was seen by him to travel, as it were, in the opposite direction. That is, he was able, in a state of hallucinosis, to see that the patterns were really my words travelling, through his eyes, to him. Furthermore the 'meaning', which could not be grasped outside the conditions of hallucinosis, was perfectly clear in a state of hallucinosis. The 'meaning' of a statement in hallucinosis is not, however, the same as its meaning in the domain of rational thought. Ordinarily, constellation, constant conjunction, and binding (by nomination) are a prelude to exploration of meaning. In the domain of hallucinosis the mental event is transformed into a sense impression and sense impressions in this domain do not have meaning; they provide pleasure or pain. In this way the unsense-able mental phenomenon is transformed into a beta-element which can be evacuated and reintroduced so that the act yields not a meaning but pleasure or pain.

The analysand in a state of hallucinosis experiences visual hallucinations which tend to be self-perpetuating. They yield pleasure and pain, both being valued, and fail to yield meaning in the sense in which that term is understood in the domain of rational thought. He tends therefore to demand, and provide, more hallucination to compensate for the missing gratification. He feels the pleasure and pain to be inadequate; the 'meaning' is likewise inadequate. The less gratification he achieves the more greedy he becomes; the more greedy, the more hallucinated. The visual element is expected to be exempt from the disabilities inherent in those senses that depend for their efficacy on proximity to the object of gratification. Meaning is lost, pain and pleasure are gained, from a state that is independent of proximity to an object and of the frustration peculiar to thoughts and their genetic association with the 'no-thing'.[1]

I suspect that what I have said of visual hallucinations is true of hallucinations with a background of senses other than visual, but

[1]It is worth contrasting this type of independence of objects, conferred by hallucinosis and the advantages of 'visual' impression, with the independence of the physical presence of objects peculiar to 'maths' and 'thinking'. Note, too, the distraction caused by the *presence* of objects.

other senses lack the quality of independence of close contact with objects.

A patient who feared guilt substituted punishment. It was achieved by hallucinosis. His circumstances were comfortable and he did not manipulate events by acting out, which he might have done, to produce a penitential life. He could presumably have forced the police to take action by committing some variety of sexual offence – sexual offences often appeared in his statements – but instead he complained incessantly though inarticulately of what he ultimately came to recognize as sexual visions, which he admitted were present throughout the sessions. For months during which I had interpreted that he was seeing visions he denied them, but they were maintained tenaciously. After their presence had been admitted he feared to lose them though their dominance was painful. The pain yielded pleasure, and therefore there was cause for him to cherish the state of which he complained. His complaints, his flow of statements, produced a painful state in analysis and then were made into a sexual link between him and me. At the stage of which I write this was a gratification and also a protection against behaviour which might yield pleasure in a more expansive way – by his becoming involved with the police, for example. But his fear of any change was so acute that it was impossible to say with any plausibility what he expected to take the place of his hallucinations were they to cease. In time, however, certain fears could be discussed. Acting-out limited the amount of hallucinatory experience and its extent because the reality component involved frustration and delay, and real pain and pleasure seemed deficient in power to satisfy.[1] This, however, was his complaint against hallucinatory gratification. Hallucinations of dreams seemed to be deficient in associations and unsuited to perform the functions of dreams, and to be felt as unrewarding. Yet he reported what he said were dreams.

In this period hallucination supplied him with punishment as it might in other circumstances have supplied him with sexual pleasure, food, or any other sensual gratification. His analysis indeed showed that the usefulness of hallucination was absolutely limited to

---

[1]In this respect, real objects, real pain and pleasure, are felt as distraction. It is worth comparing *this* type of distraction with the frustration experienced by a calculator who has to think out mathematical problems only in the presence of objects which are the essence of his calculation. [Cf. previous footnote. *Ed.*]

elements with a background of sense-able realizations: this was their virtue and their defect.

Their moral value seemed to be that they punished him by providing him with ill-deserved pain to compensate for having been once used as the source of ill-deserved pleasure. In the analytic session they seemed as a barrier against any appreciation of the realities of the session. Yet some interpretations were grasped sometimes. I found it difficult to establish any rule that would govern the time at which interpretations could be understood but I did note that the interpretation had to be exact. He could not correct or adjust an inexactitude so as to bring the interpretation into line with the realization it was intended to illumine. It had to remain uncorrected and unabsorbed because it was wrong.

The sessions were occupied in verbalization of his visual images. His verbalizations were peppered with locutions such as 'tomorrow', 'yesterday', 'last week', all of which could be taken to mean 'not now'. Splitting in time was very common and psychoanalytic objects were scattered over a range of years. Corresponding to this was a denial of the present which amounted to a denial of the passage of time. It was as if a moment of time had been stretched out like a piece of elastic to cover an enormous area.

There had been an occasion when he smelled coffee in the house where I was working. He had once seen me caught in a rain shower without a coat or umbrella. Both these facts appeared in fragments spread out over many years. It would be an exaggeration to say they were expressed unmistakably. I have no doubt, or, more accurately, by an 'act of faith' I am confident, that the scraps of sentences and intonations when put together were signs that he had had both these experiences as I have described them. Were it possible for him to witness my having coffee and being caught in the rain, to 'take it in' and then fragment what he had thus taken in, to evacuate these fragments and leave them scattered over a wide space of time, then that would be what he was doing. The two facts appear in the analysis as if they have been embedded in the elastic moment of time that has been stretched out. How far is it safe to use such descriptions as a valid basis for conjecture? I can imagine that this patient's grasp of fact is so slight that he has not enough with which to provide a cover for his psychotic mechanisms. Further, I can suppose that the obtrusion of psychotic mechanisms is such that the 'skin' or 'sanity' is stretched to breaking-point. Either description is likely to be so limited as to lead to a multiplicity of theories to serve a single configuration. But an illumination for the psychoanalyst does not necessarily provide illumination for someone not sharing the experience or illuminate for the patient who shares the experience but who transforms it under hallucinosis.

This problem prompts comparison of interpretation with the matter interpreted, or comparison of the category of associations with the category of the interpretation; the Grid is an instrument by which this can be effected. If some relationship between the categories could be established it might be possible to discover the nature of the relationship between psychotic association and the appropriate interpretation. This involves a further look at projective transformation.

The views expressed about memory and desire and the need for their regulation as the psychoanalyst's preparation for his work provide a starting-point for reconsidering the nature of the projective transformation. Hallucinosis, which can be *observed* by divesting oneself of memory and desire, must have had some corresponding mechanism in the events that led to its inception. If the analyst can take certain steps that enable him to 'see' what the patient sees, it is reasonable to suppose that the patient has likewise 'taken steps', though not necessarily the same ones, to enable him to 'see' what he sees.

4

Opacity of memory and desire

The 'act of faith' (*F*) depends on disciplined denial of memory and desire. A bad memory is not enough: what is ordinarily called forgetting is as bad as remembering. It is necessary to inhibit dwelling on memories and desires. They are two facets of the same thing: both are composed of elements based on sense impressions; both imply the absence of immediate sensual satisfaction; one supposes a store of sensual objects, the memory being the container, and the other a conjunction of sensually satisfying objects. The invariants are an inside and an outside composed of objects which are sensible. The more the psychoanalyst occupies himself with memory and desire the more his facility for harbouring them increases and the nearer he comes to undermining his capacity for *F*. For consider: if his mind is preoccupied with what is or is not said, or with what he does or does not hope, it must mean that he cannot allow the experience to obtrude, particularly that aspect of it which is more than the sound of the patient's voice or the sight of his postures. What sounds the patient makes, or what spectacle he presents, relates to O only in so far as O has evolved into the K domain.

Uninhibited exercise of memories and desires is indistinguishable from, inseparable from, and analogous to, making pre-conception impossible by virtue of leaving no unsaturated element (the desire or the memory precludes preconception if it occupies the 'space' that should remain unsaturated). If the mind is preoccupied with elements perceptible to sense it will be that much less able to perceive elements that cannot be sensed. Yet obviously anxiety cannot be said, except by analogy, to be smelled or touched or felt. Even so, anxiety comes nearer to being 'sensed' than many more subtle aspects of the personality which do nevertheless exist. It is important that the analyst should avoid mental activity, memory and desire, which is as harmful to his mental fitness as some forms of physical activity are to physical fitness.

'Past' and 'future' represent a realization related to another realization represented by the terms 'internal' and 'external'. The past is something contained 'within' the 'memory', and the 'future' something that cannot be so contained. 'Memories' can be regarded as possessions; desires, though just as much 'in' the mind as are memories, and therefore just as much 'possessions', are spoken of as if they 'possessed' the mind. A certain class of patient feels 'possessed' by or imprisoned 'in' the mind of the analyst if he considers the analyst desires something relative to him – his presence, or his cure, or his welfare. I have said if the patient 'considers' the analyst desires something, but in fact to say in this context that the patient 'considers' is to use an approximation that may be misleading because its penumbra of associations conceals more than it reveals of the state of mind of the patient. The patient is in a state of mind for which there is no verbal apparatus and the psychoanalyst is constantly faced by the need to produce his own apparatus for investigation while he is carrying on the investigation. If the psychoanalyst has not deliberately divested himself of memory and desire the patient can 'feel' this and is dominated by the 'feeling' that he is possessed by and contained in the analyst's state of mind, namely, the state represented by the term 'desire'.

A means of representing mental phenomena without words (which are unsuitable because of their background of sensible experience) is required. The patient uses words that represent visual images, or he may be mute for long periods, or use words that are evocations of emotion, sometimes powerful emotions, but challenge the psychoanalyst to detect a content and express it in ordinary English. Evocations of anger, anxiety, fear, pity, hate, and loyalty to himself often include words that give the total a particular coloration: wreath, upset, cemetery, may be words scattered through the flow in such a way as to suggest bereavement; or solicitors, damages, illness, to suggest legal proceedings.

In this way he appears to be having an experience that he is not able to represent in terms of ordinary speech. He could be described therefore as suffering from a speech disorder were it not that the disturbance would appear to be inadequately or eccentrically described in such terms; reciprocally, to ordinary view, it seems eccentric to say that a stammerer suffers from a psychosis. But in fact the descriptions of the psychotic patient as having a speech disorder and the stammerer as being psychotic both have substance, and in both eccentricity depends on the vertex. 'Stammer' and 'psychosis' are vertices displaying the same configuration in a manner that illuminates characteristics just as binocular vision demonstrates qualities that require stereoscopy to make them manifest.

Freud, in a letter to Lou Andreas-Salomé,[1] suggested his method of achieving a state of mind which would give advantages that would compensate for obscurity when the object investigated was peculiarly obscure. He speaks of blinding himself artificially. As a method of achieving this artificial blinding I have indicated the importance of eschewing memory and desire. Continuing and extending the process, I include understanding and sense perception with the properties to be eschewed. The suspension of memory, desire, understanding, and sense impressions may seem to be impossible without a complete denial of reality; but the psychoanalyst is seeking something that differs from what is normally known as reality; a criticism that applies to what is ordinarily meant by reality does not indicate undesirability for the purpose of achieving contact with psychic reality, namely, the evolved characteristics of O. This procedure is valid in psychoanalysis and other sciences; *F*, likewise, is an essential component of scientific procedure however rigorous.

There is the possibility of suppressing one or all of these functions of memory, desire, understanding, and sense either together or in turn. Practice in suppression of these faculties may lead to an ability to suppress one or other according to need, so that suspension of one might enhance the effect of domination by the other in a manner analogous to the use of alternate eyes.

Before considering the distinction to be made between total suppression, sleep or other recognized states we must consider in more detail what is meant by understanding or memory or desire. I accept Freud's view of memory and its relationship with notation (Freud, 1911b). Since all memory has a background of sense impressions, the appropriate category is row C. As there are a number of respects in which memory and desire seem to have a similar configuration

[1]Letter from Freud to Lou Andreas-Salomé, 25 May 1916 (in E. L. Freud, 1961).

I propose to consider only the C3 function of memory. What of a 'memory' of a gratification that was *missed?* – an unfulfilled desire must be classed as a desire.[1] If the constellation of thought to which it belongs is associated with feelings of grievance, regret, or remorse, such a desire may have to be regarded by the psychoanalyst as dominating or possessing the memory. A practising psychoanalyst has to decide whether he is psychoanalytically witnessing the operation of a *particular* internal object or not. Does the patient feel like that, or does what he feels like approximate to the formulations of Melanie Klein? I am concerned with developing a mode of thought which is such that a correct clinical observation can be made, for if *that* is achieved there is always hope of evolution of the appropriate theory. Defective observation means that a correct interpretation is an accident. The memory can become possessed by a desire; it can cease to be felt as a possession but itself becomes a possessor of the personality that harbours it. The category is no longer C3. What then is it? The unwelcome answer is that so long as progress, growth, is taking place, no one knows.

The probability is that either a process of rationalization leads to its conversion to categories D → F and columns 2, 4, 5, 6, n − 1, n, or it becomes fixed in row C and column 2. The need to resist the impact of changing circumstances requires that the C2 memory should become more and more independent of, and impervious to, the world of reality (sensible). These are developments in the category C3(2) and are, according to intensity, memories of sense impressions designed to act as a barrier *against* sense impressions; it would seem likely to lead to a development akin to hallucinations. The solution of the problem is made nearer by giving 'projective identification' a direction and greatly increasing the vertices and destinations. Not enough attention is paid to the unconscious as itself a destination of the projected object nor yet to the evacuation from the mental world into the sensible world and so out of the mental system.

Desire is similar to memory in that both have a background of sense impressions. But desire relates to that which is felt not to be possessed; it is 'unsaturated'. There is therefore a correspondence between desire as an unsaturated term and the evolution of O it represents. The problem in discussing O is that the discussion can only be

[1] To be a desire the idea must be felt to be unfulfilled.

about evolved characteristics of O (K) whereas *F* is related to O itself.

The problem of differentiating desire from memory lies in the fact that it is 'located' in a 'place' which cannot be determined any more than can the 'place' where parallel lines of a railway-track meet. 'Where' is a term with a background of sense impressions. The difference between desire and memory has no background of sense impressions and cannot be discussed adequately in terms that have such a background. Nevertheless, in psychoanalytic practice it is possible to decide when memory is being experienced by the patient and when desire: one is the 'past' tense and the other the 'future'. The decision depends on the fact that the experience the analyst has of the patient's experience is different from the patient's experience. Investigation of the problems involved depends on *F*. This means that the understanding of the patient and the identification with him that have been regarded as sufficient hitherto must be replaced by something quite different. The transformation in K must be replaced by the transformation in O, and K must be replaced by *F*. In transformations in K, the point on which attention is focused lies on the line of intersection of the evolution of O with $T\alpha$ to produce $T\beta$. In transformation in O, the attention is focused beyond the intersection and in O. $T\alpha$ and $T\beta$ are therefore projections onto a surface from a point at O (infinity), and although O (infinity) is inaccessible to K it is perfectly accessible to T in O. The analyst has to *become infinite* by the suspension of memory, desire, understanding. The emotional state of transformations in O is akin to dread as it is represented by the formulation:

> Like one that on a lonesome road
> Doth walk in fear and dread;
> And having once turned round walks on,
> And turns no more his head;
> Because he knows a frightful fiend
> Doth close behind him tread.[1]

The 'frightful fiend' represents indifferently the quest for truth or the active defences against it, depending on the vertex.

The menace to 'reality' is felt to derive from: (1) the suppression of memory, desire, and understanding, for such suppression undermines sense-based experience which is the reality with which the

---

[1]Samuel Taylor Coleridge, *The Rime of the Ancient Mariner*.

individual is familiar; (2) the increase of power of *F*, which reveals and makes possible experiences that are often painful and difficult for the individual analyst and analysand to tolerate; and (3) the peculiar type of relationship between one element and another in the O domain. Included in this is a relationship that is indifferently expressed as spatial or temporal. Thus, in my quotation, the walker is being 'overtaken' by dread; he walks a 'lonesome road'. It may seem improbable that dread should be associated with analytic progress towards a more realistic outlook.

I shall therefore discuss the phenomenon at greater length.

First it is to be noted that the submergence of memory, desire, and understanding appears not only to run flat contrary to accepted procedure but also to be close to what occurs spontaneously in the severely regressed patient.[1] The analyst who tries this disciplinary activity will find it disturbing despite his own analysis, however thorough and prolonged it might have been. It is necessary to consider why this should be so.

Desire, memory, and understanding are based on sensuous experience, expressed in terms whose background is precisely the same experience and which are designed for use related to that experience. They are vitiated by the same defect as are formulations based on a background of inanimate reality when they are applied to biological reality. Anxiety, depression, persecution are not *sensed* (though common usage sanctions an analogical use of the term 'sensed' in a context in which it is not appropriate). The nearer the analyst comes to achieving suppression of desire, memory, and understanding, the more likely he is to slip into a sleep akin to stupor. Though different, the difference is hard to define. The sharpening of contact with O cannot be separated from an increase of perception, in particular of elements of K; this sensuous sharpening is painful although partial and mitigated by the general obliteration of sensory perception. The residual sensory perception, often auditory and restricted to particular kinds of sound, is responsible for inducing a sharp and painful reaction (similar to the startle reaction seen in babies).

Furthermore, the sacrifice of pleasure and pain is a deprivation

---

[1]There are real dangers associated with the appearance; this is why the procedure here adumbrated is advocated only for the psychoanalyst whose own analysis has been carried at least far enough for the recognition of paranoid-schizoid and depressive positions.

that is not easily tolerated in prospect and is disliked by the analysand when he senses it in the analyst. The deprivation corresponds to displacement of the pleasure–pain principle from its dominant position. This would not matter were it not for a simultaneous apparent deposition of the reality principle, for that is based on a background of realizations which are perceptible to the psyche through the mediation of the senses. The disciplined increase of *F* by suppression of K, or subordination of transformations in K to transformations in O, is therefore felt as a very serious attack on the ego until *F* has become established. If psychoanalytic method is narrowly conceived of as consisting in the accumulation of knowledge (possessiveness), in harmony with the reality principle, and divorced from the processes of maturation and growth (either because growth is not recognized or because it is recognized but felt to be unattainable and beyond the control of the individual), it becomes a potent stimulus of envy. A further source of distortion is the tendency to link *F* with the supernatural because of lack of experience of the 'natural' to which it relates. The tendency is to introduce a god or devil that *F* is to reveal (or that is to 'evolve' from O). The element F,[1] which should remain unsaturated, becomes saturated and unfitted for its purpose. The progressive stages in the disciplinary exercise proposed for the analyst are repellent rather than attractive. The more the analyst becomes expert in excluding memory, desire, and understanding from his mental activity, the more he is likely, at least in the early stages, to experience painful emotions that are usually excluded or screened by the conventional apparatus of 'memory' of the session, analytic theories, often disguised desires or denials of ignorance, and 'understanding' (which consists more often than not of column 2 elements). I exclude consideration of painful experiences in so far as they lie in unresolved conflicts in the analyst, for these do not differ from similar experiences in the practice of accepted methods; I have nothing to add to what is already known of counter-transference and the complications to which it may give rise. But it may be as well to glance at some of the more common experiences, if only as a warning to anyone disposed to practise the approach I advocate.

In the first place, the analyst will soon find that he appears to be ignorant of knowledge which he has hitherto regarded as the

[1][F as a Grid Element, a Concept, as distinct from *F* ('Faith'). *Ed.*]

hallmark of scrupulous medical responsibility. It is disconcerting to find that one is without an idea, say, that the patient has been married, or has children, or of certain events deemed by the analysand to have been of great significance. If the patient has paranoid trends and displays a tendency towards litigation, it may seem to be running an unwarranted risk to be ignorant of matters that could, in a court of law, be regarded as significant and as evidence of ordinary medical care for detail. This would indeed be the case if there were not cogent reasons for *not* 'remembering' such detail. As it is, I think that whatever the risks may be, the obligation is for the analyst to conduct the case in accordance with his lights – and not in accordance with the supposed risks to himself. In this method the experience the analyst gains bears little resemblance to the files and case-histories with which psychiatry is familiar. It may appear to differ from what would be expected in the light of accepted analytic theory. Thus an analyst may feel, to take a common example, that his married patient is unmarried; if so, it means that psychoanalytically his patient *is* unmarried: the emotional reality and the reality based on the supposition of the marriage contract are discrepant. If this seems to suggest the analyst must preserve his capacity for memory, I maintain that he always does (as does the patient, however regressed), but error is more likely to arise through inability to *divest* oneself of memory than through forgetfulness. If the analyst does not remember that his patient is married, the fact that he *is* is irrelevant until the patient says something that reminds the analyst of this fact.

I have spoken of the 'fact' that the patient is married. Sooner or later it will be necessary to abandon locutions which, though helpful when adumbrated (i.e. used to bind a constant conjunction), become unable to fulfil the function for which they are intended. To take the present instance as an example: provided one does not consider too deeply what is meant, no difficulty is experienced in using the phrase, or the idea that is represented by the phrase, 'the patient is married'. But in psychoanalysis such matters as the patient's marriage have to be considered deeply. Is an overt practising homosexual with several children and a wife with whom he has entered into the marriage contract married? In psychoanalysis the answer does not depend only on what is meant by marriage, because marriage is but one 'element' among many: for example, the 'meaning' of having several children, or a wife or husband with whom a legal marriage has been contracted. In such a context the value can be seen of regarding both the term 'marriage' (the verbal expression) and the fact of several children, and a wife or husband, as 'statements' whose Grid category can be determined. If one considers the 'fact' of marriage it soon becomes necessary to suppose a number of different kinds of fact, such as a fact of 'external reality' or a fact of 'psychic reality'. Such terms are useful but they are themselves statements, and the belief that an event belongs to a category of 'events of external reality' leads to confusion and contradiction. It is simpler to regard the patient's statements as having a category in the vertex of the analyst and to observe that they do not, in the analyst's view, 'mean' that the patient is married (i.e. they are not column 3 elements) but that they have a particular category and that it is from the analyst's assessment of the category that the 'meaning' derives. *His* unsaturated elements are saturated. What the patient *thinks* he means is, as far as the analyst is concerned, irrelevant, but what the statement is, and to what use it is put, *is* relevant. What matters is that to statements of a particular category the patient begins to add statements of a different category. The patient whose statements have at no time suggested to the analyst that he, the patient, is married, now, at a particular point in his analysis, introduces statements that indicate that he *is;* that is to say, he behaves in a way that makes the analyst regard his statements as belonging to new categories including column 6 (he is asserting that he has actually *done* something, resorted to the kind of statement that consists in actually doing something, e.g. getting married).

Now it is clear that if the psychoanalyst has allowed himself the unfettered play of memory, desire, and understanding, his pre-conceptions will be habitually saturated and his 'habits' will lead him to resort to instantaneous and well-practised saturation from 'meaning' rather than from O.

When the psychoanalyst anticipates some crisis, and especially if he has, or thinks he has, good grounds for anxiety, his tendency is to resort to memory and understanding to satisfy his desire for security (or to resort to 'saturation' to avoid 'unsaturation'). If he gives in to this tendency he is proceeding in a direction calculated to preclude any possibility of union with O. This is understood by the psychotic patient, who does not resort to resistances but relies on being able to evoke the resistance-proliferating elements in his analyst; in other words, to stimulate the analyst's desires (notably for a successful outcome of the analysis), his memories, and his understanding, thereby intending that his analyst's state of mind will not be open to the experience of which he might otherwise be a witness.

This digression brings us back to the question of what is to be regarded as a fact. It appears to mean that the analysis should reinforce doubts of 'facts' which are part of 'memory'. The tendency to try to recall some supposed 'cause' of the crisis and to desire some different and more pleasing situation must be resisted. At best it can only recall some episode supposed to be the 'cause'. The 'recalled memory' saturates the psychoanalyst's pre-conceptions and obscures the issues at the one point where clarity of judgement and scope for its exercise are able to coincide – the current session.

To repeat: the capacity to forget, the ability to eschew desire and understanding, must be regarded as essential discipline for the psychoanalyst. Failure to practise this discipline will lead to a steady deterioration in the powers of observation whose maintenance is essential. The vigilant submission to such discipline will by degrees strengthen the analyst's mental powers just in proportion as lapses in this discipline will debilitate them. This view departs from commonly accepted practice and it may be as well, therefore, to consider the theoretical basis implicit in accepted practice.

The idea that patient A comes five times a week and has been doing so for months or years is based on a background of sense impressions and a view of the individual's continuity as an individual which is primitive and crude. It is the emergence of primitive number as a method of asserting 'constant conjunction', of asserting that the object is recurrent, that the 'breast' is something that reappears. But we are not concerned with the patient's anatomy; a belief that no cellular changes take place in twenty-four hours is unwarranted on any but a crudely macroscopic view. The mental phenomena with which we are confronted cannot possibly have remained unaltered even if no analysis had been done. The mental phenomena should reveal invariance and it should be possible to observe the invariants embedded in these phenomena, but an invariant is a characteristic not of permanence but of transformation. It must be sought for in transformation. A psychoanalyst who remembers that A is the same person as A was yesterday indulges a column 2 element. Nor is there any reason for the analysand to believe that the analyst is the same person as the analyst of the previous day. Such belief is suspect as the sign of a collusive relationship intended to prevent emergence of an unknown, incoherent, formless void and an associated sense of persecution by the elements of an evolving O.

Desire, memory, understanding thus have the column 2 function of keeping *F* at bay and preventing the transformation in K from becoming transformation in O. Ostensibly they represent a compromise, for not only do they preclude *F* and transformations in O, but they substitute transformations in K which give a similitude of transformation in O and make the pre-conception (D) in K serve as a saturation rather than as a means to a saturation. 'How I wish I had the chance to swim!' expresses the idea that a particular state of completion (wishing to swim) has been achieved and precludes the unsaturation that would be felt were the individual to *wish* to swim. Of all the hateful possibilities, growth and maturation are feared and detested most frequently. This hostility to the process of maturation becomes most marked when maturation seems to involve the subordination of the pleasure principle and the emergence of the reality principle. The change cannot be regarded as hated because it involves loss of pleasure, for the activity of the pleasure principle means activity of pain. Similarly, the continuation of pleasure when the dominance of the pleasure principle is in abeyance is not precluded by the dominance of the reality principle. But the change from pleasure principle to reality principle does mean abandonment of control over the proportion of pain to pleasure and leaves it to forces that are outside the personality. At-one-ment, or unity with O, is in prospect fearful; no experience challenging this preconception prevails because it is embodied in memory and desire, belongs to K, and does not transform into, though it may mark the inception of, O.

The central point appears to be the painful nature of change in the direction of maturation. It is probably idle to ask why it should be painful, why intensity of pain bears so little relationship to intensity of recognizable danger, and why pain is so feared. There is no doubt that mental pain in particular is feared in a way that would be appropriate if it corresponded directly with mental danger. The relationship of pain to danger is, however, obscure. In this it is not peculiar, for any relationship of one element of the personality with another seems difficult to determine. A science of relationships has yet to be established and one would look to find some discipline analogous to mathematics to represent the relationship of one element in the structure of the psychic personality with another. It is possible to argue that mathematical formulations can be fully appreciated because there is always some more concrete background to which they can be seen to relate, *even though that background may itself be only mathematical.* Something similar may be possible in the relationship of elements of the structure of personality. Envy is typical of other elements of the personality in that everyone would be prepared to admit its existence. Yet it does not smell; it is invisible, inaudible, intangible. It has no shape. It must have invariance, or it could not be so widely and surely recognized; and if it has invariants it must be invariant with regard to some kind of operation and therefore there must be an underlying group of such operations.

5

Theories: particular instance or general configuration

Controversy is the growing-point from which development springs but it must be a genuine confrontation and not an impotent beating of the air by opponents whose differences of view never meet. What follows is a contribution to bringing different psychoanalytic views together in agreement or disagreement.

Hearing psychoanalytic controversy I have felt that the same configuration was being described and that the apparent differences were more often accidental than intrinsic; different points of view are believed to be significant of membership of a group, not of a scientific experience. Yet everyone knows that what is important is not the supposed use of a particular theory but whether the theory has been understood properly and then whether the application has been sound.

It may be objected that to establish this would involve consideration of every individual analyst and of the circumstances of every individual interpretation. Even so, many difficulties could be obviated by more precise definition of the point of view (vertex). It is permissible for an observer to say that he has no evidence of infantile sexuality provided he also adds that he is an aeronautical engineer and does not take anything but a cursory view of children. What is *not* permissible is that he should say that he has no evidence of infantile sexuality without mentioning his vertex. I hope that there will be evolved a method of designating the vertex with brevity and precision. The following is a loose description, by way of a prelude to something more scientific.

To attain to the state of mind essential for the practice of psychoanalysis I avoid any exercise of memory; I make no notes. When I am tempted to remember the events of any particular session I resist the temptation. If I find myself wandering mentally into the domain of memory I desist. In this my practice is at variance with the view that notes should be kept or that psychoanalysts should find some method by which they can record their sessions mechanically or should train themselves to have a good memory. If I find that I am without any clue to what the patient is doing, and am tempted to feel that the secret lies hidden in something I have forgotten, I resist any impulse to remember what happened or how I interpreted what happened on some previous occasion. If I find that some half-memory is beginning to obtrude, I resist its recall no matter how pressing or desirable its recall may seem to be.

A similar procedure is followed with regard to desires: I avoid entertaining desires and attempt to dismiss them from my mind. (It is not enough to try to do this in the session because that is too late: the habit of desiring must not be allowed to grow.) For example, I think it a serious defect to allow oneself to desire the end of a session, or week, or term; it interferes with analytic work to permit desires for the patient's cure, or well-being, or future to enter the mind. Such desires erode the analyst's power to analyse and lead to progressive deterioration of his intuition. Introspection will show how widespread and frequent memories and desires are. They are constantly present in the mind and to follow the advice I am giving is a difficult discipline. There are exceptions, all of a simple and obvious kind.

Some matters can be easily recorded and need not burden the mind, as, for example, the times of sessions. It would be absurd if the analyst forgot to keep them and they are easily recorded on a timetable. The same may be true of age, members of the family, past illnesses, and other such facts as fancy might dictate. But these are to be recorded, together with addresses and telephone numbers, because they can then be forgotten and because they lend themselves to record. While it can be precisely stated that the patient is married and has four children it is not easily stated that his state of mind is that of a married man with four children because there is no such state of mind. Furthermore, such a 'memory', and the remembrances that such a note would provide, would greatly obscure observation of the patient's state of mind suppose it were to be more nearly what one might expect of a bachelor.

Matters that can be recorded with the means at present at our disposal, including mental means, are sensuous experiences, and the transformations they undergo issue in formulations which have all, mathematical formulations included, a sensuous background. The central phenomena of psychoanalysis have no background in sense data. Even the signs that accompany anxiety, for example increased respiration, would be more appropriate to smelling a danger, if that danger had a scent and our olfactory powers were well developed, than to detecting an endo-psychic phenomenon. An apparatus that might be useful where a danger is sensible is useless or obstructive when the danger derives from a background that is mental and not sensible. Therefore, keep records for events whose background is sensible, such as the time at which a patient is to appear, but not for phenomena of central concern to the psychoanalyst, since their background is not sensible.

How, then, are we to 'observe' and 'record' the patient's state of mind? Since I wish to discuss this but do not know the answer, I shall say 'by *F*'.

Freud said that he had to "blind myself artificially to focus all the light on one dark spot".[1] This provides a useful formulation for describing the area I wish to cover by *F*. By rendering oneself 'artificially blind' through the exclusion of memory and desire, one achieves F; the piercing shaft of darkness can be directed on the dark features of the analytic situation. Through *F* one can 'see', 'hear', and 'feel' the mental phenomena of whose reality no practising psychoanalyst has any doubt, though he cannot with any accuracy represent them by existing formulations.

The vertex I have thus far attempted to represent in this description may later be more accurately defined. Even as it is, I hope that my description will serve to make certain advantages clear. For example, it is easier for another psychoanalyst to appreciate my work if he knows the vertex and can thus anticipate what he thinks are its merits and defects. He does not have to engage in a barren argument about the theories I use (in a context of which he can know nothing) if he is given some idea of the state of mind in which I apply them.

It can be seen that with one vertex theories might be useful that are not useful with another; that if the vertex were altered, other

---

[1]In the letter referred to earlier in Chapter 4.

theories would be required to illuminate the phenomena discussed. Conversely, another psychoanalyst could understand that I might 'see' the oedipal situation in a context in which he might not.

The rules are relatively easy for a psychoanalyst to obey; if they are obeyed, dissimilar people with dissimilar patients may yet have a similar experience and so tend less often to mistake for general laws what are in fact only particular instances of old ones.

The experience to which I refer is the contact with the evolved aspects of O, the realization that I have variously described as ultimate reality, the thing-in-itself, or truth. Logically, in so far as logic affords a model for the approach I am making, the absence of memory and desire should free the analyst of those peculiarities that make him a creature of his circumstances and leave him with those functions that are invariant, the functions that make up the irreducible ultimate man. In fact this cannot be. Yet upon his ability to approximate to this will depend his ability to achieve the 'blindness' that is a prerequisite for 'seeing' the evolved elements of O.

Reciprocally, his freedom from being 'blinded' by the qualities (or his perception of them) that belong to the domain of the senses should enable the analyst to 'see' those evolved aspects of O that are invariant in the analysand. The further the analysis progresses the more the psychoanalyst and the analysand achieve a state in which both contemplate the irreducible minimum that is the patient. (This irreducible minimum is incurable because what is seen is that without which the patient would not be the patient.)

Suppose the patient proliferates endless stories, coherent, plausible, and apparently true. After some analysis it becomes evident that something is wrong: the associations vary from accounts of episodes alleged to have happened and quite likely to have happened, to accounts that sound no less convincing but that reveal flaws. From internal evidence it is clear that the event could not have happened. But for the incongruities, the tone of assurance of the narrative would have lulled all suspicion. If the narration is challenged, the patient admits the fault and at once begins to proliferate further fabrications which invite the analyst either to withdraw his comments and acknowledge the truth of the patient's assertions, or to say openly that he is lying.

It is not relevant to describe details of this case. By regarding the patient's statements as transformations and categorizing them by means of the Grid, one can do something towards understanding what is taking place. I have advocated (in *Elements of Psycho-Analysis*) exercises of this kind, but it must not be supposed that understanding of this nature is required. On the contrary, such 'understanding' can be seen to have as its background memory and desire and should therefore be avoided. The importance of the exercise is to facilitate the analyst's capacity for conjecture, not to intrude upon an analytic session. If the analysis is conducted as I advocate, the 'evolution of O' becomes manifest in the chains of fabrications such as I have described. It should be possible to observe a wide spectrum of categories of lies and what they represent. The flow of associations demands a high degree of inventiveness and speed (especially in sealing off any breach in the fabrications), and a measure of verbal facility that may give an impression of intelligence, especially if memory and desire distort judgement of the category. I am concerned here not with the diagnosis, prognosis, treatment, or cure, but with the O of psychoanalysis.

From one vertex it might seem that the analysand was 'blinding' the analyst by flooding him with illumination – so many facts that the 'obscure' point could not be 'seen'. Is this statement distinguishable from the state produced if the analyst is not successful in ridding himself of memory and desire? Only the psychoanalytic session can provide the answer. Extra-analytic activity stimulates doubt and curiosity in the analyst. Such a patient stimulates memory and desire by appearing to satisfy but without doing so; the analyst is tacitly invited to 'remember' all he is told.

A number of questions, of which the following are a few, are posed by this behaviour:

1. Are the patient's statements lies? Is 'lie' the most appropriate term to use? If not, what is the correct formulation?
2. Why does the patient transform in fabrications and what does he thus transform?
3. Does the fabrication differ from myth? It is often a plausible and coherent narrative, but it seems to declare itself to be category 3 when in fact it would appear to be C2. What, then, are the emotional experiences that are to be covered up and not allowed to emerge?

4. How do the patient's statements differ from other false statements? Respect for the truth appears to have low value compared with other vertices. What, then, is the vertex? –K? How does this compare with Plato's objections to the poet in society? With regard to other false statements it is usually supposed that there is either a mistaken idea that the lie is correct, or a belief that some reward attaches to being able to mislead. Some statements appear to be without reward to either party, but perhaps there is a pleasure in creation even though creation can be achieved only by a lie. Is it a *folie à deux* – a collaboration? Certainly with *F* it could be a sadomasochistic collusion to 'poison' or be 'poisoned'.

These questions can be answered only in analytic contact with the patient. The Grid, or some improved version of it, facilitates mental gymnastics in preparation for it.

6

The mystic and the group

It seems absurd that a psychoanalyst should be unable to assess the quality of his work. In attempting an assessment he has available popular repute (notoriously fickle and unreliable, and unsuited for use as a foundation for any judgement), anxiety, or a sense of satisfaction and well-being about a piece of work that appears to him to be well done. This last is probably as reliable a foundation as any, but is subject to doubt and misgiving. The only other person well placed to have an opinion is the analysand. His opinion is likewise a matter for scrutiny. The friendly or hostile feelings revealed converge towards a point where there should be a wise and compassionate, though critical, judgement. Instead there is an intuition, 'That is truth, accept it.[1]' Such formulations are not regarded as scientifically adequate and one craves something better. The craving cannot be satisfied unless it is recognized that standpoints such as religion, art, science, as we understand them today, are as unsatisfactory as the formulations truth, beauty, god, or future life.

The formulation is the end-product of a transformation; all transformations are associated with a particular vertex. The psychoanalyst is faced at an early date in his own development and at an early stage in the development of psychoanalysis itself with problems that arise because no vertex at present recognized is adequate. It is as absurd to criticize a piece of psychoanalytic work on the ground that it is 'not scientific', as it is to criticize it because it is 'not religious' or 'not artistic'. It is not any of these things. Its failure to be so is a criticism; but its 'success' at being any of them would not remove the reproach.

[1][Prince André, in *War and Peace*, by Leo Tolstoy. *Ed.*]

The critical formulation for which there is no substitute is that it is 'not psychoanalysis'.

It would seem that we are as far as ever from a positive result to the discussion; 'psychoanalysis' must be regarded as a term binding a constant conjunction. Years must pass before we understand what are conjoined and what the conjunction means. Can it be done in verbal terms? Are there any other terms?

It has been said in criticism of psychoanalysis that it cannot be regarded as a science because it cannot be mathematized. Available mathematics do not provide the psychoanalyst with appropriate formulations. The same is true of available verbalizations, but this has been obscured because ordinary conversation has served fairly well for the analysands who have come for analysis hitherto. This situation has been altered by the advent of so-called severe cases on the one hand, and by the needs of communication between psychoanalytic colleagues on the other. It is clear that a development is required that will help psychoanalysis in a manner analogous to that in which modern mathematics has helped the development of physics. In the meantime we are thrown back on existing verbal, mathematical, and artistic formulations, and the exceptional individuals capable of employing them. Genius has been said to be akin to madness; it would be more true to say that psychotic mechanisms require a genius to manipulate them in a manner adequate to promote growth (or life, which is synonymous with growth).

The group needs to preserve its coherence and identity; efforts to do so are manifested in conventions, laws, culture, and language. It also needs the exceptional individual and therefore needs to make provision for the exceptional individual. This might be simple if exceptional individuals declared themselves in unexceptionable terms, and if the nature of their impact on the group, its laws and conventions, could be judged as life-giving or the reverse. The possibility of such discrimination is doubtful and, centuries after, it may still be debated whether an individual of this kind exerted a beneficial or deleterious effect. The same is true of ideas; furthermore, groups are hostile or friendly, favourable or unfriendly, to the development of the new person or idea.

The 'exceptional individual' may be variously described as a genius, a messiah, a mystic, and his following may be large or small. The negative group declares itself an enemy of promise in a manner that may not be discernible to ordinary individuals, but is apparently clear to the gifted individual who seeks an atmosphere more congenial to the exercise of his gifts. For convenience, I shall use the term 'mystic' to describe these exceptional individuals. I include scientists, and Newton is the outstanding example of such a man; his mystical and religious preoccupations have been dismissed as an aberration when they should be considered as the matrix from which his mathematical formulations evolved.

The mystic may declare himself as revolutionary, or he may claim that his function is to fulfil the laws, conventions, and destiny of his group. It would be surprising if any true mystic were not regarded by the group as a mystical nihilist at some stage of his career, and by a greater or less proportion of the group. It would be equally surprising if he were not in fact nihilistic to some group, if for no other reason than that the nature of his contribution is certain to be destructive of the laws, conventions, culture, and therefore coherence of a group within the group if not of the whole group. In this it is evident that the character of the group (which I do not discuss) cannot be excluded from the facts of the evolution of a mystic in a group. The disruptive force of the mystical nihilist, or of the mystic whose impact on a particular group is of a disruptive or nihilist character, extends to and depends on the Language of Achievement, be it expressed in action, speech, writing, or aesthetic. Usually the spread of the disruptive force is limited by the vehicle of communication. The phenomena of destruction remain the same but reception of their message varies, often being restricted to relatively few.

Melanie Klein writes of symbol formation as if it were a particular function that could disintegrate or be disordered and give rise to deep disturbance in a personality; there are realizations that correspond to this theory, but I think the area of disturbance should be regarded as greater than her theory implies. For example, the psychotic patient does not always behave as if he is incapable of symbol formation. Indeed, he often talks or behaves as if he is convinced that certain actions, which to me are innocent of any symbolic significance, are obviously symbolic. They mean, apparently obviously, some message which is of personal and particular concern to him. This 'meaning' is quite different from the meaning one assumes to lie behind a constant conjunction that is public – not private to one individual. The former is, and appears to belong to, a private communication made by God (or Devil or Fate); when the psychotic symbol is met with in practice, its significance seems to be less that it symbolizes something, more that it indicates that the patient is in private rapport with a deity or demon. The symbol, as it is usually understood, represents a conjunction which is recognized by a group to be constant; as encountered in psychosis it represents a conjunction between a patient and his deity which the patient feels to be constant.

The 'symbol' can be an attempt of the personality to use its experience to formulate a theory, which may then be used when the appropriate realization presents itself, or an attempt to use an external event (e.g. a meeting with an acquaintance) to yield an interpretation *as if it were* a symbol. Thus an adverse circumstance can be used as a 'symbol' (not 'sign') of God's wrath, or past experiences can be represented by symbols whose genetic base is in their *sensuous* background. The emotional experience is thus made manageable by being symbolized, whether it is in origin felt to be a response to a painful external stimulus, or whether the external experience is felt to be the confirmation of a painful internal psychic experience.

The inescapable bestiality of the human animal is the quality from which our cherished and admired characteristics spring. 'Man is a political animal' means that he has the mental counterpart of the physical characteristics of a herd animal. As psychoanalysts, we are concerned with the mental counterpart of such physical characteristics as can be discerned in the individual when in semi-isolation from his group but closely involved in a situation likely to stimulate his 'pair' characteristics. Birth, dependence, pairing, and warfare – these are the basic situations to which the basic emotional drives correspond.

This summary of the human condition adds nothing new to what is already familiar, in greater detail, to every psychoanalyst. The summary is intended as a reminder that the analytic situation itself, and then the psychoanalytic occupation or task itself, are bound to stimulate primitive and basic feeling in analyst and analysand. Therefore, if the technique I propose for ensuring vivid appreciation of the emotional facts is as sound as I think it, these fundamental characteristics, love, hate, dread, are sharpened to a point where the participating pair may feel them to be almost unbearable: it is the price that has to be paid for the transformation of an activity that is *about* psychoanalysis, into an activity that *is* psychoanalysis. The activity that is psychoanalysis evokes desires to know how the group is reacting to the pair relationship; this desire often masquerades as a wish for validation, popular repute, or approval.

We thus return to the original problem and the impulse to repudiate the approach I have adumbrated: the more reminiscence is indulged, the farther one is removed from a form of anxiety; one's historical identity is asserted, one was such and such and had certain recognized and remembered associates; one has done as well as, or less well than, so and so. It is doubtful whether these 'historical' reminiscences would be corroborated by any of the characters who figure in one's own story, but they serve to deny the painfulness of the actual predicament that is the source of embarrassment. It is difficult, short of hallucination, to do anything about the present predicament: reminiscence becomes a C2 category orgy to keep out the painful insights that follow on denial of sensuous experience.

There is one form of denial of sensuous experience that has been a commonplace since Freud pointed out that analysis must be conducted in an atmosphere of deprivation. It has not been recognized that to achieve this it is not enough to hope that analysis of the analyst and denial of the patient's wishes will serve. Anyone who considers it possible to achieve a suitable frame of mind by a few minutes of psychological tidying up before starting work cannot have grasped the nature of the discipline necessary to be an analyst or the nature of the insights that become available to the analysed analyst if he brings 'artificial blindness' to bear on his dark spots. It may well be that analysts who attempt the approach advocated in Chapter 4 on 'Memory and Desire' will find that the intuitions achieved by it cause them to feel the need for further analysis. It is possible that the test of sensuous deprivation involved in eschewing memory and desire will bring to light a need for analysis that exists because the analytic experience has not been sufficient, or it may be that it indicates an *additional* demand that would not have occurred had the analyst remained content with the 'atmosphere of deprivation' as it has been understood hitherto. The point is of moment because, if the abandonment of memory and desire brings a need for increased stamina, analysts may have to accept that advances in insight have to be matched by further analysis. Such a contingency imposes revision of training and maintenance of capacity for a psychoanalytic career.

Though it is easy to envisage the need for further analysis, it is not certain that the further analysis must be similar to analysis as experienced and understood when we undergo our first analysis. The importance of the unconscious must not blind us to the fact that in addition to our unconscious memories and desires, dealt with psychoanalytically, there is a problem to solve in the handling of our conscious memories and desires. What kind of 'psychoanalysis' is required for the conscious?

The psychotic *is* conscious of what we feel requires analysis; to approach this problem it will be necessary to discuss memory and desire relative to loss of contact with reality. It has been supposed that the psychotic severs links with reality as a step to a sexual life in phantasy, but it is equally intended to establish freedom from sexual and allied stimulation. He appears to achieve a result resembling the neurotic patient's contact with the unconscious as it is known in classical analysis. The psychotic seems to have the same relationship and attitude to what he has *not* been able to repress, and what therefore remains conscious, that other patients have to the unconscious. The neurotic patient is concerned to show that neurotic elements in his behaviour are rational and does his best to rationalize them. The psychotic can 'see' that any action has a symbolic meaning and that the conjunction of the elements is not fortuitous but has a meaning which is clear *to him*. This is possible provided he has severed all links with anything that shows the conjunction to be fortuitous and devoid of meaning, that is, in my terminology, unsaturated – a D category element. The premature saturation involved in this has the paradoxical effect that all acts are symbolic, and yet the patient is incapable of symbol formation in the way open to the normal personality who can allow his elements to remain unsaturated. Contact with reality is unwelcome because it tends not only to show that an element is unsaturated but also to saturate the element in ways that are painful to the personality. As all his 'symbols' have an obvious meaning they can hardly be regarded as symbols at all and nothing is left that can fulfil the function that symbols fill for the non-psychotic personality.

How does this differ from the state produced by the elimination of memory and desire?

First, I am advocating only a partial severance with reality. Second, it is a deliberate, conscious act of discipline. Third, it has a purpose that would appear to differ from the purpose of the psychotic manoeuvre. He wishes to destroy contact; I wish to establish it. Furthermore, he is primarily concerned with destruction of sensuous contact and its concomitant saturation, whereas I am anxious to diminish sensuous contact to bring psychic reality into focus. The psychotic fears and hates that result; it is an extension of reality.

The domain of personality is so extensive that it cannot be investigated with thoroughness. The power of psychoanalysis demonstrates to any practising psychoanalyst that adjectives like 'complete' or 'full' have no place in qualifying 'analysis'. The more nearly thorough the investigation, the clearer it becomes that however prolonged a psychoanalysis may be, it represents only the start of an investigation. It stimulates growth of the domain it investigates. This difficulty I mean to exploit in this way: if it is true that the proportion of the known to the unknown is so small at the *end* of analysis, it must be even smaller *during* analysis. Therefore to spend time on what has been discovered is to concentrate on an irrelevance. What matters is the unknown, and on this the psychoanalyst must focus his attention. Therefore 'memory' is a dwelling on the unimportant to the exclusion of the important. Similarly, 'desire' is an intrusion into the analyst's state of mind which covers up, disguises, and blinds him to the point at issue – that aspect of O that is currently presenting the unknown and unknowable though it is manifested to the two people present in its evolved character. This is the 'dark spot' that must be illuminated by 'blindness'. Memory and desire are 'illuminations' that destroy the value of the analyst's capacity for observation as a leakage of light into a camera might destroy the value of the film being exposed.

To consider objections to the elimination of memory: it may seem impossible to have a link with a patient without remembering who he or she is; but such recognition does not depend on memory, nor does psychoanalysis. It depends on a background of an experience the peculiarity of which I shall indicate by a series of approximations. We are familiar with the experience of *remembering* a dream; this must be contrasted with dreams that float into the mind unbidden and unsought and float away again as mysteriously. The emotional tone of this experience is not peculiar to the dream: thoughts also come unbidden, sharply, distinctly, with what appears to be unforgettable clarity, and then disappear leaving no trace by which they can be recaptured. I wish to reserve the term 'memory' for experience related to conscious attempts at recall – expressions of a fear that some elements, 'uncertainties, mysteries, doubts'[1] – will obtrude.

Dream-like memory is the memory of psychic reality and is the stuff of analysis. That which is related to a background of sensuous experience is not suitable to the phenomena of mental life which are shapeless, untouchable, invisible, odourless, tasteless. These psychically real (in the sense of belonging to psychic reality) elements are what the analyst has to work with.

It may appear that this contradicts the psychoanalytic theory of dreams unless it is remembered that the dream is the *evolution* of O where O has evolved sufficiently to be represented by sensuous experience. The sensuous elements of a psychotic dream do not represent anything. They *are* a sensuous experience.[2]

Anyone who has made careful notes of what he considers to be the facts of a session must be familiar with the experience in which such notes will, on occasion, seem to be drained of all reality: they might be notes of dreams made to ensure that he will not forget them on waking. To me it suggests that the experience of the session relates to material akin to the dream, not in the sense that dreams might be part of the preoccupation of the session but that the dream and the psychoanalyst's working material both share dream-like quality.

The *reality* of the psychic experience – the O in the human personality – is such that the more the analyst is in contact, the more real will be that part of it that he has been able to interpret. It will be clear to him that he is formulating only one aspect of a multi-dimensional experience, but what will dwell in his mind will be that multi-dimensional experience. Once he has interpreted it, that facet ceases to be of moment. He reads his notes with a sense of an emotional experience powerfully present in his mind, but it is of an experience of the as-yet-unknown. It is against this powerful sense that he reads the note of an event which ceased to be of importance once it was formulated; the attempt to remember or record destroys the capacity for, and interrupts the exercise of, observation of the psychoanalytically significant events.

---

[1]John Keats, 'Letter to George and Thomas Keats', 21 December 1817. [See Chapter 13. *Ed.*]

[2]The use of the sensuous experience to represent a psychic reality differentiates the neurotic dream and its symbolic quality from the psychotic dream.

Conversely, the sacrifice of memory and desire is conducive to the growth of dream-like 'memory' which is a part of the experience of psychoanalytic reality. The transformation of the emotional experience into mental growth of analyst and analysand contributes to the difficulty of both to 'remember' what took place; in so far as the experience contributes to growth, it ceases to be recognizable; if it does not become assimilated it adds to those elements that are remembered and forgotten. Desire obstructs the transformation from knowing and understanding, to being; that is to say, $K \rightarrow O$.

7

Container and contained

An advantage of believing that observations are the foundation of scientific method is that the conditions in which they are made can be stated and then produced. The simplicity of this has its appeal for the psychoanalyst: an analytic situation is presumed to exist and interpretations of the observations made in that situation are then reported. It is possible to believe that the analysis has a location in time and space: for example, the hours arranged for the sessions and the four walls of the consulting-room; that at such times and in such a place the analyst can make observations which he cannot do if the domain has not these limitations, or if 'psychoanalytic observations' do not conform to the conventional view of an observation. If I pictorialize the statement 'the conventional view of an observation' to be a container, like a sphere, and the 'psychoanalytic observation' as something that cannot be contained within it, I have a model that will do very well not only for the 'conventional view', to represent my feelings about a 'psychoanalytic situation', but also for the 'psychoanalysis' that it cannot contain. It will also serve as a model for my feelings about certain patients: I cannot observe Mr X because he will not remain 'inside' the analytic situation or even 'within' Mr X himself.

I have found theories of acting-out enlightening, but not enlightening enough; none of the theories known to me 'contains' the 'facts' by which I seek to be enlightened. My 'facts' gird against the framework of definition and theory which I seek to erect around them. The patient who is acting out cannot be 'contained' within existing formulations.

This is a characteristic of the mental domain: it cannot be contained within the framework of psychoanalytic theory. Is this a sign of defective theory, or a sign that psychoanalysts do not understand that psychoanalysis cannot be contained permanently within the definitions they use? It would be a valid observation to say that psychoanalysis cannot 'contain' the mental domain because it is not a 'container' but a 'probe'; the formulation that I have tried to further by using the symbols ♀ and ♂ minimizes this difficulty by leaving ♀ and ♂ as unknowns whose values are to be determined.

I would pursue this train of thought further by discussing something more practical and particular. It is a matter where action[1] seems to be called for, namely, the institutionalization of psychoanalysis comprising publication, selection, training, and qualification.

In recent years there has grown up the use of the term Establishment; it seems to refer to that body of persons in the State who may be expected usually to exercise power and responsibility by virtue of their social position, wealth, and intellectual and emotional endowment. (This list is not in order of priority of attainments). I propose to borrow this term to denote everything from the penumbra of associations generally evoked, to the predominating and ruling characteristics of an individual, and the characteristics of a ruling caste in a group (such as a psychoanalytic institute, or a nation or group of nations). Because of my choice of subject it will usually be used for talking about the ruling 'caste' in psychoanalytic institutes.

The Establishment has to find and provide a substitute for genius. One of its more controversial activities is to promulgate rules (known in religious activities as dogmas, in scientific groups as 'laws', e.g. of nature or perspective) for the benefit of those who are not by nature fitted to have direct experience of *being* psychoanalytic (or religious, or scientific, or artistic) so that they may, as it were by proxy, have and impart knowledge of psychoanalysis. Group members will not through incapacity be denied a sense of participation in an experience from which they would otherwise feel for ever excluded. At the same time these rules (or dogmas) must be such that they attract rather than repel, help rather than hinder, the membership of genius which is essential to the group's continued existence and vitality. A Freud can discover and establish psychoanalysis, but it must be maintained by a continued supply of 'genius'. This cannot be ordered; but if it comes the Establishment must be able to stand the shock. Failing

[1]I shall include psychoanalysis itself in the category of 'action' for reasons given under the heading of 'Language of achievement' in Chapter 13.

genius, and clearly it may not materialize for a very long period, the group must have its rules and a structure to preserve them. Thus an environment exists ready, as Nietzsche said of the nation, to fulfil its proper function, namely, to produce a genius. Similarly, it may be said of the individual that he should be ready to produce a 'flash of genius'. Let us therefore consider this phenomenon.

The term 'genius' does not carry the associations I want, so I propose to use the term 'mystic', leaving it to be supposed that the mystic has characteristics usually associated with genius, and that the person represented by the term 'genius' or 'mystic' may with equal propriety be described by the term 'messiah'.

The mystic is both creative and destructive. I make a distinction between two extremes that coexist in the same person. The extreme formulations represent two types: the 'creative' mystic, who formally claims to conform to or even fulfil the conventions of the Establishment that governs his group; and the mystic nihilist, who appears to destroy his own creations. I mean the terms to be used only when there is outstanding creativeness or destructiveness, and the terms 'mystic', 'genius', 'messiah' could be interchangeable.

The problem posed by the relationship between the mystic and the institution has an emotional pattern that repeats itself in history and in a variety of forms. The pattern may appear in the relationship of a new phenomenon to the formulation that has to represent it. It appears in the relationship of widely dissimilar groups to their mystics; it reveals itself in the history of the Christian heresies, the heliocentric theories, the relationship of the rabbinical directorate of the Kabbalah to revolutionary mystics such as Isaac Luria, the political reformer, and the Establishment.

My object is to show that certain elements in the development of psychoanalysis are not new or peculiar to analysis, but have in fact a history that suggests that they transcend barriers of race, time, and discipline, and are inherent in the relationship of the mystic to the group. The Establishment cannot be dispensed with (though this may appear to be approximately achieved in Sufism and in the theory of Marxism) because the institutionalized group, the Work group[1] is as essential to the development of the individual, including the mystic, as he is to it. Homeric psychology indicates a stage of mental

[1][See *Experiences in Groups and Other Papers*, in Volume IV. *Ed.*]

development in which the distinction between man and god is ill defined; in the individual psyche, little distinction between ego and superego is recognized. The Work group, under the religious vertex, must differentiate between man and god. Institutionalized religion must make man conscious of this gulf in himself and in the counterparts of himself in the group of which he is a member.

The institutionalization of psychoanalysis requires a psychoanalytic group which has 'Establishment' as one of its functions. It is itself a replica, in the external world, of an object in which the desired separation has been effected. But its function is then to effect this separation in the personalities of its members. It is thus both a model of a state that is desired, and an institution whose function it is to make the individual aware of the gap between himself (his idealized, superegoized self) and himself (his unregenerate, un-psychoanalysed self).

One result of separation is no direct access of the individual to the god with whom he used formerly to be on familiar terms. But the god has undergone a change as a part of the process of discrimination. The god with whom he was familiar was finite; the god from whom he is now separated is transcendent and infinite.

To restate the above in terms appropriate to a background of human experience: Freud and his associates mix on terms of equality such as exist between any human colleagues in a common venture. Freud, merely by being a person of outstanding stature, stimulates the tensions and emotional drives appropriate to a primitive group and stimulates them still further by his work. The primitive stages of the analytic group contribute to the obtrusion of tensions and emotional drives appropriate to the primitive group, as Freud observed through his study of the individual. I doubt that he appreciated the force of the messianic hopes aroused. The primitive stage makes way for the stage of discrimination described in the religious group: a distinction is made, otherwise there will not be recognition of the real distinction that exists between a mystic (in my sense) and ordinary human beings.

This distinction cannot be achieved adequately by saying that it is inseparable from idealization. Idealization in the group is a reality-based activity which is essential for the growth of discrimination in the individual. The individual himself must be able to distinguish between himself as an ordinary person and his view that he is omniscient and omnipotent. It is a step towards recognition of a distinction between the group as it really is and its idealization as an embodiment of the omnipotence of the individuals who compose it. Sometimes the separation fails and the group is not only seen to be ideally omnipotent and omniscient but believed to be so in actuality. The individual's realization of a gulf between his view of himself as omnipotent and his view of himself as an ordinary human being must be achieved as the result of a task of the group itself as well as in individual analysis. Otherwise there is a danger that a state of mind is transferred (by projective identification) to the group and *acted out* there – not altered. Some details of this situation must be described.

In the first stage there is no real confrontation between the god and the man because there is really no such distinction. In the second stage the infinite and transcendent god is confronted by the finite man. When the function of the group is to *establish* the separation there is no question of reunion. In the third stage the individual, or at least a particular individual – the mystic – needs to reassert a direct experience of god of which he has been, and is, deprived by the institutionalized group. Before I turn to this it is necessary to glance at some peculiarities of the group that has been institutionalized and of life in it.

The individuals show signs of their divine origin (just as the gods of the previous stage show signs of human origin). The individuals may be regarded as being incarnations of the deity; each individual retains an inalienable element which is a part of the deity himself that resides in the individual. He can be regarded as constantly attempting to achieve union with the deity, or he can be regarded as divine in a somewhat low-grade way. This last shows signs of being related genetically to the stage where no real distinction exists between god-like human beings on the one hand and very human gods on the other. Finally, the individual strives for reunion with the god from whom he feels consciously separated. This is reflected in the actualities of the human relationship and contributes to the hatred of the group for a state in which individuals cannot have direct access, or even a sense of direct access, to the great man (as they might once have had to Freud). Individuals cannot reconcile themselves to a discrimination that means conscious separation of themselves from a belief in their Freud-like qualities and recognition that Freud, a genius (mystic), no longer exists. Another Freud cannot be created no matter how essential he may be.

The group and mystic are essential to each other; it is therefore important to consider how or why the group can destroy the mystic on whom its future depends and how or why the mystic may destroy the group. I shall indicate the nature of the questions at issue since it is vital that the problem should be seen to exist. It is inherent both in the nature of man as a political animal and in the nature of psychoanalysis as the explosive force.

The relationship between group and mystic may belong to one of three categories. It may be commensal, symbiotic, or parasitic. The same categorization may be applied to the relationship of one group with another. I shall not trouble with the commensal relationship: the two sides coexist and the existence of each can be seen to be harmless to the other. In the symbiotic relationship there is a confrontation, and the result is growth-producing though that growth may not be discerned without some difficulty. In the parasitic relationship the product of the association is something that destroys both parties to the association. The realization that approximates most closely to my formulation is the group–individual setting dominated by envy. Envy begets envy, and this self-perpetuating emotion finally destroys host and parasite alike. The envy cannot be satisfactorily ascribed to one or other party; in fact it is a function of the relationship.

In a symbiotic relationship the group is capable of hostility and benevolence, and the mystic contribution is subject to close scrutiny. From this scrutiny the group grows in stature and the mystic likewise. In the parasitic association even friendliness is deadly. An easily seen example of this is the group's promotion of the individual to a position in the Establishment where his energies are deflected from his creative–destructive role and absorbed in administrative functions. His epitaph might be "He was loaded with honours and sank without a trace". Eissler (1965), without mentioning the general principle involved, shows the dangers of the invitation to group or individual to become respectable, to be medically qualified, to be a university department, to be a therapeutic group, to be anything in short, but *not* explosive. The reciprocal attitude in the mystic is that the group should thrive or disintegrate but must *not* be indifferent. The attitudes are not conscious and deliberate; they are essential. Without them the group is not a group, nor the 'mystic' a mystic. An analytic parallel is the psychoanalytic interpretation which is death to the existing state of mind, the state of mind that is being interpreted. Worse than being right or wrong is the failure of an interpretation to be significant, though to be significant is not enough; it merely ensures that it exists. It must also be true. The parasitic group can be primarily concerned to destroy the mystic, or mystic (messianic) ideas, but if it fails to do so it must 'establish' his or their truth.

Eissler discusses 'applied' psychoanalysis. I suspect that applied psychoanalysis, even if 'applied' to curing people, is a method of bringing psychoanalysis under control and rendering it harmless to the Establishment. I have expressed this in another context and in a different approach by a rule that the analyst should not permit himself to harbour desires, even the desire to cure, since to do so is inimical to psychoanalytic development. Development itself is not an object that can be 'desired'. The painful nature of the dilemma is essential.

The recurrent configuration is of an explosive force with a restraining framework. For example, the mystic in conflict with the Establishment; the new idea constrained within a formulation not intended to express it; the art form outmoded by new forces requiring representation.

It is essential that the language should be preserved. To this end, rules are produced under which words and definitions are to be used. The *Oxford Dictionary*, linguistic philosophy, mathematical logic, are tributes to the work that is incessantly proceeding for this purpose. On this work ordinary men and women with ordinary ability depend to do work that otherwise would be done only by exceptional people. Thanks to Faraday and other scientists ordinary people can illuminate a room by the touch of a switch; thanks to Freud and his co-workers ordinary people hope by psychoanalysis to be able to illuminate the mind. The fact that the world's work has to be done by ordinary people makes this work of scientification (or vulgarization, or simplification, or communication, or all together) imperative. There are not enough mystics, and those that there are must not be wasted.

The more successfully the word and its use can be 'established', the more its precision becomes an obstructive rigidity; the more imprecise it is, the more it is a stumbling-block to comprehension. The new idea 'explodes' the formulation designed to express it. Sometimes the emotion is powerful but the idea weak. If the formulation survives it can be repeated. If it can be repeated under severe conditions it becomes stronger until it communicates meaning without disintegration. Conversely, the formulation may destroy its content. In his play, *Major Barbara*, George Bernard Shaw describes the apotheosis of the dictum "No man is good enough to be another man's master" as a method of rendering the emotional content ineffectual.

It may be that the distinction between creative and nihilistic mystic is no more than a temporary expedient depending on the need to express one view of the mystic rather than the other. The most powerful emotional explosion known so far, spreading to many cultures and over many centuries, has been that produced by the formulations of Jesus. The effects are still felt and present grave problems of containment even now, though some measure of control has been established. Jesus at first expressly disavowed any aim other than fulfilment of the laws of his group. The rabbinical directorate failed to solve the problem of containment, a failure associated with disastrous consequences for the Jewish group. The disaster attributed to Christian teachings did not terminate at any finite point, as for example at the crucifixion; after Alaric had sacked Rome, four hundred years later, Saint Augustine felt the reproaches against the Christians to be sufficiently serious to require refutation in his *City of God*.

The problems of mystical revelation that centre on having, or claiming to have, a direct relationship with the deity remain. The need for the Establishment to do what the rabbinical directorate had failed to do soon became evident. Complaints by the disciples that miracles were being done by unauthorized or, as we might say, 'lay', people, suggest awareness that we expect to find associated with an Establishment. That, and evidence of a need to establish a structured hierarchy ('who shall sit at the right hand'), is too slender to be more than a starting-point for conjecture. Something must have contributed to the efflorescence of structure, hierarchy, and institution. The institution is evidence of the need for the function that the rabbinical directorate had failed to provide. Although in many respects the Church was more successful, the long history of heresy (see Knox, 1950) shows that the structure required to contain the teaching of Jesus was, and still is, subjected to a great strain. It has not, however, been without its successes, and even today complaints can be heard, which are really a tribute to the success of the institutionalizing process, of the lack of enthusiasm, drive, and 'spirituality' of the Church.

Though we may contrast the success of the Church favourably with the failure of the rabbinical directorate, the force of the mystical revelation has not yet spent itself. There are signs that the Oedipus myth, and the elements that in the Christian religion touch on paternity and sonship, both have a configuration suggesting an underlying group of which these elements are representative. I have used the sign O to denote this 'ultimate reality'. Any formulation felt to approximate to illumination of O is certain to produce an institutionalizing reaction. The institution may flourish at the expense of the mystic or idea, or it may be so feeble that it fails to contain the mystical revelation.

A formulation may approximate to 'illumination' of O. Many mystics express their experience of direct access to the deity in terms of light, but light is not the only model used. Jewish mystics in particular find the voice a telling representation of the experience. Saint Paul found light *and* voice necessary to represent the experience. It is significant that psychoanalysts seeking direct access to an aspect of O, though it is not only to that part of O that informs god-like characteristics, conduct their affairs through language. To be confined to one medium of communication only is too restrictive even if it has the flexibility and capacity for development of language. Psychoanalytic observation certainly cannot afford to be confined to perception of what is verbalized only: what of more primitive uses of the tongue?

The suspension of memory and desire promotes exercise of aspects of the psyche that have no background of sensuous experiences. Paradoxically, the release of these aspects of the psyche enables them to reveal elements such as the non-verbal muscular movements of the tongue, as in stammer. The dominance of sensuous experience promotes expressions such as 'seeing' or 'hearing'; the falseness introduced by such formulation contributes to those differences that seem so significant but are in fact unimportant. Intuitive power cannot develop because it is hindered by such obtrusions of 'sense'. The institutionalizing of words, religions, psychoanalysis, – all are special instances of institutionalizing memory so that it may 'contain' the mystic revelation and its creative and destructive force. The function of the group is to produce a genius; the function of the Establishment is to take up and absorb the consequences so that the group is not destroyed.

8

Vertices: evolution

Some psychoanalytic tensions appear in a simpler, less disguised form if we use as a model the impact of the thought of Jesus on the Jewish group and on later religious institutions. The stress on miracles of healing represented an urge to 'medicalize' the institution intended to serve the teaching of Jesus. Healing retains its dominance in Christian Science, Lourdes, faith-healing. An example in the early Christian group of a problem of institutionalizing is the query put to Jesus by the disciples who wanted to have a ruling on recognition of those who cast out devils in Jesus's name. His attitude appears to have been against rigid qualification for membership of the group – 'those that are not against me are for me'. Although this reply cannot now be interpreted with sureness and may have been referable to the favourable (for Christianity) effect of turpitude in the opponents of Christianity, it shows the recurrent configuration of the problem of selection (lay versus professional, or out-group versus in-group). These conjectures illustrate the configuration to which I want to draw attention.

Psychoanalysis cannot escape ideas of cure, treatment, illness, in psychoanalysts and patients alike. Eissler warns against a structure that is too rigid and too limited to permit development. At the opposite extreme the Sufis have no rigid institution yet have endured; their solution would open the way for an 'expanding universe' of psychoanalysis but it would not be long before members of the psychoanalytic movement could not understand each other.

The importance of unconscious motivation has tended to screen the importance of conscious motivation. An analyst or a particular group of analysts may stress a medical view possessing, in my terms, a common vertex; an observer of the group would expect to find that its vertex is recognized by certain invariants such as ideas of disease, treatment, prognosis, pathology, and cure. The unconscious counterparts of such a vertex will have been laid bare in the psychoanalysis of the individuals, but this should not blind us to the conscious aspects of this vertex.

Suppose a group in whom the need or desire to make money is obtrusive. The unconscious counterpart of this will likewise have been laid bare in the analysis of the individuals. The greater the need or the 'desire', the easier it would be to detect a particular application of psychoanalytic theory (what Eissler calls 'applied' psychoanalysis as opposed to 'anthropic').

Other groups may display similarly obtrusive vertices: a wish for power, influence, propaganda, education, research, or poverty. It is evident that, in our present stage of development, if we achieve 'psychoanalytic' psychoanalysis, the vertex of the group will make a difference to the findings of the group. So far, analysts have seemed to act on the assumption that motives should be analysed and may, therefore, be safely left without further consideration. This view ignores the varieties of development opened up by the analytic experience.

The oedipal situation, or its even more primitive roots, would have a different configuration according to whether the vertex of the group was psychoanalytic, religious, financial, legal, or some other. This itself increases the variety of experiences opened up within the limits of even rigid psychoanalysis. The messianic expectation, formulated and institutionalized in the Christian religion, may represent the evolved aspect of an element which is represented also at its evolved stage by the Oedipus myth.

Similarities in the configurations suggest a common origin and common disorders associated with the problem of containing the mystic and institutionalizing his work. The emotional impact of ♀♂ will be proportionately greater the more closely it is related to the forces represented by the messianic hope, the Oedipus myth, the Babel myth, and the Eden myth; the greater the emotional impulse the greater the problem. These myths are evolved states of O and *represent* the evolution of O. They represent the state of mind achieved by the human being at his intersection with the evolving O.

Where Eissler speaks of applied psychoanalysis I shall speak of psychoanalysis conducted from a particular vertex. If an analyst or group of analysts regards the making of money as an essential part of psychoanalytic practice, that is to say that they regard it as an essential part of practice which is an equally essential part of cure, then I think that the vertex should be described as money-making, and the discoveries that are made in such analysis will bear the stamp of the financial vertex.

If the vertex is religious I should expect the discoveries to bear the stamp of that vertex. In time, the configurations associated with the various vertices would evolve to a point where they could be formulated. I should then expect the rigidity conferred by the formulation to be resisted by the fluidity of the O represented by the formulation. Just as there is at present an unbridged gap between the animate and the inanimate, which makes the transformation of the inanimate into the animate impossible, so there is a gap between the formulation of the configuration and the underlying realization approximating to it. The configuration that represents the relationship between the mystic and the institution can be recognized in, and be the representation of, the relationship between the emotional experience and the representative formulation (words, music, painting, etc.) designed to contain it. The same configuration can be seen in the relationship between the Dionysian emotional experience and the Apollonian representation. Direct access to the O of the mystic and the O of the Dionysian orgy is both contained and restrained by the religious dogmas substituted for them in the minds of 'ordinary' people.

Most analysts have felt at some time that the 'universe of discussion' in psychoanalysis is expanding so fast that we no longer maintain what a soldier calls 'lateral communication'. To take one instance about which I am able to have an opinion: the gap between what some regard as analysis and what I, as a Kleinian, regard as analysis is very wide and widening. This is attributed to differences in theory. I do not believe that what separates scientists is their difference in theory. I have not always felt 'separated' from someone who differs from me in the theories he holds; that does not seem to me to afford a standard of measurement by which the gap can be measured. Conversely, I have felt very far separated from some who, apparently, hold the same theories. Therefore, if the 'gap' is to be 'measured' it will have to be in some domain other than that of theory. The differences in theory are symptoms of differences in vertex and not a measure of the differences.

9

Ultimate reality

So far this book has been concerned with the formulation of a theory, the few 'facts' mentioned being illustrative models intended to give body to what might otherwise be an exercise in the manipulation of abstractions. It leads up to the formulation of a theory which has as its realization a background of psychoanalytic practice. The theory formulates a recurrent pattern of emotional experience of wide distribution. It does not replace any existing psychoanalytic theory, but is intended to display relationships which have not been remarked.

However thorough an analysis is, the person undergoing it will be only partially revealed; at any point in the analysis the proportion of what is known to what is unknown is small. Therefore the dominant feature of a session is the unknown personality and not what the analysand or analyst thinks he knows.

All psychoanalytic progress exposes a need for further investigation. There is a 'thing-in-itself', which can never be known; by contrast, the religious mystic claims direct access to the deity with whom he aspires to be at one. Since this experience is often expressed in terms that I find useful to borrow, I shall do so, but with a difference that brings them closer to my purpose. The penumbra of associations is intended to help those who look for my meaning.

In any object, material or immaterial, resides the unknowable ultimate reality, the 'thing-in-itself'. Objects have emanations or emergent qualities or evolving characteristics that impinge upon the human personality as phenomena. Of these qualities the personality may be consciously or unconsciously aware; they differ from the ultimate reality.

'Ultimate reality' is a term with a penumbra of associations, which makes it psychologically helpful, but this fact makes it unsuitable to represent something that by definition is unknowable. The same objection applies to the term 'godhead'. Meister Eckhart expresses his sense that the godhead evolves to a point where it becomes apprehensible by man as the Trinity.

By contrast the godhead is formless and infinite. Milton expresses a similar idea in the description of the world of waters dark and deep which has been "won from the void and formless infinite", though here the emphasis is less on the evolution characteristic of the godhead, and more on the capacity of the apprehending object to apprehend.

The religious approach postulates an emanation of the deity and an incarnation of the deity. Both formulations are needed to represent states of mind in which there is an interaction between states of an object that is sometimes whole, sometimes split into fragments dispersed within a multiplicity of objects. For the analyst, the doctrine of the incarnation yields the rewarding model, so I shall concentrate on it first.

The psychoanalyst witnesses the behaviour of a being who is usually, but not always, lying on a couch and talking. The analyst may take in the scene as a whole or any part of it. 'Whole' or 'part' is an aspect of an ultimate reality that has evolved until it intersects the personality of the observer (see Chapter 3 above).

The scientific approach, associated with a background of sense impressions, for example the presence of the psychoanalyst and his patient in the same room, may be regarded as having a base. In so far as it is associated with the ultimate reality of the personality, O, it is baseless. This does not mean that the psychoanalytic method is unscientific, but that the term 'science', as it has been commonly used hitherto to describe an attitude to objects of sense, is not adequate to represent an approach to those realities with which 'psychoanalytic science' has to deal. Nor is it adequate to represent that aspect of the human personality that is concerned with the unknown and ultimately unknowable – with O.

The criticism applies to every vertex, be it musical, religious, aesthetic, political; all are inadequate when related to O because, with the possible exception of the religion of the mystic, these and similar vertices are not adapted to the sensually baseless. The realities with which psychoanalysis deals (for example fear, panic, love, anxiety, passion) have no sensuous background, though there *is* a sensuous background (respiratory rate, pain, touch, etc.) that is often identified with them and then treated, supposedly scientifically. What is required is not a base for psychoanalysis and its theories, but a science that is not restricted by its genesis in knowledge and sensuous background; it must be a science of at-one-ment. It must have a mathematics of at-one-ment, not identification. There can be no geometry of 'similar', 'identical', 'equal'; only of analogy.

The Platonic theory of Forms and the Christian dogma of the Incarnation imply absolute essence which I wish to postulate as a universal quality of phenomena such as 'panic', 'anxiety', 'fear', 'love'. In brief, I use O to represent this central feature of every situation that the psychoanalyst has to meet. With this he must be at one; with the *evolution* of this he must identify so that he can formulate it in an interpretation. Certain states of mind obstruct this and of them I shall say more later.

An aspect of O that evolves is signified by number. Participating in the evolution can be the object, which may multiply or decrease, and the observer, who feels that the object multiplies or decreases. Ignoring the object so as to discuss only the observer, one may say that he *feels* that the object increases or decreases. The constant conjunction signified by number excites curiosity to know which, what, when, why, or how. 'The need to know' (whether the change (±) is in the objects observed or in the 'feeling') may be activated. The 'number' is assumed to relate to an aspect of the object observed, but it may with equal propriety be regarded as relating to the feeling. I shall be discussing mostly the 'number' as being the name of the feeling, but to avoid confusion I shall distinguish between, say, R3 (external reality) and Ψ3 (psychic reality), the latter being the sign for a feeling of 'threeness' which may or may not be contemporaneous with 'threeness' as an aspect of the observed object.

When I speak of 'number' in the context of feelings, the term has too many associations for my purpose. I shall therefore use (ξ), denoting a 'mathematical object'[1] as the name of a 'feeling'.

The following illustrations, taken from religion, politics, conversational intercourse, and so on, may act as an introduction to 'psychic' mathematics:

---

[1]Borrowed from Frege (1950).

'The majority of people . . .'
'Thousands (millions) all over the world . . .'
'The Trinity'
'Four or five people . . .'
'For weeks (months, years) they waited for . . .'

In these examples, numbers, used to represent a feeling in the observer, may be categorized in accordance with the principles of the Grid as intended to evoke curiosity (category 4) or as a barrier against statements that might evoke a psychological disturbance (category 2).

These 'numbers' have been transformed from $\Psi(\xi)$ to $R(\xi)$, so that they represent realizations which approximate to them. These realizations can become extremely complex. Thus Euclidean geometry has been regarded as a representation to which space, as ordinary people know it, is the approximate realization. Euclidean geometry then becomes the background realization that approximates to axiomatic algebra, which represents *it*.

Axiomatic algebra appears to be entirely independent of its sensuous background and can be developed accordingly; on the theory developed here, although it may start by representing feelings that provide the background, axiomatic algebra, the example I have taken, becomes entirely independent of that background of feelings. The H formulations (Grid category) begin to lack 'body'. What does it mean that these formulations lose 'body', cease to represent a 'feeling'? The number 'three' or 'ten' can easily represent a 'feeling' that there are three or ten objects present. The names three and ten do not seem to represent constant conjunctions in the way that 'cat' does. 'Cat' has a sensuous background; so has $R(\xi)$; but $\Psi(\xi)$ has not unless we reverse a process of transformation through Euclidean geometry back to ordinary space.

Non-sensuous phenomena form the totality of what is commonly regarded as mental or spiritual experience. $\Psi(\xi)$, which represents non-sensuous realizations, seems to be relatively easily adapted for manipulations to represent *sensuous* realizations, but not for manipulations to represent non-sensuous realizations. If 'three' represents a nonsensuous realization of 'threeness', why can it not, in combination with 'ten', 'five', etc., be made to represent anxiety or love or hate?

Certain problems may be handled by mathematics, others by economics, others by religion. It should be possible to transfer a problem that fails to yield to the discipline to which it appears to belong to a discipline that *can* handle it. If Euclidean geometry cannot handle multi-dimensional problems they may be transferred to algebraic geometry. In this way certain problems may be transferred within their own discipline so that their solution can be attempted. The mathematics evolved by the manipulation of 'numbers' has so far proved very successful in matching the formulation with the realization it represents. But the numbers representing feelings have not evolved so that they can handle the realizations of the domain from which they appear to have sprung.

Before we consider the transference of problems from one discipline to another, or of the procedures proper to one discipline to procedures proper to another discipline, we shall examine the peculiarities of catastrophic change.

10

Visual images and invariants

From the material discussed it should now be possible to detect a pattern that remains unaltered in apparently widely differing contexts. It would be useful to isolate and formulate the invariants of that pattern so that it could be communicated.

Freud's formulations do just that. Thinking, developed through psychoanalysis, has led to discoveries that were not made by Freud, but that reveal configurations resembling those in discoveries he *did* make. Can his formulations be replaced by others that reveal as nearly as possible *all* the configurations that are similar and not merely those instances that his formulations were intended to illuminate?

If his Oedipus theory is used in conjunction with the Eden myth, the Babel myth, and a version of messianic expectation, it can continue to illuminate the mind's workings as it does now and to display elements of an underlying configuration that widen significantly the area illuminated. The deity's hostility to curiosity remarked by Milton's Satan (Book IV, *Paradise Lost*) can be matched in Babel by the attack on speech (the infliction of confusion of tongues); in Oedipus by Tiresias and his warning; in the messianic story by the attack on the son by the father. The same pattern is reflected in the self-inflicted punishments of the Sphinx and Oedipus. Each version emphasizes a different facet; together they suggest a common configuration. The attempt to differentiate emotional elements is curiously unsuccessful. Thus 'omnipotent good', 'evil', 'pursuit of knowledge through curiosity', 'impending disaster', 'arrogance', and so on, each attempt seems to weaken the impact that the elements have when they are part of the narrative as a whole; they undergo a transformation similar to that undergone by the dream upon being consciously recalled, or by a work of art when it is replaced by a reproduction. The transformation depends on a change of vertex. The vertex of the myth-maker is not mine as I attempt this reformulation; the vertex of the dreamer is not that of the dreamer awake; the vertex of the artist is not that of the interpreter of the work of art. Similarly, the vertex of the psycho-analyst, and changes of vertex corresponding to moment-to-moment changes in a session, effect the transformations made manifest in associations and interpretations.

First, there must be a difference of vertex to make correlation possible. It must ultimately take place in the individual. (For the moment I assume that correlation is a necessary part of confrontation and that confrontation is a necessary part of analysis.) Schizophrenic defences are mobilized against confrontation; violence makes confrontation impossible because both sides of a confrontation are annihilated.

Second, the vertex must not be too distant or too near, otherwise correlation becomes impossible. How is 'distance' measured between the vertex of the analysand and the vertex of the analyst? If the analyst wants to make a living and the analysand wants to be 'cured', how is the 'distance' between these vertices to be 'measured'? A man and a woman can have such different outlooks that their temperaments are described as incompatible; or views so similar that they cannot stimulate each other. Is there any sense in which their views can be so 'far apart' that the distance can be 'measured', that a phrase used metaphorically can be treated so that the metaphorical sense is replaced by a literal sense?

Under this vertex the views of patient and analyst are separated; the 'gap' separating them is bridged by something that I call linear or planar, or a line or film. Very different is the gap that is bridged by a relationship between container and contained. The following will serve as a model for a theoretical formulation of this kind of link: a man speaking of an emotional experience in which he was closely involved began to stammer badly as the memory became increasingly vivid to him. The aspects of the model that are significant are these: the man was trying to contain his experience in a form of words; he was trying to contain himself, as one sometimes says of someone about to lose control of himself; he was trying to 'contain' his emotions within a form of words, as one might speak of a general attempting to 'contain' enemy forces within a given zone.

The words that should have represented the meaning the man wanted to express were fragmented by the emotional forces to which he wished to give only verbal expression; the verbal formulation could not 'contain' his emotions, which broke through and dispersed it as enemy forces might break through the forces that strove to contain them.

The stammerer, in his attempt to avoid the contingency I have described, resorted to modes of expression so boring that they failed to express the meaning he wished to convey; he was thus no nearer to his goal. His verbal formulation could be described as like the military forces that are worn by the attrition to which they are subjected by the contained forces. The meaning he was striving to express was denuded of meaning. His attempt to use his tongue for verbal expression failed to 'contain' his wish to use his tongue for masturbatory movement in his mouth.

Sometimes the stammerer could be reduced to silence. This situation can be represented by a visual image of a man who talked so much that any meaning he wished to express was drowned by his flood of words.

I hope that I have conveyed my meaning to the reader by virtue of the verbal transformations of visual images. However, the communication is not satisfactory; the visual images are too concrete to be suitable for expressing the relationship of the mystic to the group; they are too evocative of a penumbra of associations which they already carry. In short, the situation is similar to that of the stammerer whose words, or lack of them, contain rather than communicate his meaning. Alternatively, the meaning is too powerful for the verbal formulation; the expression is lost in an 'explosion' in which the verbal formulation is destroyed.

To consider the essentials: the communication is about a relationship between meaning and its expression, between emotion and its expression. But I am aware that it is not a relationship between any 'things'; it is a pattern of relationships in the way that mathematicians speak of mathematics as expressing relationships. I have in the past used the symbols ♀ and ♂ to express a relationship between container and contained; for the present I shall continue to do so.

The theory is that an object is placed into a container in such a way that either the container or the contained object is destroyed. In pictorial terms the container is represented by a mouth or vagina, the contained by breast or penis. The relationship between these objects, which I shall represent by the male and female signs ♂ and ♀, may be commensal, symbiotic, or parasitic.

By 'commensal' I mean a relationship in which two objects share a third to the advantage of all three. By 'symbiotic' I understand a relationship in which one depends on another to mutual advantage. By 'parasitic' I mean to represent a relationship in which one depends on another to produce a third, which is destructive of all three.

Take another simple visual model: a man wishing to communicate his annoyance is so overwhelmed by emotion that he stammers and becomes incoherent. The invariants under the theory I wish to formulate are the forms of speech that the man uses to convey his meaning; these I regard as being intended to 'contain' what he has to say and therefore to correspond to the sign ♀. The annoyance he strives to communicate I regard as being what should be contained in his speech, and therefore it is appropriately represented by ♂. If the man remained coherent, this could correspond to an overwhelming of the content by the container: his speech would in this case be so restrained that it could not express his feelings. But suppose he expressed himself 'perfectly':

one could then imagine that his emotions had served to develop his ability for well-chosen speech and that his capacity for speech had helped his emotional development. This contrasts with development leading to incoherence. Such a failure is the outcome of a 'parasitic' relationship between the contained (or rather, *not* contained) material and the speech devised to contain it: 'container' and 'contained' have produced a third 'object' – incoherence – which makes expression, and the means of expression, impossible. In so far as the imaginary episode led to a development of powers of expression and of the personality that strove to express itself, the relationship could be described as symbiotic. 'Commensal' is illustrated by supposing that the episode occurred in an age and society (as in Elizabethan England) in which language had reached a point of development where the ordinary man was inspired to speak it well: that which was to be expressed and the vehicle for its expression profited from the culture to which they belonged.

11

Lies and the thinker

The distinction between truth and lie constantly confronts the psychoanalyst who has to apply, in a rough and ready practical way, ideas that have been the centre of discussion over the centuries, but the rough and ready application may be too crude to do the work required of it. The analyst seeks ideas sufficiently accurate and robust to survive the emotional storms they should illuminate.

To the problems of understanding the psychoanalyst can bring something that is unknown to the philosopher of science because he has experience of the dynamics of *misunderstanding;* he is concerned *practically* with a problem that the philosopher approaches *theoretically*. Investigations of understanding and misunderstanding impinge on problems associated with truth and untruth. The reality of the problem becomes apparent when the analyst must ask himself, can a liar be psychoanalysed?

The problem can be formulated in Grid terms without moral overtones. Category 2 (reserved for formulations known by the initiator to be false, but maintained as a barrier against statements that lead to a psychological upheaval), would seem provisionally to offer a home to the lie. Such a categorization supposes that an experience has been permitted to continue to a point where the patient thinks he knows his formulation to be untrue; but is it true that he maintains it because it would be disturbing to his development not to do so? The lie could be uttered because in the view of the liar it would be profitable to him or injurious to another: is it correct in such a case to say it would be true, and if true significant, that inability to profit himself or injure another would lead to his having a psychological upheaval?

As I think it would be true, I must indicate why and in what way it is reasonable to categorize the lie in 2. I am concerned with patients who come for analysis – not with those who do not. It is clear to such a patient that he risks exposure of the lie; he must either have great confidence in his capacity (or lack of it in the analyst) or feel some dissatisfaction with the lie. However these are random conjectures,, and beg the question at issue, which must be answered in the course of an analysis, the very practicability of which is under debate. The extreme case would seem to offer the best chance of being able to observe the essential characteristics, or, as I prefer to call them, the invariants, of the liar. Present considerations make it unlikely that the psychoanalyst would treat such a case by choice. The supposition that he was going to cure such a patient would lead him to hesitate about accepting him. Therefore the probability is that the lying is so well concealed that he stumbles into such a collaboration unwittingly. This makes it possible that the same may be true of the patient; so at the outset one must be prepared to find that the supposition that the patient thinks he risks exposure, or minds it if he does, is not in fact the case.

The need for a category for statements known by the patient to be untrue arises when, for example, a patient, who has been shown in the course of analysis that there are a number of explanations of the fact that he is late, continues to repeat apologies. The analyst is challenged to accept them, at the risk of showing himself unmindful of the truth, or to reject them and assume the role of being the patient's conscience. A statement may be made not to mislead but to fill the function of evocation. Thus a lying report may be evocative or provocative, accusatory or defensive, to name only a few of the more obvious uses. In such a case, 2 is not the correct category because the statement is intended to lead to emotional upheaval. In short, the lying statement is not category 2 but category 6; its nature must be indicated by some usage such as minus L (–L) or minus K (–K).

The term 'lie' thus has limited value for use in the course of analysis. It focuses attention on something that is not invariant; on the other hand, –L or –K, together with the appropriate Grid category, leaves it open to saturation by appropriate 'meanings', should approximate realizations present themselves to the analyst and analysand.

If we suppose now that the emotional upheaval against which the lie is mobilized is identical with catastrophic change, it becomes easier to understand why investigation uncovers an ambiguous position which is capable of arousing strong feelings. These feelings relate to an outraged moral system; their strength derives from risk of change in the psyche. As the episode that I describe occurs frequently and can be resolved only in a way that seems to set the pattern for the resolution of subsequent recurrences, it is necessary to dwell on certain features which have an importance that may escape notice.

The patient can be seen to make a decision between the lie and the truth. The frequency with which this 'decision' is automatically made in favour of the statement known to be untrue will determine the nature of the case. I focus attention on the position that now arises for the analyst.

By definition and by the tradition of all scientific discipline, the psychoanalytic movement is committed to the truth as the central aim. If the patient constantly formulates –L and –K statements, he and the analyst are, in theory at least, in conflict. In practice, however, the situation does not present itself so simply. The patient, especially if intelligent and sophisticated, offers every inducement to bring the analyst to interpretations that leave the defence intact and, ultimately, to acceptance of the lie as a working principle of superior efficacy. In the last resort he will make consistent progress towards a 'cure' which will be flattering to analyst and patient alike. The alternative he offers is bleak: progressive deterioration, loss of mutual esteem both private and public, hostility, and, in extreme cases, threats of legal action. Against this the analyst has to balance a hope of retaining his integrity.

Some forms of lying appear to be closely related to experiencing desire. Long stories, with every appearance of truth, are spun out extempore as if the virtuosity of the exercise gave pleasure. One would expect such fabrications to be idealizations, and some are, but the liar's state of mind is not ordinary and the divergence from the usual is screened by the plausibility of his lies. They are usually C category formulations and may present more difficulty to an analyst whose mind is built on sensuous experience than to one who is used to discounting memory. As the problems of the psychoanalysis of the liar differ so much from those of the psychoanalysis of one whose outlook is scientific, it is worth considering shortly what is meant by the scientific approach. In ordinary speech it is taken to mean an assumption that the truth is of overriding importance and that reason should be harnessed to its elucidation. As a preliminary to attempting a more sophisticated formulation, the opposite view may be stated in terms of fable, thus:

> The liars showed courage and resolution in their opposition to the scientists who with their pernicious doctrines bid fair to strip every shred of self-deception from their dupes, leaving them without any of the natural protection necessary for the preservation of their mental health against the impact of truth. Some, knowing full well the risks that they ran, nevertheless laid down their lives in affirmations of lies so that the weak and doubtful would be convinced, by the ardour of their conviction, of the truth of even the most preposterous statements. It is not too much to say that the human race owes its salvation to that small band of gifted liars who were prepared even in the face of indubitable facts to maintain the truth of their falsehoods. Even death was denied and the most ingenious arguments were educed to support obviously ridiculous statements that the dead lived on in bliss. These martyrs to untruth were often of humble origin whose very names have perished. But for them, and the witness borne by their obvious sincerity, the sanity of the race must have perished under the load placed on it. By laying down their lives they carried the morals of the world on their shoulders. Their lives and the lives of their followers were devoted to the elaboration of systems of great intricacy and beauty in which the logical structure was preserved by the exercise of a powerful intellect and faultless reasoning. By contrast the feeble processes by which the scientists again and again attempted to support their hypotheses made it easy for the liars to show the hollowness of the pretensions of the upstarts and thus to delay, if not to prevent, the spread of doctrines whose effect could only have been to induce a sense of helplessness and unimportance in the liars and their beneficiaries.

It is not necessary to elaborate this phantasy further; this sample should indicate the vertex I wish to establish but, in so far as it does so, it throws up difficulties. It is easy to imagine that there are such things as facts independent of the mind. A belief that led a man to throw himself off a cliff in confidence that his capacity to fly would preserve him from injury would contribute to his injury because the reality of his belief, the O of his belief, is, from the vertex of survival, of less consequence than the O of throwing himself from a cliff. But O, without such a vertex, is an absolute, inhering in ('incarnate' in) everything and unknowable by man. The belief that he would fly off uninjured can be compared with the belief that he would break his neck. Depending on the vertex, the two beliefs can be regarded as valuable and precedence accorded to one of them. But to what scale of values is the value of the belief related? Ruskin defined 'valuable' as life-giving. This may do, in that the oedipal theory and primal scene afford a link (as does the theorem of Pythagoras, by the use of Cartesian co-ordinates, for the conversion of geometry to algebraic formulation) between life instincts and death instincts, and that which is valuable or life-giving and its opposite.

If value is to be the criterion, difficulty arises because there is no *absolute* value: the individual does not necessarily believe it is better to create than to destroy; a suicidal patient may seem to embrace the opposite view.

The determination of the system of beliefs, the vertices, aims, complaints, and 'cures', is often mistaken by the patient for an attempt to establish a correct system. The investigation of category 2 is to see in what respect its pains compare with those of other systems and in what way the relationships differ. Such insights laid at the disposal of the patient seem to give him the opportunity to correct errors. The contemplation of various systems enables the analyst to reconsider and correct his own system. Category 2 involves conflict with impressions of reality; sometimes these may not matter, but beyond a certain point the conflict between the need to know and the need to deny becomes acute and may usher in attacks on linking to stop stimulation which leads to conflict. But this presupposes an aim on the part of the liar, and therefore a pattern that can be detected. This is not the case with some liars. Hence it is not possible to rely on picking up a symptom, such as a wish to please the analyst, that will betray the pattern.

For satisfaction, the liar needs an audience; this makes him vulnerable, since his audience must set a value on his fabrications. It is therefore necessary that the analyst-victim should attach importance to the patient's statements as formulations of a truth. It must be possible to observe incoherent elements and to detect a pattern that brings together the disparate elements, showing a coherence and a meaning that they did not have without it. So far, this description does not differ from that of the transformation from the paranoid-schizoid to the depressive position; it is superior to a narrative formulation which betrays the lying element of the story only by the weakness of the causative links. The Ps ⇌ D reaction reveals a whole situation which seems to belong to a reality that pre-exists the individual who has discovered it. The lying discovery lacks the spontaneous bleakness of the genuine Ps ⇌ D. The lie requires a thinker to think. The truth, or true thought, does not require a thinker – he is not logically necessary.

Provisionally, we may consider that the difference between a true thought and a lie consists in the fact that a thinker is logically necessary for the lie but not for the true thought. Nobody need think the true thought: it awaits the advent of the thinker who achieves significance through the true thought. The lie and its thinker are inseparable; the thinker is of no consequence to the truth, but the truth is logically necessary to the thinker. His significance depends on whether or not he will entertain the thought, but the thought remains unaltered.

In contrast, the lie gains existence by virtue of the epistemologically prior existence of the liar. The only thoughts to which a thinker is absolutely essential are lies. Descartes's tacit assumption that thoughts presuppose a thinker is valid only for the lie.

The paranoid-schizoid state may then be seen as peculiar to the thinker who is in a state of persecution by thoughts that belong to a non-human system, the O domain. The O domain may be said to be, *vis-à-vis* the thinker, in a state of evolution. This evolving system intersects with the personality of the individual thinker. The impact of the evolving O domain on the domain of the thinker is signalized by persecutory feelings of the paranoid-schizoid position. Whether the thoughts are entertained or not is of significance to the thinker but not to the truth. If entertained, they are conducive to mental health; if not, they initiate disturbance. The lie depends on the thinker and gains significance through him; it is the link between host and parasite in the parasitic relationship.

The relationship between the lie, the thought, the thinker, and the group is complex. The thinker may express the truth in a lying group; the group may not want its ideas disturbed and will be dominated by category 2 mechanisms and formulations. The relationship between such a group and such a thinker will be one of envy and hate. If the thinker is expressing lies, the relationship of the thinker to his lies will be parasitic, and lies and thinker will destroy each other. If the lie is of the 'sun rises at dawn' type, the relationship between lie and thinker is commensal – such a thought *requires* a thinker and the thinker is essential. But the relationship, at least in our present age, is commensal. The thought that the world will endure may be a lie but it may be essential to keep at bay ideas that the world is on the verge of coming to an end. Such a relationship between lie and thinker is symbiotic.

The link between one mind and another that leads to destruction of both is the lie. The term 'link' gives an inadequate idea of the realization it is intended to represent. The lie is not restricted to the domain of thought, as the word 'lie' would ordinarily imply, but has its counterpart in the domain of being; it is possible to *be* a lie and being so precludes at-one-ment in O.

In psychoanalysis the liar is a significant fact and gains significance from the lying nature of what he says. The parasitic relationship between liar and environment, corresponding to the parasitic relationship between the thinker and the lie, denudes the environment of significance. The analyst who accepts such lies is acting as host; if he does not, he contributes to the feelings of persecution by 'being' an unthought thought, a thought without a thinker. The thought to which a thinker is not necessary is also a thought that the thinker would not regard as likely to contribute to *his* significance. On the contrary, once he has expressed a truth the thinker is redundant.

To summarize, I formulate two definitions:

1. True thought requires neither formulation nor thinker.
2. The lie is a thought to which a formulation and a thinker are essential.

The lie is peculiar to a relationship between the host mind and the parasitic mind and destroys both. The thinker can harbour thoughts if he does not need thoughts to contribute to his significance, and can tolerate thoughts that do not do so. If essential to the thought, the thinker conflicts with other thinkers who feel themselves to be essential to the thought. The envy, jealousy, and possessiveness aroused are the mental counterparts of toxic elements in physical parasitism.

They contribute to the destructive nature of the culture that develops from the development of the lie. The need for each individual to claim his contribution to the thought as unique and essential, differentiates the emotional climate from that in which the inevitability of the thought and the unimportance of the individual who harbours it do not gratify the narcissism of the individual and therefore lack emotional appeal. Work that corroborates the discovery of others has a lack of appeal. Even if it requires a thinker it does not require a *particular* thinker and in this resembles truths – thoughts that require no thinker.

Since the analyst's concern is with the evolved elements of O and their formulation, formulations can be judged by considering how necessary his existence is to the thoughts he expresses. The more his interpretations can be judged as showing how necessary *his* knowledge, *his* experience, *his* character are to the thought as formulated, the more reason there is to suppose that the interpretation is psychoanalytically worthless, that is, alien to the domain O.

12

Container and contained transformed

In this chapter I repeat the configuration in formulations that appear to be descriptions of events in psychoanalysis or history but have not the status of historical narrative. They are C category elements, images derived from a background of experience or reported experience, reassembled for my purpose.

Description 1: The signs ♂ and ♀ I call the contained and the container. The use of the male and female symbols is deliberate but must not be taken to mean that other than sexual implications are excluded. These signs designate a relationship between ♀ and ♂ The link may be commensal, symbiotic, or parasitic.

Description 2: A word contains a meaning; conversely, a meaning can contain a word – which may or may not be discovered. The relationship is established by the nature of the link. A constant conjunction of elements in a psychoanalysis can be 'bound' by the attribution to it of a word, a theory, or other formulation. The word by which it is bound can have such a powerful pre-existing penumbra of associations that it squeezes the meaning out of the constant conjunction it is supposed to mark. Conversely, the constant conjunction can destroy the word, theory, or other formulation that the formulation is intended to 'contain'. For example, a man is attempting to express such powerful feelings that his capacity for verbal expression disintegrates into a stammer or a meaningless, incoherent babble of words.

Description 3: The container (♀) extracts so much from the contained (♂) that the contained is left without substance. A psychoanalysis is so long continued that the patient can get no further meaning from it. A converse example would be the continuation until the patient had no more patience, tolerance, fortitude, or money left. The container can squeeze everything 'out of' the contained; or the 'pressure' may be exerted by the contained so that the container disintegrates. An illustration would be the word used as a metaphor until the background is lost and the word loses its meaning.[1]

Description 4: The marriage *in* which the sexual relationship ♀♂ plays such a part that there is *no room* for any of the other activities in which the married couple might engage. Conversely, the other (i.e. 'other than sexual') activities play such a part that there is *no room* for sexual fulfilment. (The metaphors used in this description exemplify the outside-inside, container–contained, ♀♂ pattern.)

♀ or ♂ may represent memory. The container ♀ is filled with 'memories' derived from sensuous experience. The sensuous background is dominant and 'memories' with such a background are tenacious. The ♂ memory is saturated accordingly. The analyst who comes to a session with an active memory is therefore in no position to make 'observations' of unknown mental phenomena because these are not sensuously apprehended. There is something that has often been called 'remembering' and that is essential to psychoanalytic work; this must be sharply distinguished from what I have been calling memory. I want to make a distinction between (1) remembering a dream or having a memory of a dream and (2) the experience of the dream which seems to cohere as if it were a whole, at one moment absent, at the next present. This experience, which I consider to be essential to evolution of the emotional reality of the session, is often called a memory, but it is to be distinguished from the experience of remembering. In memory, time is of the essence. Time has often been regarded as being of the essence of psychoanalysis; in the growth process it has no part. Mental evolution or growth is catastrophic and timeless. I shall use 'memory' with its ordinary conversational meaning; it represents something that is out of place in the psychoanalyst's conduct of a psychoanalysis. A patient's close relatives are burdened with memories which

[1]See H. W. Fowler's *Dictionary of Modern English Usage*, 2nd edition, 'Metaphor' 2D.

make them unreliable judges of the patient's personality and unfit to be the patient's analyst.

So far, I have examined the configuration as it appears in the limits of words themselves; its appearance in more complex formulation indicates the degree of its persistence. The psychoanalytic situation provides and evokes examples of the configuration; it pervades difficulties which analysand and analyst find in communication. There are emotional experiences to be conveyed or represented, some of great intensity. Therefore, we find instances of the configuration in the subject-matter and in the psychoanalytic procedure designed to deal with it.

Description 5: The patient will be at a loss to convey his meaning, or the meaning he wishes to convey will be too intense for him to express properly, or the formulation will be so rigid that he feels that the meaning conveyed is devoid of any interest or vitality. Similarly, the interpretations given by the analyst (♂) will meet with the apparently co-operative response of being repeated for confirmation, which deprives ♂ of meaning either by compression or by denudation. Failure to observe or demonstrate the point may produce an outwardly progressive but factually sterile analysis. The clue lies in the observation of the fluctuations which make the analyst at one moment ♀ and the analysand ♂, and at the next reverse the roles. When this pattern is observed the links (commensal, symbiotic, or parasitic) within the pattern must also be observed.

The more familiar the analyst becomes with the configuration ♀, and ♂, and with events in the session that approximate to these two representations, the better. The essential experience is not the reading of this volume but the matching of the real event in the psychoanalysis that approximates to these formulations. The frequent references made to events that occur 'in analysis', or 'in the past', or 'inside' or 'outside', should aid recognition of the realizations to which these signs relate. The recognition of the category of link that is operating may be more difficult unless a lead-in can be obtained by considering the kind of event that takes the place of ♀ or ♂. Thus an extremely greedy patient may want to obtain as much as he can from his analysis while giving as little as possible; we should expect this to show itself by frequent events in which the container was denuding the contained object, and vice versa. The patient might show that he made enormous demands on his family but resented doing anything for it. Many patients might show behaviour of this kind on relatively rare occasions, but some might show it in many activities and in striking degree as, for example, by habitual incoherence while demanding great precision of interpretation from the analyst. This kind of patient cannot well be described in terms of narrative recording actual events, first, because any such formulation is suspect for reasons I have given in discussing memory, and, second, because it is impossible to predict what form his greed will take. Therefore the psychoanalyst who may have such a patient, or a patient showing such patterns of behaviour relatively rarely, or anything between these extremes, needs formulations of theory that enable him to have as wide a spectrum of observation as possible so that these configurations do not pass unnoticed. If these formulations are too abstract they lack body. Accordingly I give them body by using C category descriptions, but these are liable to produce so great a penumbra of associations that the formulations become saturated and narrow the psychoanalyst's perspicacity.

Descriptions 1–5 could include claustrophobia, agoraphobia, and acting-out as illustrations of the configuration.

Acting-out, as it is ordinarily understood, takes place 'in' the analysis and the analysis is then itself a part of acting-out. The claustrophobic-agoraphobic patient identifies himself with an object which is inside or outside a container. An ability to see the configuration reveals relationships within the patient's personality that otherwise would remain unknown. When a patient can be said to be acting out, the analysis is 'in' a situation of which the boundaries are unknown. If the behaviour characterized as 'acting-out' is brought to the analysis it can be accompanied by claustrophobic symptoms in the patient. The coherence of these symptoms may not be detected if the underlying configuration is not realized. As this last point touches on group behaviour I shall make my next description a formulation in terms of history. The description will appear to be complex because I intend to broaden the scope of the configuration, but its complexity will be less if it is borne in mind that the description has the same fundamental configuration even if at first sight it appears that this is not so. It may help if I explain that new ideas may appear to be presented in this description; their novelty or otherwise is a function of the reader's personality and must not be supposed to inhere in the communication.

Description 6: This section is mostly recapitulation and expansion of the model of mystic and group. Some mystics attract notice but others do not because the conditions are not propitious. The same is true of ideas; the idea which I consider to be the counterpart of the mystic or genius, I call the 'messianic idea'. The idea that is messianic may be confused with the person; he may believe he is the messiah. The person, I call 'the mystic'; the idea, I call the 'messianic idea'. The terms 'mystic' and 'genius' are interchangeable. Mystics appear in any religion, science, time, or place. Such persons 'contain' the 'messianic idea', or the 'messianic idea' may 'contain' the person who is sought to incarnate, represent, or manifest the messiah in a manner analogous to the meaning that is felt to 'contain' the word that is to represent it.

The society in which the mystic appears has been described by Nietzsche as a body whose function it is to produce a genius. It is also the function of the society to make the mystic or messianic idea available to the members of the group. This is effected by laws (in society), dogma (in religion), rules or laws (in mathematics or science). The governing body of the society I call the Establishment; the counterpart in the domain of thought would be the pre-existing disposition or pre-conception.

The mystic makes direct contact with, or is 'at one' with, God. This capacity is not attributed to the ordinary member of the group. The Establishment must pronounce dogmatically, make laws or rules, so that the advantages of the mystic's communion with God or ultimate truth or reality may be shared at one remove by the ordinary members. This the Establishment may fail to do through lack of discrimination, leading to the furtherance of false views, or through rigid adherence to an existing framework, so that a parasitic link is set up between mystic and group, ♂ and ♀. The life is then squeezed out of the mystic or messianic idea, or the society is disrupted.

Description 7: The conflict between the mystic and his group is exhibited in its most exaggerated, and therefore most easily studied, form in the account of Jesus and his relationship with the group. He himself claimed, in a manner typical of many mystics, that his teachings were in conformity with the existing Establishment: "Think not that I am come to destroy the law or the prophets: I am not come to destroy but to fulfil" (Matthew 5:17. A.V.). This claim is often associated with an awareness of the disruptive force that is being brought to bear upon the group from within. The mystic does not always claim to conform to the group. He may appear in the guise of a destroyer from within or without. He does not claim peaceable intentions or methods. A distinction is sometimes made between the nihilistic mystic, who disrupts the community, and the creative mystic, who denies violent methods particularly against his own group. I wish to stress the disruptive quality of the mystic, whether he claims to be disruptive or not, for it is this disruptive quality that is associated with the group's hostility to the mystic, and vice versa. It is, furthermore, the quality that I wish to emphasize in this description.

The reaction of the Establishment is to prevent the disruption, and this it does by incorporating the mystic within itself. This is expressed in the biblical illustration by the temptation in the wilderness where the rewards of conformity are clearly stated. Conformity can be renunciation of the messianic idea or acceptance of the role of the messiah. Alternatively, the mystic can be destroyed and an attempt made to ensure the same fate for his ideas.

The functions of containment – I use the word with its military implication of one force containing another – had to be assumed by the split factions of the group, one ostensibly against, and the other for, Jesus. Gradually a fresh group was formed and a fresh Establishment to contain the mystic or rather the messianic idea. The Jewish group learned to handle the mystic with consequences that were less disastrous for itself. The Christian group, though finding a different solution of the problem, achieved a similarly satisfactory result. Neither system was free from recurrences of the problem. One Christian Establishment restored the disrupted structure and ensured its continuity by taking over the festivals of paganism, and thus mollifying the hostility that might otherwise have followed the loss of holidays and feasts that were beloved and valued. The theme could be stated as bigger and brighter paganism, with gods refurbished and rejuvenated as saints and devils. (Milton expresses this very clearly in his representation of Pandemonium in Books I and III of *Paradise Lost*.)

The problems of the Christian Establishment developed in the lifetime of Jesus. They were: delineation of the borders of the group, selection and training, and stabilization of the hierarchy.

To take the last point first. In the account in Mark's Gospel (10:35–45), the problem was clearly posed by James and John with their request for status. In his reply Jesus seems to suggest a kind of initiation or test, but the alacrity with which the two accept the conditions makes it hard to know what the initiation was, though it is clear that Jesus regarded its performance as beyond them. He also adumbrates a change in the function of the Establishment as it existed among the Gentiles of that time. The proposal put forward by James and John seems to be for status, and status appears to be a substitute for qualification. Their desires were to be satisfied as it were *ex officio*. The reply given by James seems to indicate that the 'position' achieved *ex officio* was an alternative preferred by the pair to undergoing the experience of the mystic himself. In this respect the rejected solution meets one of the requirements of society, namely, to make the fruits of the mystic's work available to ordinary members who do not have the mystic's qualifications for at-one-ment with the deity.

The problem of membership of the group and how to decide whether or not a man was to call himself a Christian[1] also arose early. Characteristically, it hinged on the question of the therapeutic efficiency of the Christian and his brand of Christianity. The problem was brought to a head through the apparently successful therapeutic effects obtained by persons not qualified members of the group (Mark 9:38). In the instance quoted, the criterion proposed by Jesus seems to be the successful cure and its attribution by the therapist to Jesus. The issues involved are: membership of the group as itself being a symbol of status; status, expressed by the locution 'in Thy name' as a therapeutic agent; therapeutic result as a criterion of membership of the group. The solution was empirical but it accepted the criterion of therapeutic efficiency. For the time being the test of membership seems to be twofold, namely, medical or therapeutic, and capacity for achieving results. This last requirement has been a problem throughout history. It might be described as a demand that the group leader

[1]The modern Israeli state has met the same problem of deciding who is, or is not, a Jew.

should be able to forestall the future, confer adequacy on someone already supposed to be suitable, and guarantee his adequacy in future contingencies.

The Christian hierarchy soon found itself faced by the same problems that had defeated the rabbinical directorate. The same forces were involved: on the one side, the need to control the messianic idea and make it available to ordinary people through dogmatic formulation; on the other side, the messianic idea or its incarnation perpetually breaking through the barriers intended to control it and threatening to disrupt the society in which it became manifest. The Reformation was a spectacular example of this (Knox, 1950).

I have used for descriptions 6 and 7 material familiar to all, for a configuration that is repeated in many forms and at many times. It is not limited to religious societies, or therapeutic or artistic or scientific societies, but is discernible in many. My intention is, however, not to express any opinion upon the nature of diverse groups. I am not purporting to write history but to formulate a pattern in picturesque C category terms; that is to say, to represent a configuration in terms that will give body to an idea that might otherwise seem to be a meaningless elaboration of abstractions. Naturally, I suppose that people other than psychoanalysts would profit from a recognition of the configuration and the underlying group to which one suspects that it belongs. But here I am concerned only as an analyst with the configuration as it might be discerned by other analysts. Descriptions 6 and 7 must not, therefore, be supposed to have a sociological or political application, but to be by way of fables or mythological constructs (C category) which, if formulated with greater precision and sophistication, represent a pattern to which the human personality would be found to approximate. The fable, constructed in terms of the group, must be regarded as a pictorialization of man's inner world (Money-Kyrle, 1961). For those familiar with Kleinian theory my description can be seen as a dramatized, personified, socialized, and pictorialized representation of the human personality. It may clarify the procedure to contrast this pictorial view with the accepted morphology of classical analysis. The theory formulated in terms of ego, super-ego, and id differs in two respects. First, it is an F category formulation whereas the pictorialized formulation I am representing verbally is a C category formulation, primitive and based on sensuously derived terminology. Second, it is a theory of which the realization that approximates to it is to be found in psychopathology and psycho-morphology. The realization approximating to the C category formulation is to be found in material that is superficial and easily accessible to the conscious. Its unconscious roots are to be discovered through psychoanalytic investigation.

The nature of the messianic idea can be only very approximately represented by the C category formulations I have been using. Jesus, Meister Eckhart, and Isaac Luria represent in different ways the problem of reconciling the messianic idea and the Establishment. The rabbinical directorate learned caution, so that when it had to adjust to the Lurianic doctrine, and to the injuries that Lurianic doctrine was alleged by its opponents to have inflicted on Judaism, it did not contribute to an explosion. Luria for his part insisted on his conservatism and related all he said to older authorities. Significantly, he left no writings and, when questioned by a disciple about his reasons for not setting out his teaching in book form, he replied: "It is impossible because all things are interrelated. I can hardly open my mouth to speak without feeling as though the sea burst its dams and overflowed. How then shall I express what my soul has received, and how can I put it down in a book?" (Scholem, 1955, p. 254). Meister Eckhart wrote extensively, but the obscurity of his writing and perhaps the matter led to the condemnation as heretical of some twenty-eight propositions from his later writings. The main question seems to centre on his forthright statements of identity with the deity – "we are transformed and changed into God". The fate of Jesus himself had been crucifixion as a criminal on the one hand, and deification on the other. Both Isaac Luria and Jesus were alike in being followed by a proliferation of hagiographical biography; much of it, in the instance of Jesus, not being included in the canon. The common features are: containment of the messianic idea in the individual; containment of the messianic individual in the group; the problem for the Establishment that is concerned with the group on the one hand and the messianic idea and individual on the other. It is now necessary to return to the word.

Description 2 (cycle 2): If it were necessary to express descriptions 6 and 7 by one word, a choice could be made from terms such as 'religion' or 'Christianity' or 'God'. If none of these terms were considered suitable, an attempt could be made to find the suitable term by introspection. This attempt is a search in the mind for the term supposed to exist, or it is a search in the meaning for the term; the latter is an instance of the meaning containing the word. The difficulties attendant on finding the word are described in the terms used by Poincaré, searching for a mathematical formula, or by Luria in the passage quoted above (p. 115). A better idea of the problem is obtained by substituting the term 'statement' for 'word' and including in its definition any act of expression whatever. In C category terms the problem is analogous to that of the sculptor finding his form in the block of his material, of the musician finding the formula of musical notation within the sounds he hears, of the man of action finding the actions that represent his thoughts. One of the peculiarities of this discussion lies in its being an example of the problem being discussed. It is an attempt to find a verbal formulation to which psychoanalytic realizations approximate. I restate the problem thus: psychoanalysis, the thing-in-itself, existed; it remained for Freud to reveal the formulation embedded in it. Conversely, once formulated by Freud, it remains for others (including Freud himself) to discover the meaning of the conjunction bound by his formulation.

It is necessary to postulate 'thinking' without supposing a thinker to be essential. I shall not at this point try to explain why. All thinking and all thoughts are true when there is no thinker. In contrast to this, for lies and falsities a thinker is absolutely necessary. In any situation where a thinker is present the thoughts when formulated are expressions of falsities and lies. The only true thought is one that has never found an individual to 'contain' it.

The messianic idea may be supposed to have a counterpart, the absolute truth, O, for which a thinker is not necessary. Falsity is the characteristic of thought within an individual, or thought within a container. It follows that all thought as it is ordinarily known, that is, as an attribute of the human being, is false, the problem associated with it being the degree and nature of the falsity. The lie is a falsity associated with 'morals'.

The messianic idea is a term representing O at the point at which its evolution and the evolution of a thinker intersect. The mystic, as seen in descriptions 6 and 7, is a thinker who claims the capacity for direct contact with O. The degree of falsity depends on whether the relationship with O is commensal, symbiotic, or parasitic. It is not often enough recognized that a patient in whom resistance is active can be reacting against what he feels to be a thought in search of a thinker. It is supposedly his own thought (classical resistance theory), but it does not have to be so.

The thought O and the thinker exist independently of each other – there is no reaction. Or, as we should ordinarily say (identifying ourselves with the thinker) the truth has not been discovered though it 'exists'. In symbiosis the thought and the thinker correspond, and modify each other through the correspondence. The thought proliferates and the thinker develops. In a parasitic relationship between thought and thinker there is a correspondence but the correspondence is category 2, meaning that the formulation is known to be false, but is retained as a barrier against truth which is feared as annihilating to the container or vice versa. The falsity proliferates until it becomes the lie. The barrier of the lie increases the need for the truth, and vice versa.

The commensal position changes when thought and thinker approximate. In more usual terms, a critical situation arises when a 'discovery' threatens. It is commonly said that messianic hopes were more than usually active at the birth of Jesus, and it is a matter for remark that more than one investigator often seems to be approaching a discovery at the time when a discovery is made. The resistance of the thinker to the unthought thought is characteristic of category 2 thinking. The crucial problem appears to be the relative strength of the messianic idea and the personality who is to 'contain' it. We must therefore reconsider the personality. To do this I shall use descriptions 6 and 7 as pictorial representations (C category) of the parts composing the totality of the individual, not the group. I am assuming that the reader keeps in mind existing theories of personality structure. It is not to be supposed that they are to be abandoned or even modified by what follows. Existing theories are F category formulations; what takes place in the consulting-room is an emotional situation which is itself the intersection of an evolving O with another evolving O. The description I am giving is, as it has been throughout this chapter, a C category formulation intended to bridge the gap between a unique event on the one hand and a generalized F category formulation on the other.

Description 3 (cycle 2): The messianic idea clothes itself in a variety of forms. Though it may take any form there appears to be difficulty for form and idea to achieve a symbiotic or commensal relationship. Therefore it is difficult to find a formulation by which I can convey my meaning to the reader, but I can point to the consulting-room or group where he may intuit it for himself. Similarly, I can direct him to observe the word 'cure' when he hears it; for 'within' this word he may be able to intuit the messianic idea. His attention should dwell on formulations in which he is described in positive terms; for 'within' these statements he may be able to intuit the 'contained' messianic idea. Whether the statement appears outwardly to be representing a summer holiday, a car, a person, or a state in time, he should be able by degrees to intuit the frequent occurrence of the messianic idea and be persuaded of its reality and his ability to feel its presence.

When I say the reader might search the consulting-room or group, I am restricting the field of search to provide a 'container' wherein the search may be pursued without difficulty and relatively quickly. Yet it is doubtful whether intuition of a constant conjunction in the domain of psychic reality can be attainable quickly or easily. Therefore there can be no short cut for the psychoanalyst; he can hope that experience may enable him to intuit the messianic idea or recognize that this hope is itself a formulation containing it.

The notion that the messianic idea is contained within the analysis, or that descriptions 6 and 7 can be used as C category statements or formulations of the individual personality, implies that the personality can be represented by a ♀♂ relationship and that the personality has a ♀♂ relationship with a psychoanalysis. Such a formulation assists the psychoanalyst to intuit a personality, external to the psychoanalysis, which is present in the psychoanalysis only by 'hearsay'; the patient becomes a voice reporting that the messianic idea is abroad. A typical complexity of the ♀♂ relation, significant for its bearing on 'acting-out', relates to beta-elements lying outside the domain of thought proper, but appearing to belong to it because they are represented 'in' the psychoanalysis by C3 statements made by the analysand. The psychoanalyst and his analysand appear, therefore, to be excluded from the domain of action and 'confined within' the domain of thought in such a way that they are not in a position to 'psychoanalyse', but only to substitute 'psychoanalysis' for psychoanalytic thinking, which is a prelude to interpretations – the psychoanalytic counterpart of action.

Psychoanalytic practice shows that the motives for any human activity are numerous and complex. They are derived from a background of sensuous desires; as fast as one is demonstrated it is apparent that further desires lie unknown. The aims of the psychoanalytic couple are arrived at by conjecture and are formulated, at least as far as the analysand is concerned, in terms representative of sensuous experience. Even the objects of curiosity are formulated in terms suitable to a sensuous background. In so far as desires can be stated they will be sensuous desires and sensuous aims, the overriding aim being to keep alive. Without exception these aims and desires are not relevant to psychoanalysis. Nor have they proved relevant in either Judaism or Christianity. Their place has not yet been taken by any formulations that are more satisfactory. So long as thinking is regarded as subordinate to the senses there is no difficulty. If thinking is a primary activity, the *aims* of contemplation or meditation are presumed to exist because thinking is tied to its genetic history as subordinate to muscular activity; similarly, muscular activity is presumed to have an aim in accord with the dominance of the pleasure principle.

It is possible that the vacuity produced by the subordination of sensuous aims to growth of a capacity for contemplation or meditation was filled, in the course of his teaching, by Jesus. But as his teaching was subjected to the twin pressures I have described, namely, annihilation by physical destruction on the one hand and divine honours on the other, we do not know what such a solution might have been. In practice the problem is shelved; thinking remains subordinate to the satisfaction of sensuous desires.

In consequence, psychoanalysis is saddled with an aim that, according to their various desires, is attributed to it by both analyst and analysand. Both are debarred from fulfilling their aim when the aim is pursued in the domain of action and the psychoanalysis is confined to the domain of thought in which thought is the only means of fulfilment. The 'conflict' is between action and thought, the counterpart (in descriptions 6 and 7) being the conflict expressed in Saint Augustine's refutation of the responsibility of Christianity for the fall of Rome. In the individual, demands for action and sensuous gratifications associated with physical survival conflict with the demand for mental 'activity'. The latter cannot justify itself in terms comprehensible to the former. The former cannot justify itself to the latter, for its apparatus of sensuous fulfilment is irrelevant to the domain of thought.

I have used the term 'conflict', in describing action and thought, as a reminder of the accepted view. The object of using ♀♂ is to differentiate the states of containment which, as with thought and action, prevent conflict by containing thought and action in a mutually exclusive commensal state. In this condition thought and action do not modify each other but persist commensally in the same personality. Actions that appear to be compulsive are in reality beta-elements confined to the domain of action and thus insulated against thoughts, which are confined to the domain of thought – including psychoanalysis. Similarly, thoughts are within the domain of thought and cannot be influenced by beta-elements confined within the domain of action. An apparent exception, not real, is provided by C3 elements in thoughts that appear to bring A category into the realm of thought but are only C category *records* of action; there is no conflict.

The domains of thought and action are so close, when the musculature used in talking is involved with beta-elements, that the distinction between them becomes confused. The same confusion arises if intolerance of frustration leads to a substitution of thought for action. The associated omnipotence of thought obstructs the proper use of the musculature, as a feeling of helplessness stimulated by ineffectual muscular action is often the genetic base of omnipotence: when one is active the other is present.

In the previous paragraphs I have given examples of ♀♂ associated with outside and inside. They have a psychological value in giving body to a formulation that might otherwise lack it, but the reader should seek further instances from his practice. According to his background a patient will describe various objects as containers, such as his mind, the unconscious, the nation; others as contained, such as his money, his ideas. The objects are many but the relationships are not.

The individual always displays some aspect of his personality that is stable and constant even though it may sometimes be very difficult to detect in the welter of evidence for instability; it may appear only in the regularity with which the patient attends his sessions. In this stability will be found the counterpart of what, in descriptions 6 and 7, I have called the Establishment. It will be maintained with great tenacity as the only force likely to contain the counterpart of the messianic idea. Reciprocally, the messianic idea is the only force likely to withstand the pressures of the counterpart of the Establishment in the individual. Fears of megalomanic identification with the messianic idea are associated with an inability to be at one with the omnipotent Father. The counterpart of the Establishment in the individual is not related to father or mother, but can be related to fragments of both.

In the ♀♂ configuration, decision is synonymous with selection for inclusion or exclusion. Thus the psychoanalyst has to decide whether to include himself in or exclude himself from various groups; to include or exclude given associations, ideas, experiences, and so on. The Establishment of the group has to decide to include or exclude certain individuals.

The personality decides to include or exclude certain characteristics or, failing that, to include or exclude awareness of their existence. Dislike of the onus of decision, or awareness of responsibility for the decision, contributes to the formulation of selection procedures by which selection, like dogma and laws of science, is made to act as a substitute for judgement or a scapegoat for the guilt attendant on overtly acknowledged exercise of responsibility.

The configuration to which I have drawn attention can be seen to have a penumbra of associations which retain an illuminating function in the circumstances on which they are brought to bear. At times the light they shed distorts by over-emphasis of the irrelevant past and occlusion of the unknown (and therefore relevant) present and future. Once the constancy of the configuration is recognized its nature can be assessed and related to psychoanalytic theory. Reciprocally, theory can be reformulated when it requires readjustment.

The primitive formulation of ♀♂ in C category terms of breast and mouth, penis and vagina, has the simplicity of all C category formulations. Although descriptions 6 and 7 appear more complex, they too share the stamp of all C category formulations. Both appear to differ from the configurations represented by the Kleinian theory of paranoid-schizoid and depressive position interplay. I am unwilling to accept this apparent cleavage. The most satisfactory formulation that displays the underlying harmony relates to the practice of psychoanalysis.

The discussion of the configuration of container and contained has occupied a considerable space in this book. It may, therefore, seem surprising if, at this stage and in relatively few sentences, I describe what is perhaps the most important mechanism employed by the practising psychoanalyst. It requires less description and is relatively more easily grasped. It is for these reasons only that it occupies what may appear to be an insignificant place in this book. It is derived from Melanie Klein's descriptions of the paranoid – schizoid and depressive positions, and to these the reader should refer.

Here, briefly, is my formulation of this matter as it concerns the practising analyst:

In every session the psychoanalyst should be able, if he has followed what I have said in this book, particularly with regard to memory and desire, to be aware of the aspects of the material that, however familiar they may seem to be, relate to what is unknown both to him and to the analysand. Any attempt to cling to what he knows must be resisted for the sake of achieving a state of mind analogous to the paranoid-schizoid position. For this state I have coined the term 'patience' to distinguish it from 'paranoid-schizoid position', which should be left to describe the pathological state for which Melanie Klein used it. I mean the term to retain its association with suffering and tolerance of frustration.

'Patience' should be retained without "irritable reaching after fact and reason" until a pattern 'evolves'. This state is the analogue to what Melanie Klein has called the depressive position. For this state I use the term 'security'. This I mean to leave with its association of safety and diminished anxiety. I consider that no analyst is entitled to believe that he has done the work required to give an interpretation unless he has passed through both phases – 'patience' and 'security'. The passage from the one to the other may be very short, as in the terminal stages of analysis, or it may be long. Few, if any, psychoanalysts should believe that they are likely to escape the feelings of persecution and depression commonly associated with the pathological states known as the paranoid-schizoid and depressive positions. In short, a sense of achievement of a correct interpretation will be commonly found to be followed almost immediately by a sense of depression. I consider the experience of oscillation between 'patience' and 'security' to be an indication that valuable work is being achieved.

13

Prelude to or substitute for achievement

> I had not a dispute but a disquisition with Dilke on various subjects; several things dove-tailed in my mind, and at once it struck me what quality went to form a Man of Achievement, especially in Literature, and which Shakespeare possessed so enormously – I mean Negative Capability, that is, when a man is capable of being in uncertainties, mysteries, doubts, without any irritable reaching after fact and reason.
>
> John Keats[1]

A number of aspects of the practice of psychoanalysis must now be discussed; I group them under the Language of Achievement. The quotation from Keats will serve as an introduction to the area to be covered. Language is loosely and widely defined to include behaviour of which it is sometimes said "actions speak louder than words". Set over against and in contrast with the Language of Achievement, I consider the language that is a substitute for, and not a prelude to, action. Language of Achievement includes language that is both prelude to action, and itself a kind of action; the meeting of psychoanalyst and analysand is itself an example of this language. This discussion is centred on the problem of bringing attention to bear on the realizations to which Freud's theories approximate.

Any session should be judged by comparison with the Keats formulation so as to guard against one commonly unobserved fault leading to analysis 'interminable'. The fault lies in the failure to observe and is intensified by the inability to appreciate the significance of

[1]'Letter to George and Thomas Keats', 21 December 1817 (in E. L. Freud, 1961).

observation. I have rarely failed to experience hatred of psychoanalysis and its reciprocal, sexualization of psychoanalysis. These are part of a 'constant conjunction'. In C category terms: the human animal has not ceased to be persecuted by his mind and the thoughts usually associated with it – whatever their origin may be. Therefore I do not expect any psychoanalysis properly done to escape the odium inseparable from the mind. Refuge is sure to be sought in mindlessness, sexualization, acting-out, and degrees of stupor. The analyst's attention must not wander from areas of material characterized either by the Language of Substitution or by the Language of Achievement; he must remain sensitive to both. I do not claim that sensitivity can be achieved easily: the mental space available to the analysand and the material observed are subject to so many transformations that such a claim suggests inexperience of the practice of psychoanalysis. The experienced analysand finds dreams a useful stand-by because analysts are rightly expected to want to hear them. Current events can be transformed to expression in sado-masochistic terms or near psychopathological jargon; there is no limit to the forms of transformation. Experience leads to an extension of the area over which the Language of Achievement operates and therefore an extension of the area in which its operation can be recognized. We must now consider the extension of the concept of vertices in relation to both individuals in the psychoanalytic couple.

It will be remembered that the term 'vertex' can be understood as similar to 'point of view' except in certain special instances. There is a psychological or mental specificity analogous to the specificity associated with the relationship of sense organs to sense impressions. To allow for this specificity it is necessary to discard the term 'point of view' and replace it by a more abstract term such as 'vertex'. Language of Achievement is always related to a vertex whether that vertex has been determined (or evolved) or not. Since we shall consider both psychoanalyst and analysand we shall have to approach our problem by moving *outside* the field usually thought of as belonging to psychoanalysis. The states of mind with which psychoanalysts deal comprise many that are generally the hunting-ground of other than psychoanalysts; for example, thieves, burglars, sexual perverts, murderers, blackmailers. Their mental world is matched by a world of external reality which caters for their states of mind by an established organization of international and commercial spying, police forces, religious organizations; the one group is matched by the other. A process of selection in Church or police force is carried out by examiners (in the instance of delinquents, by varieties of courts of law). It is intended to separate the good from the bad. Who or what is to exercise the power, and what voice is to utter the Language of Achievement is a matter of consequence and has been accepted as such whether the field in which the struggle is carried on is the individual, or agglomerations of individuals. Psychoanalysts accept their field to be the individual. The supposition that inhibitions should be decreased seems to be based on a view of the individual analogous to a view of the group in which democracy is a bad form of government but none the less the best.

The analyst and the analysand each have a vertex (or vertices) which, if it were known, would indicate the organization each regarded as best. Freud's scheme of id, ego, super-ego suggests one view of the organization of the personality, though there is nothing to suggest that the scheme represents a preference and not an observation.

The idea that is nourished by love develops from matrix to function in Language of Achievement; from which it can be transformed into achievement. But if the idea is subjected to splitting it may split again repeatedly, each split growing and having to be split again. Thus one gets not development but division and multiplication – cancerous, not qualitative, increase. There appears to be a great increase in ideation, but there is not, because all the ideas turn out, on inspection, to be the same one. The emotional matrix from which this springs is not envy and gratitude, but envy and greed. The idea is split over and over again and is felt to produce a quantity of splits – 'mental faeces'. Envy and gratitude, on the other hand, stimulate a desire for gain, but enable the individual to establish a good relation between what has been gained and that which has enabled him to gain it. The repudiation of the debt owed to his 'predatory' personality, and the need to continue repudiating it, exclude other parts of the personality from activity. The greed of the super-ego leads to the usurpation of the domain of reality (scientific facts) by the 'moral' outlook, and of 'scientific' laws by 'moral' laws.

The model for cancerous growth is not splitting of the object but splitting of the envy, each 'bit' then growing independently of every other 'bit'. Ostensibly these 'bits' appear as 'different' ideas. In fact they are a cover: ideas → impulses → *One* impulse. In this respect sessions can be regarded as repeating themselves, and the unchanging quality of the sessions should betray itself despite the multitudinous changes in disguise. Sometimes this state is described as a negative therapeutic reaction when it would be more accurately described as 'proliferation of fragmented envy'. If the envy were to assume an aspect of whole object it could be seen as envy of the personality capable of maturation and of the object stimulating maturation. The stimulating object is the breast (♀) or mouth (♂). They replace each other. The stimulating quality in turn replaces the stimulating object. A series of transformations is thus initiated, each a substitution for the previous one and each subject to splitting. Berkeley's criticism of Newton's mathematics is psychologically well based because it is *not* the mathematics of growth that is represented by the infinitesimal calculus and its use of concepts of infinitely small positive and negative increments – "the ghosts of departed quantities". It is psychologically more nearly true to regard Newton's formulation as *measurement* of restoration of whole objects than as measurement of growth. Is mathematics the Language of Achievement or of Restoration? What is required is not the decrease of inhibition but a decrease of the impulse to inhibit; the impulse to inhibit is fundamentally envy of the growth-stimulating objects. What is to be sought is an activity that is both the restoration of god (the Mother) and the evolution of god (the formless, infinite, ineffable, non-existent), which can be found only in the state in which there is *no* memory, desire, understanding.

BOOK REVIEWS

1966

The review of K. R. Eissler, *Medical Orthodoxy and the Future of Psycho-Analysis* (New York: International Universities Press, 1965), was published in the *International Journal of Psycho-Analysis, 47* (1966): 575–579.

The review of R. Slovenko (Ed.), *Sexual Behavior and the Law* (Springfield, IL: Thomas, 1964), was published in the *International Journal of Psycho-Analysis, 47* (1966): 579–581.

Review of K. R. Eissler's *Medical Orthodoxy and the Future of Psycho-Analysis*

Questions of importance for psychoanalysts have been debated in this able book by Eissler. The subject may seem to British readers not to concern them; a great deal of hard-hitting criticism is directed against American institutes of psychoanalysis, American failings (in the author's view), and American psychoanalytic 'heresies'. Ostensibly he is arguing in favour of the lay analyst – which again may appear to a British psychoanalyst to be a subject no longer for debate, but which to me appears only to be one facet of the problem of the relationship between group and mystic which has now become vital for the psychoanalytic group. On an adequate solution of this the future of psychoanalysis hangs, and the adequate solution demands, as a prerequisite, adequate debate. This is not possible unless psychoanalysts are prepared to spend time studying the history and dynamics of the relationship between the mystic and the group. Eissler's book should be read against the background of this seldom and inadequately discussed phenomenon. The central point is the impact of an explosive force on a pre-existing framework. This configuration is recurrent, and can be detected in the impact of new ideas on an old vocabulary, formula, or deductive system; or of the genius, mystic, or messiah upon the group in which his presence becomes manifest.

The group and mystic are essential to each other: it is therefore important to consider how or why the group can destroy the mystic on whom its future depends and how or why the mystic may destroy the group. The reader will not expect me to do more than indicate the nature of the questions at issue. I do not wish to pronounce upon it, but to say why it is vital that the problem should be seen to exist and to be inherent – both in the nature of man as a political animal, and in the nature of psychoanalysis as the explosive force.

The relationship between group and mystic may be seen to belong to one of a few major categories. It may be commensal, symbiotic, or parasitic. The same categorization may be applied to the relationship of one group with another. I shall not trouble with the commensal relationship. The two sides co-exist and the existence of each can be seen to be harmless to the other. In the symbiotic relationship there is a confrontation, and the result is growth-producing – though that growth may not be discerned without some difficulty. In the parasitic relationship the product of the association is something which destroys both parties to the association. The realization which approximates most closely to my formulation is the group-individual setting dominated by envy. Envy begets envy and this self-perpetuating emotion finally destroys host and parasite alike. The envy cannot be satisfactorily ascribed to one or the other party; in fact it is a function of the relationship.

In a symbiotic relationship the group should be capable of hostility and benevolence, so that the mystic contribution is subject to close scrutiny. From this scrutiny the group grows in stature, and the mystic likewise. It is not useful, therefore, to consider the relationship in terms of hate or love – for both can be beneficial. But in the parasitic association, even apparent friendliness is deadly. An easily seen example of this is the group's promotion of the individual to a position in the Establishment where his energies are deflected from his creative-destructive role, and absorbed in administrative functions. His epitaph might be "He was loaded with honours and sank without a trace." Eissler, without specifically mentioning the general principle involved, shows how sensitive he is to the dangers of the invitation to group or individual to become respectable, to be medically qualified, to be a University Department, to be a therapeutic group, to be anything, in short, but NOT explosive. The reciprocal attitude in the mystic is that the group should thrive or disintegrate, but must not be indifferent. Put thus, it may seem that I mean these attitudes to be conscious and deliberate. I do not think of them as anything but essential, Without them the group is not a group, or the 'mystic' a mystic.

Eissler discusses at length 'applied' psychoanalysis. I sympathize with his anxiety – though I may be misunderstanding him in doing so. My suspicion of applied psychoanalysis, even if 'applied' to curing people, is that it is a method of bringing psychoanalysis under control, and rendering it harmless to the Establishment. I have expressed this in another context and in making a different approach; as a rule no analyst should permit himself to harbour desires; even the desire to cure is inimical to psychoanalytic development or the development of psychoanalysis. Development itself is not an object that can be 'desired'.

A formulation may approximate to 'illumination' of reality: I must, however, point out that while many mystics have felt the need to express their experience of direct access to the deity in terms of light,[1] light is not the only model that is used. The Jewish mystics in particular appear to find the *voice* a more telling representation of the experience. St Paul, as befits a Jew and a Christian, seems to have found light *and* voice necessary for adequate representation of the experience; he also objected to the Greeks (Acts Ch. 17, v. 21) for being insufficiently institutionalized. It may therefore be a matter of some consequence that analysts, who, in my opinion, are bound to be seeking direct access to an aspect of reality – even though it cannot be said to be only to that part of reality that informs godlike characteristics that a contact is sought – conduct their affairs in a medium which, for establishing the mystical revelation, is only used for that purpose generally by the Jews. I suggest that to be confined to verbal contact only – even if only in metaphor – is too restrictive.

Eissler quotes a procedure adopted by Aichhorn (whose clinical acumen he praises highly) for watching strangers to whom he is close, for a period, with a view to forming a conjecture about their next act. As he describes it, Aichhorn was playing a game not unlike that of a boy imitating Sherlock Holmes. He speaks of it with approval, attributing to it some of Aichhorn's flair for understanding instantly and accurately the personality of the delinquents with whom he dealt. But he deprecates the possibility of making any parallel procedure part of a formal training course. But why not? I welcome the introduction into training of Baby Observation; I think it would be all the better for an injection of the good humour of the 'Holmesian' technique. The baby should be observed with all the enthusiasm of Holmes on the track of a desperate criminal. Pessimistically Eissler doubts the success of any approach, even Aichhorn's, to the delinquent. I suggest

[1]For example, Milton in Book III of *Paradise Lost*; Dante in *Paradiso*, Stanza xxxiii; the Christian mystics generally.

that the lack of success will continue so long as the investigation is carried out with predisposition to see the object of the investigation as a 'delinquent' – matter what his life may have been – and to do so with the humourless attitude which seems to be inseparable from having suffered a psychoanalytic training course. Indeed, anyone who has not been reduced to revolt by the course must either be insensitive to his environment or in an analysis which increases his robustness to a remarkable degree. Who does not remember, at the end of the day, entry into a hot and smoke-filled room with the expectation of an hour and a half of boredom from a tired psychoanalyst and a dozen equally tired colleagues? Exceptions were rare and welcome, but haunted by the suspicion that relief must depend on the meretricious nature of the seminar or lecture.

The personal analysis, which in any case can hardly be expected to be pleasant, is not the trouble. The relief which comes with the understanding of one's problems makes the pain involved tolerable. The extra-analytic training however, can hardly be excused. The subject is of profound interest in itself. It is one of the few domains of human effort – peace be to the nuclear scientists – in which any real progress is being made. Can there then be any justification for boredom and lack of imagination in the training course hallowed by the authority of institutionalized psychoanalysis? Eissler doubts the suitability of the limited field from which selection has to be made to provide our training candidates. He gives cogent reasons for his doubts. He might well have given more had he considered how candidates drawn from the same field acquit themselves when called upon to train others. Can this discrepancy possibly be right?

The question demands a serious rather than a polemical answer. I should certainly be unwilling to wound people who have devoted themselves to the pursuit of psychoanalysis, but I am fortified by the thought that people who are devoted to their subject are rarely boring without the fault, whatever it may be, being shared by the bored. Certainly there must be austerity and hard work, frustration and anxiety: I am also suspicious of enthusiasm and its fellows. We do not expect our candidates to be free from defects at one end of the scale or the other. Nor does anyone suppose that a few years of analysis makes us as psychoanalysts approximate to what we might regard as desirable in analysts, teachers, administrators. How then are we to give effect to our suspicions when they are the fruit of legitimate self-criticism?

I believe the answer is similar to the answer that we accept as analysts when we regard psychoanalysis as the method of choice in any given problem. For this reason I regard Eissler's approach, scrutiny by the group of itself – through books such as his – as offering the best hope. It is for this reason I make this contribution.

In my Grid[1] I made a preliminary attempt at forging an instrument to help with all such problems by a method of categorization. At the same time I have suggested substituting the term 'vertex' for 'point of view'. Put in other terms, I think the problem should be approached by determining the Grid category of the vertex.

Eissler might describe this – to take as example the particular problem he poses – as considering the point of view of the medically trained man *vis-à-vis* the point of view of the layman or 'anthropic' scientist. In the example of the impact of the thought of Jesus on the Jewish group, and subsequently on the various other groups formed by the different religious institutions of history, it is possible to see some of our present tensions in a simpler, less disguised, and therefore purer culture. It is clear that the stress on miracles of healing could easily have represented a powerful urge to 'medicalize' the institution intended to embody the teaching of Jesus. Even to-day, the healing aspect retains its force in Christian Science, Lourdes, faith healing. An example of a problem of institutionalizing in the early Christian group is the query put to Jesus by the disciples who wanted to have a ruling on recognition of those who cast out devils in Jesus's name. The attitude of Jesus appears to have been against any rigid qualification for membership of the group on the ground of survival of the group. ("Those that are not against me are for me.") Although this reply cannot be interpreted with any sureness at this length of time, and may well have been referable to the favourable (for Christianity) effect of turpitude in the opponents of Christianity, it shows sufficiently the recurrent nature of the configuration of the problem of selection and lay versus professional or out-group versus in-group. My object is not, however, to make conjectures about ancient history, but to educe illustrations which, between them, can serve to convey the configuration to which I want to draw attention. Similarly with the vertex and the part it plays in determining the configuration of the group.

---

[1]W. R. Bion (1963), *Elements of Psycho-Analysis* [Volume V].

As Eissler points out, psychoanalysis cannot escape from the consequences of Freud's association with medicine; it is to be expected that ideas of cure, treatment, and illness would play a big part in psychoanalysts and patients alike. Eissler does well to draw attention to the dangers of making permanent a structure which is too rigid, and too limited, to permit the development of psychoanalysis or – as I think – of the mystic who is, and provides, the stimulus for growth. At the opposite extreme would seem to lie the Sufis who have no rigid institution. They have endured; they appear to feel no need for an institution, and no obstruction to growth in their lack of it. Can their example suggest anything of interest to the psychoanalysts in their problem? It is possible to propose that any candidate should be free to go to any psychoanalyst who would have the right to declare the candidate fit to be a psychoanalyst when he, unaided, thought so. This solution would seem to lay the way open for the production of an 'expanding universe' of psychoanalysis in which it would not be long before members of the movement could not understand each other. I would be prepared to argue that this prediction is not so far from fulfilment under the present dispensation, were it not for the fact that the degree of mutual comprehension which exists may be considered to be remarkable when allowance is made for the nature of the subject, the apparently infinite variety of human personalities, and the fact that the psychoanalytic approach tends to magnify differences the more thorough and the less macroscopic the result that is sought. Obviously there should be no ruling on what is discovered, but only on how it is discovered.

I propose to consider motivation without stressing the difference between conscious and unconscious. An analyst, or a particular group of analysts, may be remarkable for stressing a medical view – for possessing, in my terms, a common vertex. That is to say, an observer of the group would expect to find that the vertex of the group would be recognized by certain invariants, say ideas of disease, treatment, prognosis, pathology, and cure. No doubt the unconscious counterparts of such a vertex will have been laid bare in the psychoanalysis of the individual members, but this should not blind us to the conscious aspects of this vertex.

Suppose now yet another group in whom the need or desire to make money was obtrusive. No doubt the unconscious counterpart of this will likewise have been laid bare in the analysis of the individuals. The greater the need or the desire, the easier it would be to detect a particular application of psychoanalytic theory – what Eissler calls 'applied' psychoanalysis as opposed to 'anthropic'.

Another group may display a similarly obtrusive 'vertex', say a wish for power or influence, propaganda, or education (public relations), or research, or poverty. To me it is self-evident – at any rate in our present stage of development – that whatever may happen if we achieve 'psychoanalytical' psychoanalysis, the vertex of the group will make a difference to the findings of the group. So far analysts have seemed to act on the assumption that motives should be analysed, and may thereafter be safely left without further consideration. Such a view is mistaken and helps to obscure the varieties of development that are opened up by the analytic experience of the individual, or the group of which he becomes an adherent. In his chapter on polemics Eissler is critical of what he feels to be the failure – one might almost say the apostasy – of certain groups of analysts. Even if he is mistaken in the particular judgements that he makes, it would require a pathological optimism to deny the possibility of groups to which his criticisms would apply. There may well be vertices which are not regarded by the group as respectable, and therefore of which it needs to be unconscious. The group tendency would be to foster unconsciousness in other groups of these defects in itself while claiming their discovery elsewhere. Since if this were successful it would deny us the opportunity for study, it is obvious that it would help if we could understand the means by which any group of analysts could collude with any other to bring about the desired result. For successful collusion to deny the vertex would remove the basis for understanding why that particular group, sharing that particular approach, also shared their particular psychoanalytic discoveries. The Oedipal situation – or whatever its even more primitive roots might be – would have a different configuration according to whether the vertex of the group was psychoanalytic, religious, financial, legal – or indeed any of the other vertices which time may show to be central rather than peripheral.

Where Eissler speaks of applied psychoanalysis I shall speak of psychoanalysis conducted from a particular vertex. If an analyst or group of analysts regards the making of money as an essential part of psychoanalytic practice – that is to say that they regard it as an essential part of practice which is an equally essential part of cure – then I think the vertex should be described as money-making and the discoveries that are made in such analysis will bear the stamp of the vertex, 'Babel'.

If the vertex is religious, I should expect the discoveries to bear the stamp of *that* vertex. I should further expect that in time the configurations associated with the various vertices would themselves evolve to a point where they could be formulated. I should then expect the rigidity conferred by the formulation to be opposed by the fluidity of the reality represented by the formulation.

It is evident that Eissler feels, as any analyst must at some time have felt, that the 'universe of discussion' in psychoanalysis is 'expanding' so fast that we are no longer able to maintain what a solider calls 'lateral communication'. He feels, to take one instance, that the gap between what he regards as analysis and what I, as a Kleinian, regard as analysis, is very wide – and widening. This he attributes to differences in theory. I do not, and never have been able to believe that what separates scientists are their differences in theory. I have not felt 'separated' from someone who differs from me in the theories he holds; that does not seem to afford a standard of measurement by which the gap can be assessed. Similarly, I have felt very far separated from some who, apparently, hold the *same* theories. Therefore if the 'gap' is to be 'measured' it will have to be in some domain other than that of theory. The differences in theory are symptoms of a difference in vertex and not a measure of the difference.

Eissler and I cannot see the same patient. Even if this were possible the patient would not be the 'same' when seen by him and when seen by me. There can be certain invariants in Eissler, the patient, and myself which ensure a relationship sufficiently constant for comparison. Of these invariants, only those are relevant which are also invariant under psychoanalysis.

I hope that I have made clear the reasons why the topics discussed in this book are of importance to everyone concerned with the growth and development of psychoanalysis. The questions raised in it demand dispassionate and serious thought, because on that will depend ultimately the chance that the day-to-day problems that have to be faced will be seen in relation to the wider problem, and therefore wisely decided. Individual solutions must vary in a movement where so much importance is attached to the individual. If members of the movement can learn from Eissler, it becomes more likely that diversity of opinion in relation to the issues involved will not menace group unity, or group unity the integrity of the individual.

Review of R. Slovenko's *Sexual Behavior and the Law*

The nature of psychoanalytic training and practice promotes a paradox which sometimes misleads psychoanalysts themselves, and usually makes confusion amongst our critics even worse. For though the discipline is severe if it is loyally adhered to, it enhances the unique qualities of the individual to a point where non-analysts at least wonder in what way such a diversity of views can be seen to cohere; I have had a better opportunity than most of appreciating the reality of the paradox.

One unfortunate result for members of the psychoanalytic movement is the impossibility of keeping up with – or even being aware of – the contributions which psychoanalysts are making in fields outside the narrow domain of psychoanalytic practice, training, and research.

Sometimes a number of psychoanalysts are engaged on work which enables them to make a contribution to some aspect of society not usually illuminated by psychoanalytic insight. This has occurred in the book under review, *Sexual Behavior and the Law*. It is therefore with some interest that one looks to see what the diversity of the individual analyst – together with the background that he shares with his fellow analysts – will lead him to put forward to society as his uniquely analytic contribution. From this we may learn something of an aspect of psychoanalysis with which we are unfamiliar, and something of the image of psychoanalysis with which our colleagues are presenting the public.

It would be helpful to give some idea of other contributions to this book, but this unfortunately I feel unable to do. As psychoanalysts we sometimes complain that our views are misrepresented by those who mistake familiarity with the words we use, for familiarity with the ideas we try to express by use of the words. I shall avoid this error by not criticizing contributions made by masters in their own field – their views can best be understood by those familiar with the field.

In this volume one expects to find that the contributions by lawyers state the legal view of sex. In fact the difficulties of doing this are not made clear; yet it is one half of the equation because it is difficult to discuss such a subject without knowing what the law-making body considers sex to be, or how it defines criminal sex. In his introduction, Slovenko states a number of definitions of sexual crime, but he admits that they apply only in some states of the Union and not others. Furthermore, some of his definitions – mostly of rape – seem to be his own summary of the legal position, rather than a quotation of an actual law. What is required is something analogous to Lord Devlin's account[1] of the legal view of Guilt; it was possible, listening to Lord Devlin, to observe the enormous gulf which separates the view he expressed from the views commonly accepted by psychoanalysts. Indeed, so much was this the case that many psychoanalysts expressed disappointment, as if they expected to hear up-to-date formulations of the psychoanalytic view of guilt, rather than to be reminded of what a member of the Establishment – to use a convenient if loose expression – thought on the subject, and the sort of theory to which he expected the realities of the law courts would approximate.

In Great Britain the courts are expected to apply the laws passed by Parliament. That is to say, they are supposed to arrive at a practical conclusion on what any given law means – not always an easy task – and then to match it with what they find. The function of the court must surely be to discover what it is they have found, before they can match it with the Law. But they do not, as is very evident from Slovenko's introduction. For example: a man is charged with rape; in the Court an extremely complex story is unfolded, as will be evident from the case of B, recounted by Arthur Hyatt Williams (p. 568). A psychoanalyst listening to the proceedings might well form an opinion about where the guilt lay, and of what the criminal was guilty – which was quite unlike the case the Court was being asked to consider.

---

[1] 1964 Ernest Jones Lecture to the British Psychoanalytical Society.

The problem arises of course because sexual impulses and sexual acts may be a part of an immense diversity of episodes, ranging from expressions of passionate and profound love to methods of earning a living by blackmail, or prostitution, espionage, complex revenge – sometimes conscious and relatively simple, sometimes requiring an analytic investigation to display its roots. Yet in the catalogue they all count as sex.

It has been said that a famous criminal, responsible for many murders as a part of the routine of his working life, was finally brought to book – all other charges having failed to stick – on the grounds of evasion of income tax. Perhaps sexual laws are devised on this principle; they may lead to the apprehension of a criminal when all other legal procedures fail. Yet this can scarcely be a justification for law as it is at present practised. The system is easy to criticize, but the remedy hard to find. Masud Khan makes a contribution on 'The Function of Intimacy and Acting Out in Perversions'. It is no criticism of the article to say it is difficult to see how the non-analyst is to profit from it or what he would make of it. Someone who has been analytically trained would find the article interesting and illuminating. He could legitimately come to his own conclusions, and match Khan's findings with his own. But although it is claimed that those who have these matters at heart will profit by a perusal of the articles in this book, it must be confessed that something more than goodwill is required of them to make their reading profitable. I can well understand that a lawyer or magistrate or schoolmaster would find such an article hard going. Yet – and here is the rub – psychoanalysis was spread by those who had little to go on except what they read of Freud's own articles. Analysis in those days was rudimentary, and it still is accessible to few. There must then be a place for these articles, and a hope that here and there they will meet with understanding and help to leaven the culture of which they form a part through publications of this kind. At least the cases cited by Hyatt Williams and Khan may be brought to light through the obtrusion of the sexual characteristics of crime. In this respect the law may be regarded as a network, in some part of which the criminal may become enmeshed. But as Rubinstein points out, the crime may be quite simple: the criminal is caught thieving, brought to court and sentenced. Nothing, one might think, could be simpler or more straightforward. No psychoanalyst could possibly take such a view, as Lothair Rubinstein points out. Once in prison the simplicity of the story evaporates. After repeated crimes and recaptures it becomes clear that a fish has been caught that does not lend itself to simple classification. One of the invaluable functions of the Institute for the Scientific Treatment of Delinquency is that it can do much by its impact on the courts to spread knowledge, in just the way it is hoped that this book will manage to do.

I have said that the layman will find psychoanalytic concepts hard going. The problem is that if the analyst resorts too readily to concepts that the layman can understand he will give a misleading impression of psychoanalytic theory. When Khan talks of a technique of intimacy it is likely that he will seem to a layman to be more easily comprehensible than in other parts of his discussion of perversion. It is difficult to see how the analyst is to evade giving an impression of banality or jargon, but the only solution would seem to be that arrived at by Freud, when he decided that the only way was to express himself as clearly as he could, without any compromise with the susceptibilities of those who would, in any case, be antagonized. The analyst cannot evade this obligation. The criminal on the other hand can, and often does. Ronald Markillie points out the effect it has on the criminal who realizes that it makes a great difference to what crime he confesses (p. 780). He has to recognize that the 'treatment' meted out by a court of law is based on a simple psychopathology, namely, that what is the matter is a lack of anxiety in the criminal, and that clearly the cure to correspond with this disease is to increase anxiety by adding the threat of punishment to any already existing fears. In addition to this, as Markillie shows, while he may be being tried for a sexual offence, what he may be punished for is disgusting the court. The rule for the criminal would seem to be, "Be criminal if you must; but be disgusting at your peril."

Markillie's article has some illuminating things to say about the sentenced man, and the use to which such a man puts the law and the sentence he receives. In my experience a patient may easily decide to use a mental hospital for what is really a purpose indistinguishable from that to which another man will put prison and the courts. There is a point at which despair of ever getting proper understanding or treatment – least of all from himself –will lead a man of pathological make-up to use the institutions of the Law, or the institutions of medical cure, as instruments for improvising a treatment he despairs of ever getting. As can be seen such a choice may go back to times when the only formulations of his distress open to the patient might be either that he was 'naughty', or that he was 'ill'. Society is asked to collude, through its institutions, with one or other view. These same institutions, the legal system being one, are however also supposed to be exempt from such collusion; even case law has to develop in such a way that potentially the citizen is able, increasingly, to see how he stands in his legal obligations to his group. In this book Wels and Freed quote Mr Justice Jackson giving a dissenting opinion – explaining that he does so precisely because the majority view fails to clarify the law and makes confusion worse. With this view the authors obviously agree (p. 176). In England the confusion often arises before the case ever gets to the courts, because the Parliamentary legal draughtsmen fail to formulate the intentions of Parliament in such a way that a reasonably competent court might be expected to arrive at a correct interpretation of the intention of the Law.

In truth, in any trial two sets of interpretations have to be made: one is of the behaviour of the supposed criminal, and the other is of the meaning of the Law. Only when both have been made can the one be matched against the other.

It must not be forgotten that the courts are not supposed to be legislating, but carrying out orders imposed on them by the sovereign body. Even when allowance is made for the development of case law, in fact the authority of the courts resides in the supposition that it has correctly interpreted the will of Parliament. The court rules are intended to ensure the court remains what I have elsewhere called a Work Group,[1] and does not become dominated by powerful, primitive urges which cause it to express impulses that are not the intention of the sovereign body that it should express. In their review of the historical sources of American Law, Wels and Freed bring out very clearly how much the courts are influenced by their historical development. Even such elasticity as common law procedure introduces into legal settlements of sexual problems is denied by the accident of the development of divorce law from canon law.

One of the consequences of this is described by R. V. Sherwin, who bluntly characterizes the behaviour of the courts as dominated by prudery. He makes out a good case for saying that the courts are frequently swayed by hostility to sex rather than by concern for the

[1][*Experiences in Groups and Other Papers,* in Volume IV. *Ed.*]

legality or otherwise of the act being tried (p. 425 et seq.). This brings his view very close to that expressed by Markillie to which I have already alluded.

The blurb describes this work as likely to be regarded as, "the most profound work on psycho-sexuality since Freud". Psychoanalysts need not be deterred by such praise. There is a great deal of comfort to be had by reading what these workers have to teach us of their experiences in that extremely complex field where intuition and understanding have to be converted into wise action.